American Heart Association

Healthy Family Meals

American Heart
Association

Healthy Family Meals

**150 RECIPES
EVERYONE
WILL LOVE**

CLARKSON POTTER / PUBLISHERS
NEW YORK

Also by the American Heart Association

American Heart Association Low-Fat, Low-Cholesterol Cookbook, Fourth Edition

American Heart Association No-Fad Diet

The New American Heart Association Cookbook, Seventh Edition

American Heart Association Low-Salt Cookbook, Third Edition

American Heart Association Quick & Easy Cookbook

American Heart Association Meals in Minutes

American Heart Association One-Dish Meals

American Heart Association Low-Calorie Cookbook

American Heart Association Low-Fat & Luscious Desserts

Copyright © 2009 by AMERICAN HEART ASSOCIATION, INC.

All rights reserved.

Published in the United States by CLARKSON POTTER/PUBLISHERS, an imprint of the
CROWN PUBLISHING GROUP, a division of RANDOM HOUSE, INC., New York.
www.crownpublishing.com
www.clarksonpotter.com

CLARKSON POTTER is a trademark and Potter and colophon are registered trademarks
of Random House, Inc.

Library of Congress Cataloging-in-Publication Data
American Heart Association healthy family meals /
American Heart Association. — 1st ed.
p.   cm.
Includes index.
1. Nutrition.   2. Low-fat diet—Recipes.   3. Salt-free diet—Recipes.   4. Heart—Diseases—Diet therapy—Recipes.
I. American Heart Association.   II. Title: Healthy family meals.
RA784.A46   2009
641.5'6311—dc22   2008051191

ISBN 978-0-307-45059-3

Printed in China

PHOTOGRAPHY BY BEN FINK

DESIGN BY JENNIFER K. BEAL DAVIS

Shrimp Tacos photograph appears on front cover; see page 89 for recipe.
Good-for-You Fried Rice photograph appears on back cover (bottom); see page 125 for recipe.
South of the Border Beef photograph appears on page 2; see page 162 for recipe.
Mini Chicken Pot Pies photograph appears on back cover (top) and page 6; see page 62 for recipe.
Ginger Beef Stir-Fry photograph appears on page 10; see page 108 for recipe.

10 9 8 7 6 5 4 3 2

First Edition

Your contribution to the American Heart Association supports research that helps make
publications like this possible. For more information, call 1-800-AHA-USA1 (1-800-242-8721) or
contact us online at www.americanheart.org.

Acknowledgments

American Heart Association Consumer Publications

Director: Linda S. Ball

Managing Editor: Deborah A. Renza

Senior Editor: Janice Roth Moss

Science Editor/Writer: Jacqueline F. Haigney

Assistant Editor: Roberta Westcott Sullivan

Senior Marketing Manager: Bharati Gaitonde

Recipe Developers

Mary Ellen Evans

Nancy S. Hughes

Annie King

Jackie Mills, M.S., R.D.

Kathryn Moore

Carol Ritchie

Cheryl Sternman Rule

Julie Shapero, R.D., L.D.

Carla Fitzgerald Williams

Roxanne Wyss

Nutrition Analyst

Tammi Hancock, R.D.

Contents

Preface

The role nutrition plays in the overall health of our children has emerged as one of our nation's top concerns. The U.S. food supply offers lots of choices, but much of what kids eat just fills them up without providing the nutrients their young bodies need. And we adults need nutritious food as well to stay healthy and productive. The general shift to a sedentary lifestyle has reduced the level of physical activity for both adults and kids. The result is that about one in every three children and two out of three adults are overweight or obese.

Today's typical American diet increases children's risk for health problems, including high blood pressure and high blood cholesterol. These are problems that have serious consequences later in life. Diseases that in the past have developed in adulthood—for example, type 2 diabetes—are becoming more and more common in children. If this trend continues, it's quite possible that the current generation of young people may be the first in American history to live shorter lives than their parents.

What can we do to improve our children's eating habits? Start with a commitment to provide children with the most nutritious foods possible—one meal or snack at a time. At the American Heart Association, we know that it's never too early—or too late—to eat well and to enjoy the benefits of a healthy lifestyle. This book, *Healthy Family Meals,* is geared to the nutritional needs and tastes of all ages so you can create one meal everyone will enjoy. It also will help you make the right food choices that—over time—will become second nature for you and your family.

You'll find 150 all-new, family-focused recipes here, including No-Guilt Macaroni and Cheese (page 181), Meat "Loaf" with Hidden Vegetables (page 112), Five-Vegetable Soup (page 43), Shrimp Tacos (page 89), and Honey BBQ Chicken Nuggets (page 93). These and the other recipes in this book shatter the idea that nutritious food has to be boring, bland, and time-consuming. We hope you'll try all our recipes—and that many will become family favorites. You'll find you can cook delicious dishes in the same time as—or less than—it takes to eat out or resort to convenience foods. Since we're all busy, we need *Healthy Family Meals* to show us how to offer a variety of appealing, nutritionally packed foods to the families we love and care for.

In addition to heart-smart recipes, *Healthy Family Meals* includes information on the American Heart Association dietary recommendations and provides strategies for healthier shopping, cooking, and dining out, as well as other family-friendly topics.

To help get your children creatively involved in the kitchen, we've devoted an entire chapter to cooking with them. Your kids can acquire hands-on experience with 10 fun recipes designed especially to teach age-appropriate cooking skills. Throughout the book, you'll also find nutrition tips and suggested substitutions to make the recipes more versatile and give you even more ideas on how to keep your family as involved and as healthy as possible.

By bringing nutritious—and delicious—food to your table, you'll give your whole family a giant head start toward a longer, more vibrant life. From the American Heart Association's family to yours, we wish you happy cooking and a lifetime of good health.

Rose Marie Robertson, M.D., FAHA, FACC
Chief Science Officer
American Heart Association/American Stroke Association

Introduction

Every family faces the challenge of integrating good nutrition and healthy eating habits into their lives—and many fail. Busy days and conflicting schedules make it easier to head for the drive-through window than the grocery store. Kids beg for french fries and refuse to eat their carrots. You're too exhausted to figure out what to feed the kids and what to feed yourself.

The kitchen, once the heart of the home, may now be more like a hub where family members cross paths on the way to the next car-pool appointment or soccer practice. You may be sacrificing good nutrition for convenience and paying the price with your health.

After a generation of easy access to junk food and a significant increase in eating out, reports of increasing obesity, type 2 diabetes, and heart disease in American children make it very clear that they should eat a heart-healthy diet from infancy on. Heart disease starts in childhood, and the best defense is a wholesome lifestyle based on good food choices and regular exercise. But it's not easy to know what to do.

If you're the one choosing the meals that go on your family's table, you're making important decisions every day. You need a plan for success, and *Healthy Family Meals* is here to help. With 150 recipes in hand that are easy, nutritious, and created with the entire family in mind, you can start to develop a healthy food culture in your home. This book will help you take three important steps:

- **You can simplify cooking for the family.** The recipes in this book are geared to the entire family's enjoyment; cook once, everyone eats! Forget about "kid food" and "grown-up" food and concentrate on *healthy* food. Plus, if meal preparation is easier and feeds the whole family at the same time, you may eat at home more often.

- **You can stock your pantry and refrigerator with healthy food.** *You* choose the snacks and beverages you want your family to eat and drink. The kids may crave ice cream, but if there's a delicious fat-free yogurt in the freezer instead, that's what they'll eat. Make all the options in your kitchen nutritious ones!

Building a Healthy Food Culture

As soon you bring your first baby home, you begin the daily process of deciding how to feed the family. In the beginning, you can choose what goes into your children's mouths. As kids get older, though, they begin to voice their preferences, and their input becomes part of the family culture. That's why making the decisions about family meals isn't always straightforward. Many factors pull you in lots of directions: time constraints, end-of-day meltdowns, picky eaters, and budgetary considerations, as well as the goal of putting a nourishing meal on the table.

The question remains how to do it all while consistently working toward a healthier, active lifestyle. Take stock of the food culture your family has created—and take control! A healthy food culture will pay long-term dividends in the well-being of your family. Eating habits are set in childhood, and for better or worse, they tend to stick with us for life. Choose fresh foods instead of processed foods, which tend to be high in harmful fats, sodium, and added sugar. Load up on fruits and vegetables. Buy fat-free and low-fat dairy products. Watch the snacks. And teach your family that what they eat is important, today and for lots of tomorrows. You *do* have the control because you are making the decisions. After all, eating well is the best investment you can make in your family's long-term physical well-being.

You may recognize the need to educate your children and adopt healthy practices for the entire family, but you also know achieving those goals can be a real challenge. So start with realistic expectations and give yourself a break. If you feel that the pressures of life have taken you too far from a healthy food culture, you can reinvent the way your family eats. It's easy to begin with just one or two small but significant changes. For example, if your family is constantly on the run and grab-and-go is your usual routine, create a new food event. Plan an "everyone-home-for-dinner" meal at least two nights a week, maybe a weeknight and Sunday night. Find the family favorite and serve it often.

Make the most of the meals you do share, both nutritionally and as family gatherings. Remember that families that eat together tend to be healthier both physically and emotionally, as many studies have shown. Also, sharing time at the table gives you the opportunity to show your children through your example that you care about good food and good nutrition. And when you make better food choices, you and your family will be better off for it.

Ten Steps to Healthy Food Choices

1. Eat a variety of VEGETABLES and FRUITS daily. Serve your family lots of different types of vegetables and fruits, especially deeply colored ones—they have the highest concentrations of nutrients. Aim to serve at least one vegetable and one fruit at every meal. Encourage your kids to eat fruits instead of drinking juices; they'll get more fiber and probably fewer calories. Limit fruit drinks with added sugar.

2. Eat WHOLE GRAINS rather than refined grain products as often as possible. Serve whole-grain and high-fiber breads, pastas, cereals, and side dishes for their fiber and important nutrients. Try to be sure at least half of the grains you eat are whole grains (check that the labels on grain products list a whole grain as the first ingredient).

3. Include FAT-FREE OR LOW-FAT DAIRY products daily. Serve fat-free and low-fat milk, cheeses, yogurt, and other dairy products. Limit whole-fat dairy products, such as whole milk and full-fat cheese. These little changes can make a huge difference in your family's health.

4. Eat FISH at least twice a week. Fish is a good source of protein and is low in harmful saturated fat. Fatty fish, especially salmon, tuna, trout, and halibut, are high in omega-3 fatty acids, which help reduce the risk of heart disease. If you're concerned about the mercury in fish and shellfish, remember that the risks from mercury exposure depend on the amount of seafood eaten and the levels of mercury in the individual fish itself. Eat a variety of fish to minimize possible adverse effects. Women who are pregnant, planning to become pregnant, or nursing—and young children—should avoid eating the fish most prone to contamination, such as shark and swordfish. For most people, however, the benefits of eating fish far outweigh the risks.

5. Eat lean POULTRY and MEATS. For poultry, choose white meat most often, discard all visible fat, and don't eat the skin. Meats can be heart-healthy if you choose lean cuts and discard all visible fat before cooking them. Grill, bake, or broil poultry and meats without adding saturated fat, and cut back on processed meats, which can be high in fat and sodium.

6. Include LEGUMES, NUTS, and SEEDS in your diet. Legumes, such as peas, peanuts and peanut butter, beans, and lentils, are a great source of fiber and meatless protein. Nuts and seeds are rich in helpful monounsaturated fats and may actually help keep down blood cholesterol levels when they are part of a diet that is low in saturated fat and cholesterol. Nuts are high in calories, so don't go overboard.

7. Use liquid vegetable OILS and soft margarines. Vegetable oils, such as olive and canola, provide heart-healthy unsaturated fats. When you can't use an oil, use fat-free spray margarines or the light spreads that are lowest in saturated and trans fats. Avoid butter and stick margarines, and limit cakes, cookies, crackers, and other commercial products made with partially hydrogenated or saturated fats.

8. Cut back on SODIUM. When shopping, be mindful of the hidden sodium in packaged and processed foods. Compare the food labels of similar products to find the ones with less sodium, choose low-sodium or no-salt-added products, and watch for high-sodium restaurant meals. Limit condiments, such as soy sauce, that are high in sodium. When cooking, use little or no salt.

9. Cut back on added SUGAR. Limit sugary foods and beverages that are low in nutrients but high in calories. Read the ingredient lists and choose products that don't list sugars in the first four ingredients.

10. Cut back on foods high in dietary CHOLESTEROL. Try to eat less than 300 mg of cholesterol each day. Common cholesterol-containing foods include whole milk, egg yolks, and shellfish.

Make Meal Time Your Family Time

Studies show that the more often you share meals as a family, the more likely your kids are to develop healthier eating habits and maintain an appropriate weight. When you prepare meals at home, you control what and how your family eats. In addition to building a strong nutritional foundation for your children, eating together gives your kids a sense of comfort in the routine. Children like knowing there's a regular time when everyone sits down together. Even if there's some bickering, the interaction at the table promotes better manners, improves vocabulary, and reinforces your family's values and culture.

If you want to enjoy sit-down meals but find it hard to make them happen, ask yourself what's in your way. Start by getting rid of obstacles and distractions: Keep the kitchen cleared of clutter! It's tempting to use the kitchen table and countertops as all-purpose catchalls, but having to clear them of "stuff" every night will make meal prep more of a challenge. Don't add unnecessary stress to meals. Remember: It's okay not to be perfect! A pretty table setting is a nice touch, but it doesn't mean as much as quality time spent together. Turn off the television when you sit down to eat, and talk instead. Ask each child in turn to tell you about his or her day. Dinner may be the only time your child can talk to you without the distractions of cell phones, carpools, reality shows, or video games.

Forget the old battle of having a child "clean the plate." Trust your kids to know when they've eaten enough. If you're concerned about wasting food, serve smaller amounts to start and then offer seconds as appropriate. Mealtime is a natural opportunity to teach kids about portion control, since ever-increasing portion size has become a major cause of overweight. As you serve meals, show your older kids what a reasonable portion should look like. Talk about how much food is appropriate to eat at one sitting, and get them thinking about the portions they're given in restaurants. Let them know it's okay to take food home from restaurants when they're given too much to eat comfortably.

Keep Kids in the Kitchen

The kitchen is where the action is, and it also can be the heart of your home, full of laughs and fun! The more you can involve your kids in preparing the family's food, the more likely they are to enjoy eating well and with a more adventurous spirit. Share the heritage and traditions of your own childhood, and start new ones with your kids. Bake Grandma's favorite cookies for special occasions, and tell kids about how food was prepared in earlier generations. A nice way to document your cooking fun is to have your kids—at various ages—create a family cookbook and draw pictures for every recipe.

As kids grow, you can progressively let them have as much control over the home cooking as is comfortable for you. "Cooking with Your Kids" on page 227 and a feature called Kids in the Kitchen will give you ideas on how to work with your children. By becoming involved, your kids will:

- Feel a sense of accomplishment and of contributing to the family.
- Show a greater interest in sitting down to a meal to show off what they helped prepare.
- Enjoy the shared time parents spend focused on them.
- Learn long-term cooking skills that will pay off for the rest of their lives.
- Develop increased self-esteem from positive experiences.
- Take away a deeper appreciation of the family food culture you create together.

And you will:

- Have the satisfaction of passing on your own heritage along with family recipes.
- Know that kids who learn to eat well at home will grow up to be healthier adults.
- Treasure those priceless moments, from watching flour-covered toddlers to sharing a proud teenager's first home-baked cake.

Expect Fabulous Food

Start right here—the recipes in this book are delicious! Browse the options, and you'll see it's no chore to eat healthy. You'll learn how to use the right ingredients and techniques to make fresh, wholesome meals—many fast enough even for your hectic nights. You'll find recipes for a wide variety of dishes that will appeal to adults as well as kids; the recipes are current, not cute. With a little planning, you'll be cooking fast and fabulous, with enough energy left over for what really matters: setting the groundwork for a strong family food culture that will nurture and nourish your kids throughout their lives.

About the Recipes

How the Recipes Are Organized

We know the center of most family meals is the main course. That's why you'll find 80 entrées to choose from in this book. Within the main dishes, you'll find the recipes organized into four chapters—Everyday Dinners, Busy Nights, Plan-Aheads, and Cook Once, Eat Twice—that will help you meet the time frame of your daily schedule. For variety, look for seafood, poultry, meat, and vegetarian recipes throughout these chapters.

- **Everyday Dinners**—These full-of-flavor family-friendly recipes are delicious dishes for every day of the week. With choices such as steak, spaghetti, salmon, and more, you'll be sure to find a variety of favorites that you and your family will love night after night!

- **Busy Nights**—Running short on time? No worries. Designed for those dinnertimes that are especially hurried, these recipes are just as tasty as Everyday Dinners but will be complete within 30 minutes or less—from start to finish. That's right, you'll have your family eating a healthy meal in practically no time at all. You'll find nearly half of our main-dish selections in Busy Nights—that's 39 recipes to choose from!

To help you incorporate additional vegetables, fruits, and grains into your family's diet, we've included a special feature called Make It a Meal, which provides suggestions for accompaniments to main dishes—side salads and soups, vegetable and grain side dishes, and even desserts. This feature will be particularly helpful on the nights you are not only pressed for time but also stuck on what "go-withs" to serve with the main dish.

- **Plan-Aheads**—Looking to get a jump start on your next meal? We call recipes that require time for marinating, slow cooking, chilling, and so on Plan-Aheads as a reminder that you will need to incorporate upfront time into your schedule.

- **Cook Once, Eat Twice**—These paired recipes give you the benefit of cooking once and eating twice, another way to help save time for a family on the go. The first recipe instructs you to make extra to use in the totally different companion recipe that you and your family can enjoy later in the week.

Using the Nutrition Analyses

Each recipe includes a breakdown of the nutrients it provides. In the same way you use the information on the Nutrition Facts label of commercial food products, compare recipes to find the dishes that best meet your family's needs.

Keep the following information in mind as you review the nutrition analyses:

- Each analysis is based on a single serving.

- Optional ingredients and garnishes are not included in the nutrition analysis unless noted. We encourage you to be creative with garnishes, especially fruits and vegetables.

- Ingredients with a weight range (⅓ to ½ cup fresh orange juice, for example) are analyzed at the average weight.

- When a recipe lists two or more ingredient options, the first is used in the nutrition analysis.

- The specific amount of an ingredient listed, not the amount sometimes shown in parentheses, is analyzed. The amounts in parentheses are guidelines to help you decide how much of an ingredient to purchase to prepare that recipe.

- Meats are analyzed as cooked and lean, with all visible fat discarded. For ground beef, we use 95 percent fat-free meat.

- Products in the marketplace come and go quickly, and the labeling changes as well. To avoid confusion, we use the generic terms "fat-free" for products that may be labeled either "fat-free" or "nonfat" and "low-fat" for products that may be labeled "low-fat" or "reduced-fat." The important thing is to read labels and purchase the products lowest in saturated fat, trans fat, and sodium that will provide good results.

- We use olive and canola oils for the analyses as specified in each recipe, but other unsaturated oils, such as corn, safflower, soybean, and sunflower, also are acceptable.

- The values listed for saturated, trans, polyunsaturated, and monounsaturated fats are rounded and may not add up to the total fat value.

- Processed foods can be very high in sodium. To keep the level of sodium in our recipes low, we call for unprocessed foods or low-sodium products when possible and add table salt sparingly for flavor. For instance, a recipe may use a can of no-salt-added tomatoes and ¼ teaspoon of table salt. The amount of sodium in the finished dish will be less than if we called for a regular can of tomatoes and no table salt.

- If meat, poultry, or seafood is marinated and the marinade is discarded, we include only the amount of sodium absorbed. For marinated vegetables and basting liquids, we include the total amount of the marinade in the analysis.

Appetizers, Snacks, and Beverages

Mango and Black Bean Salsa

1 medium mango, chopped

1 cup canned no-salt-added black beans, rinsed and drained

1/2 cup canned no-salt-added corn, drained

1/4 cup chopped red onion

1/4 cup chopped red bell pepper

1/4 cup snipped fresh cilantro

1 to 1 1/2 teaspoons seeded and finely chopped fresh jalapeño

1/2 teaspoon grated lime zest

2 tablespoons fresh lime juice

1/2 teaspoon salt-free all-purpose seasoning blend (optional)

1/8 teaspoon garlic powder

1/8 teaspoon salt

This homemade salsa is a delicious and easy way to add more fruit and vegetables to your family's diet. The mango and beans punch up the flavor and give an extra boost of nutrients and fiber.

In a medium bowl, stir together the ingredients. Serve immediately for peak flavor or cover and refrigerate for up to one day before serving.

COOK'S TIP ON HOT CHILE PEPPERS: Wear disposable plastic gloves when working with hot chile peppers, such as jalapeños, because the oils from the peppers can irritate your eyes and skin. If you prefer not to wear gloves, be sure to wash your hands thoroughly with warm, soapy water to remove the oils.

NUTRITION TIP: Serve this salsa with baked tortilla chips (see the Nutrition Tip on page 165) as an appetizer or snack. Also try it as an accompaniment to grilled chicken or seafood or instead of salad dressing.

PER SERVING

Calories	24
Total Fat	0.0 g
Saturated Fat	0.0 g
Trans Fat	0.0 g
Polyunsaturated Fat	0.0 g
Monounsaturated Fat	0.0 g
Cholesterol	0 mg
Sodium	15 mg
Carbohydrates	5 g
Fiber	1 g
Sugars	2 g
Protein	1 g

Dietary exchanges: 1/2 carbohydrate

Candy Apple Dip

SERVES 4 | 2 TABLESPOONS DIP AND ½ CUP APPLE SLICES PER SERVING

DIP

- 1 cup fat-free frozen whipped topping, thawed in refrigerator
- 2 tablespoons peanut butter
- 2 tablespoons fat-free caramel apple dip

- 2 medium apples, such as Gala, Fuji, or Granny Smith, or firm pears, cut into medium slices

A creamy, peanutty, caramel-topped gooey fruit treat, this kid-friendly snack offers lots of nutritional value, too!

In a small bowl, whisk together the dip ingredients. Serve with the fruit.

PER SERVING	
Calories	154
Total Fat	4.0 g
Saturated Fat	1.0 g
Trans Fat	0.0 g
Polyunsaturated Fat	1.0 g
Monounsaturated Fat	2.0 g
Cholesterol	0 mg
Sodium	78 mg
Carbohydrates	27 g
Fiber	3 g
Sugars	19 g
Protein	3 g
Dietary exchanges: 1 fruit, 1 carbohydrate, 1 fat	

Fruit Pockets

SERVES 4 | 1 FRUIT POCKET PER SERVING

- 5 ounces strawberries, sliced
- 4 ounces blueberries
- 1 small banana, cut into ¼-inch slices
- ⅓ cup fat-free tub cream cheese, room temperature
- 1 tablespoon plus 1 teaspoon all-fruit raspberry spread
- ⅛ teaspoon ground nutmeg
- 2 6-inch whole-wheat pita pockets, halved

Here's a fun and easy way to fix a healthy snack that delivers whole wheat, fruit, and dairy at the same time.

In a medium bowl, gently stir together the strawberries, blueberries, and banana.

In a small bowl, stir together the cream cheese, raspberry spread, and nutmeg.

Gently open the pocket of each pita half. Spread the cream cheese mixture inside. Spoon in the fruit.

PER SERVING	
Calories	164
Total Fat	1.5 g
Saturated Fat	0.5 g
Trans Fat	0.0 g
Polyunsaturated Fat	0.5 g
Monounsaturated Fat	0.0 g
Cholesterol	2 mg
Sodium	266 mg
Carbohydrates	34 g
Fiber	4 g
Sugars	11 g
Protein	7 g
Dietary exchanges: 1 starch, 1 fruit	

Pick-Up-Sticks Tuna Wraps

SERVES 4 | 2 WRAPS PER SERVING

1 6-ounce can low-sodium chunk light tuna in water, drained and flaked

2 tablespoons light mayonnaise

2 tablespoons fat-free sour cream

2 tablespoons sweet pickle relish, undrained

½ teaspoon curry powder

½ teaspoon celery seeds

8 large lettuce leaves, such as romaine, Bibb, or iceberg

1 medium red bell pepper, cut into thin strips

½ cup matchstick-size carrots (about 1 medium)

Crisp lettuce and veggies provide a perfect foil for creamy tuna salad. (See photograph on page 18.)

In a medium bowl, combine the tuna, mayonnaise, sour cream, relish, curry, and celery seeds. Spoon onto each lettuce leaf. Top with the bell pepper and carrots. Roll the lettuce jelly-roll style over the filling or serve open face.

PER SERVING	
Calories	116
Total Fat	3.5 g
Saturated Fat	0.5 g
Trans Fat	0.0 g
Polyunsaturated Fat	1.5 g
Monounsaturated Fat	1.0 g
Cholesterol	17 mg
Sodium	159 mg
Carbohydrates	9 g
Fiber	2 g
Sugars	5 g
Protein	12 g
Dietary exchanges: ½ carbohydrate, 2 lean meat	

Sweet and Crunchy Trail Mix

SERVES 6 | ½ CUP TRAIL MIX PER SERVING

2 cups crunchy high-protein cereal

¼ cup dried sweetened cranberries

½ cup slivered almonds, dry-roasted

1 to 2 teaspoons grated orange zest

Just combine and shake to fix this quick, portable snack. The mix provides complex carbs and protein for both short- and long-term energy.

KIDS IN THE KITCHEN:
Have the kids measure everything, seal the bag, and shake it. Go one step further and have them fill snack-size resealable plastic bags with single portions to take to school or to have on hand so they can grab a quick snack during the week.

In a large resealable plastic bag, combine the ingredients. Seal the bag tightly. Shake until well blended.

PER SERVING	
Calories	140
Total Fat	5.5 g
Saturated Fat	0.5 g
Trans Fat	0.0 g
Polyunsaturated Fat	1.5 g
Monounsaturated Fat	3.5 g
Cholesterol	0 mg
Sodium	73 mg
Carbohydrates	19 g
Fiber	4 g
Sugars	9 g
Protein	5 g
Dietary exchanges: 1½ starch, 1 fat	

Wonton Berry Baskets

SERVES 12 | 2 WONTON BASKETS PER SERVING

Butter-flavor cooking spray

24 wonton wrappers

2 tablespoons sugar

1/2 teaspoon ground cinnamon

2 6-ounce containers fat-free plain yogurt

1/4 cup frozen orange juice concentrate, thawed

2 tablespoons light brown sugar

1 teaspoon vanilla extract

6 ounces fresh strawberries, sliced

4 ounces fresh blueberries

2 tablespoons sliced almonds, dry-roasted

PER SERVING

Calories	105
Total Fat	1.0 g
Saturated Fat	0.0 g
Trans Fat	0.0 g
Polyunsaturated Fat	0.5 g
Monounsaturated Fat	0.5 g
Cholesterol	2 mg
Sodium	33 mg
Carbohydrates	21 g
Fiber	1 g
Sugars	10 g
Protein	4 g
Dietary exchanges: 1½ carbohydrate	

These tasty treats offer just the right balance of textures: crisp wontons, creamy yogurt, soft fruit, and crunchy almonds. Delicious and unusual, they're also great fun for kids—and good for your heart!

Preheat the oven to 400°F. Lightly spray two 12-cup mini-muffin pans with cooking spray.

Place the wonton wrappers in a single layer on a flat surface, such as a large cutting board or piece of aluminum foil. Lightly spray both sides of the wrappers with cooking spray. Place a wrapper in each muffin cup. Press down gently in the middle of each wrapper so it molds to the shape of the cup and the tips point out attractively.

In a small bowl, stir together the sugar and cinnamon. Sprinkle over the wonton wrappers.

Bake for 6 to 7 minutes, or until golden brown. Transfer the pans to cooling racks. Let cool for at least 15 minutes before removing the baskets from the pans.

Meanwhile, in a medium bowl, stir together the yogurt, orange juice, brown sugar, and vanilla. Spoon about 1 tablespoon mixture into each cooled basket. Arrange 2 or 3 strawberry slices, 4 or 5 blueberries, and 3 or 4 almond slices attractively on top of each.

> COOK'S TIP: If you don't need all the baskets filled to serve at one time, store the empty baskets and the almonds in separate airtight containers at room temperature. Cover and refrigerate the yogurt mixture, strawberries, and blueberries in separate containers. Use within four days.

Pick-Your-Own Pita Chips

Perfect for TV-time munching, these crisp whole-wheat snacks come together in a flash.

Italian Pita Chips

1 tablespoon dried Italian seasoning, crumbled

1 teaspoon shredded or grated Parmesan cheese

1/8 teaspoon garlic powder

1 6-inch whole-wheat pita pocket, cut into 8 wedges and separated into 16 pieces

Olive oil cooking spray

Preheat the oven to 350°F.

In a small bowl, stir together the Italian seasoning, Parmesan, and garlic powder.

On a baking sheet, place the pita wedges close together with the rough (inner) side up. Lightly spray with cooking spray. Sprinkle with the Italian seasoning mixture.

Bake for 12 to 15 minutes, or until browned and crisp. Remove from the baking sheet and let cool on a cooling rack.

PER SERVING

Calories	42
Total Fat	0.5 g
Saturated Fat	0.0 g
Trans Fat	0.0 g
Polyunsaturated Fat	0.0 g
Monounsaturated Fat	0.0 g
Cholesterol	0 mg
Sodium	87 mg
Carbohydrates	8 g
Fiber	1 g
Sugars	0 g
Protein	2 g
Dietary exchanges: ½ starch	

NUTRITION TIP: Try all three pita versions here, and then experiment with different flavor combinations to come up with your family's favorites. As long as you stick with ingredients that don't add sodium, saturated fat, or too much sugar, your imagination is the only limit.

Cocoa-Cinnamon Pita Chips

1½ teaspoons sugar

½ teaspoon unsweetened cocoa powder

½ teaspoon ground cinnamon

1 6-inch whole-wheat pita pocket, cut into 8 wedges and separated into 16 pieces

Butter-flavor cooking spray

Prepare as directed on page 26, replacing the Italian seasoning, Parmesan, and garlic powder with a mixture of sugar, cocoa powder, and cinnamon and replacing the olive oil cooking spray with butter-flavor cooking spray.

PER SERVING

Calories	48
Total Fat	0.5 g
Saturated Fat	0.0 g
Trans Fat	0.0 g
Polyunsaturated Fat	0.0 g
Monounsaturated Fat	0.0 g
Cholesterol	0 mg
Sodium	80 mg
Carbohydrates	10 g
Fiber	1 g
Sugars	2 g
Protein	2 g

Dietary exchanges: ½ starch

Blueberry Pita Chips

2 tablespoons all-fruit blueberry spread, mashed with a fork

½ teaspoon ground cinnamon

1½ teaspoons water

1 6-inch whole-wheat pita pocket, cut into 8 wedges and separated into 16 pieces

Prepare as directed on page 26, replacing the Italian seasoning, Parmesan, and garlic powder with a mixture of blueberry spread, cinnamon, and water and omitting the cooking spray. Brush the mixture on the top side of the pita wedges. Increase the baking time to 15 to 17 minutes.

PER SERVING

Calories	61
Total Fat	0.5 g
Saturated Fat	0.0 g
Trans Fat	0.0 g
Polyunsaturated Fat	0.0 g
Monounsaturated Fat	0.0 g
Cholesterol	0 mg
Sodium	80 mg
Carbohydrates	14 g
Fiber	1 g
Sugars	4 g
Protein	2 g

Dietary exchanges: ½ starch, ½ fruit

Frozen Fruit Pops

SERVES 14 | 1 POP PER SERVING

8 ounces strawberries, halved

½ cup apricot nectar and ½ cup apricot nectar, divided use

1 tablespoon light brown sugar

½ teaspoon almond extract

2 medium bananas, cut into 1-inch pieces

1 teaspoon fresh lemon juice

1 teaspoon vanilla extract

PER SERVING

Calories	35
Total Fat	0.0 g
Saturated Fat	0.0 g
Trans Fat	0.0 g
Polyunsaturated Fat	0.0 g
Monounsaturated Fat	0.0 g
Cholesterol	0 mg
Sodium	1 mg
Carbohydrates	9 g
Fiber	1 g
Sugars	6 g
Protein	0 g

Dietary exchanges: ½ fruit

NUTRITION TIP: For a festive fruit drink, put a frozen fruit pop in a glass. Pour in 8 ounces of sparkling water, and garnish with a slice of lemon or lime.

Make these fruit-rich treats with your kids as a weekend project, then enjoy them as no-guilt snacks after school or work for the rest of the week. The strawberries, apricot nectar, and bananas are loaded with potassium—essential for growing bodies and healthy blood pressure.

Put the strawberries, ½ cup apricot nectar, brown sugar, and almond extract in a blender. Blend for about 15 seconds, or until smooth, scraping the sides occasionally with a rubber scraper. Pour into a small container with a pouring spout, such as a small liquid measuring cup or small pitcher. Rinse the blender container with cold water.

Put the bananas, lemon juice, vanilla, and remaining ½ cup apricot nectar in the blender. Blend for about 15 seconds, or until smooth, scraping the sides occasionally. Pour into a separate small container with a pouring spout.

Pour a scant ounce (scant 2 tablespoons) of each mixture into each of fourteen 2-ounce frozen pop molds or 2-ounce paper cups. Using the point of a sharp knife, make one quick, deep swirl in each. If the molds included tops and sticks, use those; otherwise, cover tightly with aluminum foil and insert a wooden pop stick in the center of each pop. Freeze for 4 hours, or until frozen solid. To serve, run the inverted molds under warm water for 15 to 20 seconds, or just until they loosen from the sides, or peel the cups away from the frozen pops.

Blueberry-Apple Slushes

SERVES 4 | 1 CUP PER SERVING

2 cups fresh or frozen blueberries
  (no thawing necessary)

2 cups ice cubes

1 large apple (about 8 ounces), any
  variety, cut into chunks (peel
  left on)

²⁄₃ cup fresh orange juice

2 tablespoons honey

¼ cup fresh blueberries (optional)

Refreshing and good for you, this fruit treat comes together in a flash and provides fiber from the apple and antioxidants from the deeply colored blueberries. (See photograph opposite.)

In a blender, process the ingredients except the ¼ cup blueberries until smooth. Serve garnished with the remaining blueberries.

PER SERVING

Calories	122
Total Fat	0.5 g
Saturated Fat	0.0 g
Trans Fat	0.0 g
Polyunsaturated Fat	0.0 g
Monounsaturated Fat	0.0 g
Cholesterol	0 mg
Sodium	2 mg
Carbohydrates	31 g
Fiber	3 g
Sugars	25 g
Protein	1 g
Dietary exchanges: 2 fruit	

Peanut Butter and Banana Smoothies

SERVES 4 | 1 CUP PER SERVING

3 very ripe medium bananas
  (speckled with brown spots), cut
  crosswise into ½-inch slices

2 6-ounce containers fat-free vanilla
  yogurt

1¼ cups fat-free milk

6 ice cubes

¼ cup creamy peanut butter

> NUTRITION TIP: Pour this protein-rich smoothie in a to-go cup for a quick and easy handheld breakfast.

Fat-free dairy products provide enough calcium and protein to make this filling smoothie a terrific breakfast.

Put the bananas on a large freezer-safe plate. Put in the freezer for 30 minutes, or until firm and very cold.

In a blender, process the ingredients for 30 seconds, or until the mixture is thick and smooth and the ice is fully incorporated.

PER SERVING

Calories	276
Total Fat	8.5 g
Saturated Fat	2.0 g
Trans Fat	0.0 g
Polyunsaturated Fat	2.5 g
Monounsaturated Fat	4.0 g
Cholesterol	3 mg
Sodium	165 mg
Carbohydrates	42 g
Fiber	3 g
Sugars	31 g
Protein	12 g
Dietary exchanges: 2 fruit, 1 fat-free milk, ½ lean meat, 1 fat	

Mulled Pomegranate-Apple Cider

SERVES 4 | 1 CUP PER SERVING

3½ cups unsweetened apple cider (not apple juice)

½ cup unsweetened pomegranate juice

4 quarter-size slices gingerroot, tapped with the side of a knife to flatten slightly

4 cinnamon sticks (each about 3 inches long)

COOK'S TIP ON GINGER-ROOT: Slightly flattening ginger-root, as in this recipe, releases more of the flavor.

Pomegranate juice adds beautiful color and a pleasant tang to this spiced autumn classic. (See photograph opposite.)

In a medium saucepan, stir together the ingredients. Bring to a simmer over medium heat. Reduce the heat and simmer for 5 minutes. Remove from the heat and let steep for 5 minutes. Discard the gingerroot. Ladle the liquid into mugs. Put the cinnamon sticks in the mugs as garnish.

PER SERVING

Calories	120
Total Fat	0.0 g
Saturated Fat	0.0 g
Trans Fat	0.0 g
Polyunsaturated Fat	0.0 g
Monounsaturated Fat	0.0 g
Cholesterol	0 mg
Sodium	25 mg
Carbohydrates	30 g
Fiber	0 g
Sugars	28 g
Protein	0 g

Dietary exchanges: 2 fruit

Strawberry-Mango Smoothies

SERVES 4 | 1 CUP PER SERVING

2 cups (about 8 ounces) frozen unsweetened strawberries

1⅓ cups fat-free half-and-half

1 cup frozen mango or unsweetened peach cubes

1 8-ounce can crushed pineapple in its own juice, undrained

⅓ cup all-fruit apricot spread

1 teaspoon vanilla extract

NUTRITION TIP: Just about any fruit and fruit juice combination will work well in this recipe.

Fat-free half-and-half gives a rich-tasting creaminess to this fruity treat, and the vanilla intensifies the sweetness.

In a blender, process the ingredients until smooth.

PER SERVING

Calories	199
Total Fat	0.0 g
Saturated Fat	0.0 g
Trans Fat	0.0 g
Polyunsaturated Fat	0.0 g
Monounsaturated Fat	0.0 g
Cholesterol	0 mg
Sodium	86 mg
Carbohydrates	47 g
Fiber	3 g
Sugars	34 g
Protein	6 g

Dietary exchanges: 2 fruit, 1 fat-free milk

Side Soups and Salads

Strawberry-Orange Soup 36

Garden Tomato Soup with Pita Sprinkles 37

Squash Soup with Apple "Bobbers" 38

Broccoli Cheese Soup 40

Creamy Carrot Soup 41

Five-Vegetable Soup 43

Strawberry Patch Salad 44

Creamy Chop-Chop Salad 45

Pear and Spinach Salad 45

Spinach and Artichoke Caesar 46

Watermelon and Blueberry Salad 48

Island Fruit Salad 48

Twisted Pasta Salad 49

Sweet Potato Pie Salad 51

Strawberry-Orange Soup

SERVES 4 | ¾ CUP PER SERVING

2 cups frozen unsweetened whole strawberries

½ teaspoon grated orange zest

1 cup fresh orange juice

1 cup (heaping 10 ounces) fat-free plain yogurt

1 tablespoon sugar

Strips of orange zest (optional)

Fruit in soup? Serve this sweet-tart fruit combo as a starter for brunch through dinner, whip it up for an easy afternoon snack, or use it as a refreshing alternative to dessert. (See photograph on page 34.)

In a blender, process the ingredients except the strips of orange zest until well blended. Garnish the soup with the strips of orange zest. Serve immediately.

PER SERVING

Calories	101
Total Fat	0.5 g
Saturated Fat	0.0 g
Trans Fat	0.0 g
Polyunsaturated Fat	0.0 g
Monounsaturated Fat	0.0 g
Cholesterol	1 mg
Sodium	49 mg
Carbohydrates	21 g
Fiber	2 g
Sugars	17 g
Protein	4 g

Dietary exchanges: 1 fruit, ½ fat-free milk

COOK'S TIP: Making this soup with frozen instead of fresh berries saves prep time and eliminates chilling time. If you prefer to use fresh strawberries, chill the soup for an hour before serving.

Garden Tomato Soup with Pita Sprinkles

SERVES 4 | 1 CUP PER SERVING

Cooking spray

1 6-inch whole-wheat pita pocket,
  separated into 2 layers

1 tablespoon shredded or grated
  Parmesan cheese

¼ teaspoon garlic powder

⅛ teaspoon paprika

2 large tomatoes (about 1 pound
  total), peeled and quartered

½ cup low-sodium vegetable broth
  and 1 cup low-sodium vegetable
  broth, divided use

1 medium garlic clove

½ teaspoon dried oregano, crumbled

⅛ teaspoon salt

⅛ teaspoon pepper

PER SERVING

Calories	74
Total Fat	1.0 g
Saturated Fat	0.5 g
Trans Fat	0.0 g
Polyunsaturated Fat	0.5 g
Monounsaturated Fat	0.0 g
Cholesterol	1 mg
Sodium	270 mg
Carbohydrates	14 g
Fiber	3 g
Sugars	3 g
Protein	4 g

Dietary exchanges: ½ starch,
  1 vegetable

Fresh tomatoes provide both vitamins and vibrancy for this soup, which pairs beautifully with the garlicky toasted pita topping.

Preheat the oven to 375°F.

Lightly spray both sides of the pitas with cooking spray. Place with the smooth side up on a baking sheet. Sprinkle the pitas with the Parmesan, garlic powder, and paprika.

Bake for 8 to 10 minutes, or until golden brown. Remove from the baking sheet and let cool completely on a cooling rack, about 10 minutes.

Meanwhile, in a food processor or blender, process the tomatoes, ½ cup broth, garlic, oregano, salt, and pepper for 15 to 20 seconds, or until slightly chunky or the desired texture. Pour into a medium saucepan.

Stir in the remaining 1 cup broth. Bring to a simmer over medium-high heat, stirring occasionally. Reduce the heat and simmer, covered, for 5 minutes, or until the flavors have blended.

Meanwhile, break the toasted pita rounds into ¾-inch pieces. Sprinkle on top of bowls of the soup.

NUTRITION TIP: Most soups are based on some kind of broth, whether it's made from chicken, beef, fish, or a variety of vegetables. Commercial broths can be very high in sodium, so compare labels when you shop to find the ones with the least added salt.

Squash Soup with Apple "Bobbers"

Cooking spray

"BOBBERS"

2 medium apples (about 12 ounces total), halved lengthwise, cut crosswise into ½-inch slices, and each slice halved crosswise

2 teaspoons firmly packed light brown sugar

½ teaspoon ground cinnamon

¼ teaspoon ground allspice

SOUP

2 teaspoons olive oil

¾ cup chopped onion

2 tablespoons grated peeled gingerroot

1 1-pound bag frozen cubed butternut squash (about 1⅓ cups)

1½ teaspoons ground cinnamon

½ teaspoon ground ginger

¼ teaspoon ground allspice

¼ teaspoon ground nutmeg

1¼ cups fat-free, low-sodium chicken broth

⅔ cup apple cider

⅛ teaspoon salt

2 tablespoons fat-free half-and-half

2 teaspoons firmly packed light brown sugar

This creamy, smooth soup packs a nutritional punch courtesy of the butternut squash. The "bobbers" are sweetly spiced, slow-cooked apple slices.

Preheat the oven to 325°F. Line a baking sheet with aluminum foil. Lightly spray with cooking spray.

For the bobbers, put the apples in a single layer on the baking sheet.

In a small bowl, stir together the brown sugar, cinnamon, and allspice. Sprinkle over the apples.

Bake for 40 minutes, or until very tender. Transfer the baking sheet to a cooling rack. Set aside.

Meanwhile, for the soup, heat a medium saucepan over medium heat for 2 minutes. Pour in the oil, swirling to coat the bottom. Add the onion. Reduce the heat to low. Cook for 8 minutes, or until the onion just begins to turn golden, stirring frequently.

Add the gingerroot. Cook for 2 minutes, stirring constantly.

Stir in the squash, cinnamon, ginger, allspice, and nutmeg. Increase the heat to medium and cook for 2 minutes, stirring constantly.

Pour in the broth. Bring to a boil, still over medium heat, stirring frequently. Reduce the heat and simmer, covered, for 15 minutes, or until the squash is tender, stirring frequently.

Stir in the apple cider and salt. Simmer, covered, for 5 minutes. Remove from the heat.

Carefully transfer the soup to a blender or food processor. Process the soup in batches until smooth, being careful not to burn yourself. (You may want to cover the lid with a dish

towel.) As you finish a batch, pour it into an extra pan or medium bowl. When all the soup has been processed, return it to the medium saucepan.

Stir in the half-and-half and brown sugar. Cook over medium heat for 5 minutes, or until heated through, stirring frequently. Serve the soup with the bobbers sprinkled on top. If you use large, shallow soup bowls, all the bobbers should fit perfectly. If your bowls are smaller in diameter, save any leftover bobbers for snacking or to replace croutons in salads.

PER SERVING

Calories	196
Total Fat	2.5 g
Saturated Fat	0.5 g
Trans Fat	0.0 g
Polyunsaturated Fat	0.5 g
Monounsaturated Fat	1.5 g
Cholesterol	0 mg
Sodium	110 mg
Carbohydrates	44 g
Fiber	5 g
Sugars	24 g
Protein	4 g
Dietary exchanges: 2 starch, 1 fruit	

COOK'S TIP: When you select your favorite apples for this recipe, consider using one Granny Smith for tartness and green color and one sweet red apple, such as Rome Beauty, Fuji, Jonathan, or Gala.

Broccoli Cheese Soup

SERVES 6 | 1 CUP PER SERVING

1½ teaspoons olive oil

2 medium carrots, thinly sliced

2 medium ribs of celery, thinly sliced

9 ounces broccoli florets, chopped (about 3 cups)

2 medium green onions, thinly sliced

3 cups fat-free, low-sodium chicken broth

1½ cups fat-free half-and-half

¼ cup all-purpose flour

⅛ teaspoon pepper

½ cup shredded low-fat Cheddar cheese

2 tablespoons shredded or grated Parmesan cheese

Chunks of nutrient-dense broccoli and carrot make this hearty soup a good starter for a light lunch or dinner.

In a large saucepan, heat the olive oil over medium-high heat, swirling to coat the bottom. Cook the carrots and celery for 2 minutes, stirring occasionally.

Stir in the broccoli and green onions. Cook for 3 to 4 minutes, or until the vegetables are tender-crisp. Stir in the broth. Bring to a simmer.

Meanwhile, in a small bowl, whisk together the half-and-half, flour, and pepper. Stir into the soup once it has reached a simmer. Simmer for 2 to 3 minutes, or until thickened, stirring occasionally.

Add the Cheddar and Parmesan. Remove from the heat. Stir until the cheeses are melted.

> **NUTRITION TIP:** Packing lunches for school or work gives you much more control over what your family eats. Make soups like this one portable by putting them in a thermos or microwaveable container.

PER SERVING

Calories	125
Total Fat	2.5 g
Saturated Fat	1.0 g
Trans Fat	0.0 g
Polyunsaturated Fat	0.0 g
Monounsaturated Fat	1.0 g
Cholesterol	3 mg
Sodium	218 mg
Carbohydrates	18 g
Fiber	2 g
Sugars	6 g
Protein	10 g

Dietary exchanges: 1 starch, 1 vegetable, 1 very lean meat

Creamy Carrot Soup

SERVES 4 | ¾ CUP PER SERVING

4 medium carrots (about 1 pound total), quartered lengthwise, cut into pieces 2 inches long

1 medium sweet onion (about 9 ounces), such as Maui, OsoSweet, or Vidalia, cut into 1½-inch chunks

2 teaspoons olive oil

¼ teaspoon ground coriander

⅛ teaspoon salt

⅛ teaspoon pepper

1¼ cups water and ½ cup water, divided use

¾ cup low-sodium vegetable broth

1 teaspoon fresh lime juice

2 teaspoons fat-free sour cream and 1 tablespoon plus 1 teaspoon fat-free sour cream, divided use

2 teaspoons finely snipped fresh cilantro

PER SERVING

Calories	72
Total Fat	2.5 g
Saturated Fat	0.5 g
Trans Fat	0.0 g
Polyunsaturated Fat	0.5 g
Monounsaturated Fat	1.5 g
Cholesterol	1 mg
Sodium	142 mg
Carbohydrates	12 g
Fiber	3 g
Sugars	6 g
Protein	2 g

Dietary exchanges: 2 vegetable, ½ fat

Here's a colorful, naturally sweet soup with a smooth texture and subtle carrot flavor that even the youngest kids in the family will love.

Preheat the oven to 425°F.

Put the carrots and onion in a single layer on a rimmed baking sheet. Drizzle with the oil.

Sprinkle the coriander, salt, and pepper over the carrots and onion. Using your fingertips, rub in the oil and spices.

Roast for 30 to 35 minutes, or until the carrots are deeply browned and tender when tested with a fork, stirring once halfway through.

Meanwhile, in a medium saucepan, combine 1¼ cups water and the broth. Bring to a simmer over medium-high heat, about 6 minutes. Leave the pan on the burner but turn off the heat. Cover to keep warm.

When the vegetables are roasted, scrape them into a food processor or blender. Add the broth mixture. Process for 2 minutes, or until smooth, being careful not to burn yourself. (You may want to cover the lid with a dish towel.) Return the soup to the pan.

Stir in the lime juice and remaining ½ cup water. Cook over medium-low heat for 3 minutes, or until the soup is hot, stirring constantly. Remove from the heat.

Stir in 2 teaspoons sour cream. Serve garnished with the remaining sour cream and cilantro.

NUTRITION TIP: Carrots and other orange vegetables are excellent sources of beta-carotene, a powerful antioxidant. In general, the deeper the color, the more nutrients a vegetable contains.

Five-Vegetable Soup

SERVES 4 | 1 CUP PER SERVING

2 teaspoons olive oil

¼ cup chopped onion

2 medium garlic cloves, minced

2 cups water

1 medium parsnip, chopped

1 large carrot, chopped

2 tablespoons no-salt-added tomato paste

½ teaspoon dried rosemary, finely crushed

2 ounces spinach, coarsely chopped

2 medium Italian plum (Roma) tomatoes, chopped

1 teaspoon balsamic vinegar

¼ teaspoon pepper

⅛ teaspoon salt

PER SERVING

Calories	72
Total Fat	2.5 g
Saturated Fat	0.5 g
Trans Fat	0.0 g
Polyunsaturated Fat	0.5 g
Monounsaturated Fat	1.5 g
Cholesterol	0 mg
Sodium	113 mg
Carbohydrates	12 g
Fiber	3 g
Sugars	5 g
Protein	2 g

Dietary exchanges: 2 vegetable, ½ fat

This simple and delicious soup is a great way to introduce younger children to new vegetables, such as the parsnip used here, because the pieces can be small and unobtrusive. Serve with crusty whole-wheat bread to soak in the soup.

In a large saucepan, heat the oil over medium-high heat, swirling to coat the bottom. Cook the onion for 3 minutes, or until soft, stirring occasionally.

Stir in the garlic. Cook for 1 minute.

Stir in the water, parsnip, carrot, tomato paste, and rosemary. Bring to a boil, still on medium high. Reduce the heat and simmer, covered, for 10 minutes, or until the parsnip is tender.

Stir in the spinach and tomatoes. Cook for 2 minutes, or just until the spinach wilts. Remove from the heat.

Stir in the vinegar, pepper, and salt.

COOK'S TIP: To remove the sand from spinach, put the leaves in a large bowl of cold water. Lift them out, discard the sandy water, and repeat the process until no sand remains in the bowl.

NUTRITION TIP: Vegetable soup makes a satisfying but low-calorie snack or light lunch. Keep it on hand for a guilt-free pick-me-up or easy after-school snack.

Strawberry Patch Salad

SERVES 4 | 1½ CUPS SALAD AND 1½ TABLESPOONS DRESSING PER SERVING

6 cups bite-size pieces mixed salad greens

8 medium strawberries, sliced

2 tablespoons sliced almonds, dry-roasted

CITRUS DRESSING

2 tablespoons fresh orange juice

2 tablespoons olive oil (extra-virgin preferred)

1 tablespoon minced shallot

2 teaspoons honey

2 teaspoons white wine vinegar

¼ teaspoon pepper (coarsely ground preferred)

The light, sweet flavor of the citrus dressing refreshes everyday greens. Almonds give a healthy crunch, and bright red strawberries add eye appeal.

Put the salad greens in a large salad bowl. Sprinkle with the strawberries and almonds.

In a small bowl, whisk together the dressing ingredients. Pour over the salad. Toss gently to coat. Serve immediately for the best texture.

PER SERVING

Calories	121
Total Fat	8.5 g
Saturated Fat	1.0 g
Trans Fat	0.0 g
Polyunsaturated Fat	1.0 g
Monounsaturated Fat	6.0 g
Cholesterol	0 mg
Sodium	22 mg
Carbohydrates	11 g
Fiber	3 g
Sugars	6 g
Protein	2 g
Dietary exchanges: ½ carbohydrate, 2 fat	

Creamy Chop-Chop Salad

SERVES 4 | 1½ CUPS PER SERVING

SALAD

- 4 cups finely chopped romaine
- 1 rib of celery, finely chopped
- 3 green onions, finely chopped
- 1 Italian plum (Roma) tomato, seeded and finely chopped

DRESSING

- ¼ cup fat-free sour cream
- 2 tablespoons light mayonnaise
- 2 tablespoons fresh lemon juice
- ¼ teaspoon chili powder
- ¼ teaspoon garlic powder

The finely chopped romaine and vegetables make this tangy salad a favorite choice for children.

In a salad bowl, combine the salad ingredients.

In a small bowl, whisk together the dressing ingredients. Pour over the salad. Toss gently. Serve immediately for the best texture.

PER SERVING	
Calories	59
Total Fat	2.5 g
Saturated Fat	0.5 g
Trans Fat	0.0 g
Polyunsaturated Fat	1.5 g
Monounsaturated Fat	0.5 g
Cholesterol	5 mg
Sodium	86 mg
Carbohydrates	7 g
Fiber	2 g
Sugars	3 g
Protein	2 g

Dietary exchanges: ½ carbohydrate, ½ fat

Pear and Spinach Salad

SERVES 4 | 1½ CUPS SALAD AND 2 TABLESPOONS DRESSING PER SERVING

ORANGE VINAIGRETTE

- ¼ cup fresh orange juice
- 1 tablespoon cider vinegar
- 1 tablespoon honey
- 1 teaspoon olive oil (extra-virgin preferred)
- ¼ teaspoon dried basil, crumbled
- ⅛ teaspoon pepper

SALAD

- 1 large pear, halved lengthwise, cored, and cut crosswise into thin slices
- 4 ounces baby spinach
- 2 tablespoons chopped walnuts, dry-roasted
- 2 teaspoons grated orange zest

Dark-green spinach, rich in vitamins A and K, provides a pretty backdrop for juicy pear slices.

In a medium bowl, whisk together the vinaigrette ingredients.

Add the pear and spinach, tossing gently to combine. Sprinkle with the walnuts and orange zest. Serve immediately for the best texture.

PER SERVING	
Calories	99
Total Fat	3.5 g
Saturated Fat	0.5 g
Trans Fat	0.0 g
Polyunsaturated Fat	2.0 g
Monounsaturated Fat	1.0 g
Cholesterol	0 mg
Sodium	24 mg
Carbohydrates	17 g
Fiber	3 g
Sugars	12 g
Protein	2 g

Dietary exchanges: 1 fruit, 1 fat

Spinach and Artichoke Caesar

PITA SQUARES

1 5-inch whole-wheat pita pocket, separated into 2 layers and cut into ½-inch pieces

Olive oil spray

¼ teaspoon garlic powder

½ teaspoon shredded or grated Parmesan cheese

DRESSING

1 tablespoon fresh lemon juice

1 tablespoon shredded or grated Parmesan cheese

2 teaspoons olive oil (extra-virgin preferred)

2 teaspoons red wine vinegar

2 teaspoons Worcestershire sauce (lowest sodium available)

1 medium garlic clove, minced

½ teaspoon dry mustard

¼ teaspoon pepper

SALAD

4 ounces baby spinach

½ cup thinly sliced red onion

½ 15¾-ounce can (about ¾ cup) quartered artichoke hearts, rinsed, well drained, and leaves separated

3 ounces button mushrooms, sliced (about ¾ cup)

Homemade pita squares make the perfect croutons for this fiber-rich salad with a Mediterranean twist.

Preheat the oven to 350°F.

On a nonstick baking sheet, place the pita pieces with the rough side up. Lightly spray with olive oil spray. Sprinkle with the garlic powder and ½ teaspoon Parmesan.

Bake for 10 minutes, or until crisp. Transfer the baking sheet to a cooling rack. Set aside and let the squares cool.

Meanwhile, in a blender or mini food processor, process the dressing ingredients until smooth.

In a large bowl, toss together the spinach and onion. Add the artichokes and mushrooms. Toss well.

Pour the dressing over all. Toss lightly. Sprinkle with the pita squares. Serve immediately for the best texture.

PER SERVING

Calories	89
Total Fat	3.5 g
Saturated Fat	0.5 g
Trans Fat	0.0 g
Polyunsaturated Fat	0.5 g
Monounsaturated Fat	2.0 g
Cholesterol	1 mg
Sodium	200 mg
Carbohydrates	13 g
Fiber	2 g
Sugars	2 g
Protein	4 g

Dietary exchanges: ½ starch, 1 vegetable, ½ fat

COOK'S TIP: Do not substitute marinated artichokes from a jar for the canned artichokes in this salad. Marinated artichokes are higher in sodium and fat than the canned, water-packed variety.

COOK'S TIP: Mincing the garlic before processing it in the blender helps makes sure the finished dressing will be smooth.

Watermelon and Blueberry Salad

SERVES 4 | ¾ CUP PER SERVING

2 cups diced watermelon, chilled

1 cup fresh or frozen blueberries, chilled, thawed and patted dry if frozen

¼ cup pineapple juice or ginger ale, chilled

1 tablespoon snipped fresh mint

1 tablespoon fresh lemon juice

This unusual salad is surprisingly refreshing because the watermelon absorbs the dressing's sweet lemony mint flavor.

In a medium bowl, gently stir together the ingredients. Serve immediately for peak flavor.

> COOK'S TIP: If you purchase watermelon cubes to use in this dish, cut them into smaller pieces before combining with the other ingredients so they'll absorb more of the liquid.

PER SERVING	
Calories	54
Total Fat	0.0 g
Saturated Fat	0.0 g
Trans Fat	0.0 g
Polyunsaturated Fat	0.0 g
Monounsaturated Fat	0.0 g
Cholesterol	0 mg
Sodium	3 mg
Carbohydrates	13 g
Fiber	1 g
Sugars	10 g
Protein	1 g
Dietary exchanges: 1 fruit	

Island Fruit Salad

SERVES 4 | ½ CUP FRUIT AND ¼ CUP SAUCE PER SERVING

LIME SAUCE

1 6-ounce container fat-free vanilla yogurt

2 tablespoons confectioners' sugar

½ teaspoon grated lime zest

2 tablespoons fresh lime juice

1 cup pineapple chunks

1 medium mango, cut into 1-inch cubes

Combining luscious fresh fruit and fat-free yogurt, this versatile dish can be served for breakfast, lunch, or dinner!

In a small bowl, stir together the sauce ingredients. Spoon onto salad plates. Using the back of a spoon, spread into a thin circle.

Arrange the pineapple and mango attractively on the sauce.

> NUTRITION TIP: Try this salad with different fruit, or use the sauce for dipping with after-school fruit snacks.

PER SERVING	
Calories	108
Total Fat	0.5 g
Saturated Fat	0.0 g
Trans Fat	0.0 g
Polyunsaturated Fat	0.0 g
Monounsaturated Fat	0.0 g
Cholesterol	1 mg
Sodium	31 mg
Carbohydrates	26 g
Fiber	2 g
Sugars	23 g
Protein	3 g
Dietary exchanges: 1 fruit, ½ carbohydrate	

Twisted Pasta Salad

SERVES 4 | ½ CUP PER SERVING

2 ounces dried whole-grain pasta, such as rotini or penne

½ medium rib of celery, chopped

1 ounce broccoli florets (heaping ¼ cup)

¼ medium yellow bell pepper, diced

4 grape tomatoes

1 medium green onion, chopped

3 tablespoons fat-free sour cream

2 tablespoons shredded or grated Parmesan cheese

2 tablespoons light mayonnaise

1 tablespoon Dijon mustard

¼ teaspoon pepper

PER SERVING

Calories	110
Total Fat	4.0 g
Saturated Fat	1.0 g
Trans Fat	0.0 g
Polyunsaturated Fat	1.5 g
Monounsaturated Fat	1.0 g
Cholesterol	6 mg
Sodium	195 mg
Carbohydrates	16 g
Fiber	3 g
Sugars	2 g
Protein	5 g
Dietary exchanges: 1 starch, ½ fat	

Combine crisp fresh veggies with creamy Parmesan dressing in this all-purpose whole-grain salad. For kid appeal, pick a fun pasta shape that pleases your family!

Prepare the pasta using the package directions, omitting the salt and oil. Drain well in a colander.

Meanwhile, in a medium bowl, combine the celery, broccoli, bell pepper, tomatoes, and green onion.

In a small bowl, whisk together the remaining ingredients.

Add the cooked pasta to the celery mixture. Pour the dressing over all. Toss to combine. Serve at room temperature for the best flavor or cover and refrigerate until chilled.

Sweet Potato Pie Salad

SERVES 4 | ½ CUP PER SERVING

3 tablespoons coarsely chopped pecans

¼ teaspoon pumpkin pie spice and ¼ teaspoon pumpkin pie spice, divided use

¼ teaspoon dark brown sugar

1½ medium sweet potatoes (about 20 ounces total), peeled, cut crosswise into ¾-inch pieces, and quartered

2 teaspoons olive oil and 1 teaspoon olive oil (extra-virgin preferred), divided use

⅛ teaspoon salt

2 teaspoons very finely chopped shallots

1 teaspoon snipped fresh parsley

PER SERVING

Calories	193
Total Fat	7.5 g
Saturated Fat	1.0 g
Trans Fat	0.0 g
Polyunsaturated Fat	1.5 g
Monounsaturated Fat	4.5 g
Cholesterol	0 mg
Sodium	151 mg
Carbohydrates	30 g
Fiber	5 g
Sugars	7 g
Protein	3 g
Dietary exchanges: 2 starch, 1 fat	

This unusual dish, seasoned with classic pie spices, offers the health benefits of sweet potatoes and crunchy pecans as a salad instead of dessert.

Preheat the oven to 425°F.

In a small bowl, stir together the pecans, ¼ teaspoon pumpkin pie spice, and brown sugar. Set aside.

Place the sweet potatoes in a single layer on a rimmed baking sheet. Drizzle with 2 teaspoons oil. Sprinkle with the salt and remaining ¼ teaspoon pumpkin pie spice.

Roast for 20 minutes, or until tender, stirring once halfway through. Transfer to a medium serving bowl. Reduce the oven temperature to 350°F.

Spread the reserved pecan mixture on the same baking sheet. Dry-roast in the oven for about 5 minutes, or until the pecans become just fragrant.

Add the pecan mixture, shallots, and parsley to the sweet potatoes. Toss gently. Drizzle with the remaining 1 teaspoon oil. Toss again. Serve at room temperature.

> NUTRITION TIP: Like other nuts, pecans are rich in healthy unsaturated fats, but they are also high in calories. Dry-roasting them gives more flavor and crunch from fewer nuts.

Everyday Dinners

SEAFOOD

Oodles of Noodles Tuna Casserole 55

Salmon with Sweet-and-Spicy Salsa 56

Tuna Kebabs with Citrusy Brown Rice Pilaf 59

POULTRY

"It's Greek to Me" Chicken 60

Mini Chicken Pot Pies 62

Turkey Surprise Meat Loaf 64

(continued on following page)

MEATS

Spaghetti and Meatballs with
Roasted Red Bell Pepper Sauce 67

Peach-Chutney Pork Roast 68

Easy Weeknight Chili 70

VEGETARIAN

Bean and Potato Enchiladas Verde 71

Build-Your-Own Pizzas 73

Popeye's Special Lasagna 74

Oodles of Noodles Tuna Casserole

SERVES 4 | 1¼ CUPS PER SERVING

Cooking spray

5 ounces (about 3¾ cups) dried no-yolk extra-wide noodles (whole-grain preferred)

1 large rib of celery, chopped (about ½ cup)

2 tablespoons finely chopped onion

2 tablespoons water

¼ large red bell pepper, chopped

1¼ cups fat-free milk

1 tablespoon all-purpose flour

¼ teaspoon pepper

1 cup shredded low-fat Cheddar cheese

1 6-ounce can low-sodium chunk light tuna in water, well drained and flaked

¾ cup frozen peas, partially thawed

2 tablespoons sliced almonds

1 tablespoon shredded or grated Parmesan cheese

PER SERVING

Calories	305
Total Fat	5.0 g
Saturated Fat	2.0 g
Trans Fat	0.0 g
Polyunsaturated Fat	1.0 g
Monounsaturated Fat	2.0 g
Cholesterol	21 mg
Sodium	294 mg
Carbohydrates	38 g
Fiber	7 g
Sugars	8 g
Protein	29 g

Dietary exchanges: 2½ starch, 3 very lean meat

Updated with ingredients to please health-conscious parents, this classic has all the elements that make it such a hit with kids: creamy cheese sauce, mild tuna, big noodles, and a crunchy topping.

Preheat the oven to 375°F. Lightly spray a 1½-quart glass casserole dish with cooking spray.

Prepare the pasta using the package directions, omitting the salt and oil. Drain well in a colander. Set aside.

Meanwhile, in a medium saucepan, stir together the celery, onion, and water. Cook, covered, over medium-high heat for 3 minutes.

Stir in the bell pepper. Cook, covered, for 1 minute.

In a medium bowl, whisk together the milk, flour, and pepper. Pour into the celery mixture. Reduce the heat to medium and cook for 3 minutes, or until slightly thickened and bubbly, stirring constantly. Stir in the Cheddar. Reduce the heat to low and cook for 1 minute, or until the Cheddar is melted, stirring constantly. Remove from the heat.

Stir in the tuna and peas. Add the cooked pasta, stirring to coat. Spoon into the casserole dish. Sprinkle with the almonds and Parmesan.

Bake for 12 to 15 minutes, or until bubbly and lightly browned.

NUTRITION TIP: Tuna comes in all sorts of packages, varieties, and flavors these days. The convenience and availability are great, but the most important factor for good health is to choose low-sodium tuna whenever you can.

Salmon with Sweet-and-Spicy Salsa

SERVES 4 | 3 OUNCES SALMON AND ¼ CUP PINEAPPLE SALSA PER SERVING

SALSA

¾ cup diced pineapple

2 tablespoons finely chopped red onion

2 tablespoons snipped fresh cilantro

2 tablespoons finely chopped red bell pepper

1 teaspoon seeded and finely chopped fresh jalapeño

2 teaspoons plain rice vinegar

Cooking spray

4 salmon fillets with skin (about 5 ounces each), rinsed and patted dry

2 tablespoons no-salt-added ketchup

1 tablespoon hoisin sauce

1 tablespoon honey

1 teaspoon plain rice vinegar

1 small garlic clove, minced

A sweet-and-spicy pineapple salsa is a great way to jazz up baked salmon, a fish that is a super source of omega-3s and is low in saturated fat and cholesterol.

In a small bowl, stir together the salsa ingredients. Cover and refrigerate until serving time, up to 8 hours.

Preheat the oven to 350°F. Line a baking sheet with aluminum foil. Lightly spray with cooking spray.

Place the fish with the skin side down on the foil.

In a small bowl, whisk together the remaining ingredients. Spread over the top and sides of the fish.

Bake for 20 minutes, or until the fish is cooked to the desired doneness. Serve with the salsa.

NUTRITION TIP: Make an extra batch of this salsa to serve with baked tortilla chips for a snack or appetizer or to spoon over baked chicken breasts. For an easy dessert, broil any extra pineapple and serve over fat-free frozen yogurt or with a light drizzle of maple syrup.

PER SERVING

Calories	190
Total Fat	4.5 g
Saturated Fat	0.5 g
Trans Fat	0.0 g
Polyunsaturated Fat	1.5 g
Monounsaturated Fat	1.0 g
Cholesterol	65 mg
Sodium	107 mg
Carbohydrates	12 g
Fiber	1 g
Sugars	10 g
Protein	25 g

Dietary exchanges: 1 carbohydrate, 3 lean meat

Tuna Kebabs with Citrusy Brown Rice Pilaf

1¾ cups water

¼ cup fresh orange juice and ¼ cup fresh orange juice, divided use

⅔ cup uncooked brown rice

1 pound tuna steaks, about ¾ inch thick, rinsed and patted dry, cut into 16 cubes

1 zucchini, about 4 inches long, cut crosswise into 8 pieces

½ medium red bell pepper, cut into 8 squares

4 small whole button mushrooms

¼ cup fresh lemon juice

2 medium garlic cloves, minced

1 teaspoon canola or corn oil

1 teaspoon soy sauce (lowest sodium available)

Cooking spray

2 medium green onions, chopped

1 medium orange, peeled and sections removed from membranes, chopped

PER SERVING

Calories	237
Total Fat	2.5 g
Saturated Fat	0.5 g
Trans Fat	0.0 g
Polyunsaturated Fat	1.0 g
Monounsaturated Fat	1.0 g
Cholesterol	51 mg
Sodium	89 mg
Carbohydrates	23 g
Fiber	3 g
Sugars	7 g
Protein	30 g

Dietary exchanges: 1 starch, ½ fruit, 3 very lean meat

How about fish on a stick instead of fish sticks tonight? These tasty kebabs feature cubes of tuna and vegetables on brown rice brightened with bits of green onions and orange.

In a medium saucepan, stir together the water, ¼ cup orange juice, and rice. Bring to a boil, covered, over medium-high heat. Reduce the heat and simmer, covered, for about 45 minutes, or until the rice is tender and the liquid is absorbed. Remove from the heat.

Meanwhile, put the fish, zucchini, bell pepper, and mushrooms in a glass dish, such as an 11 × 7 × 2-inch baking dish.

In a small nonmetallic bowl, stir together the lemon juice, garlic, oil, soy sauce, and remaining ¼ cup orange juice. Pour half the mixture over the fish and vegetables, turning with tongs to coat. Cover and refrigerate for 30 minutes, turning once after 15 minutes. Reserve the unused mixture.

Lightly spray the grill rack with cooking spray. Preheat the grill on medium high. Soak four 12-inch wooden skewers for at least 10 minutes in cold water to keep them from charring, or use metal skewers.

Drain the fish and vegetables. Discard the marinade. Thread each skewer as follows: fish, zucchini, bell pepper, fish, mushroom, fish, zucchini, bell pepper, fish.

Grill the kebabs for 6 to 8 minutes, or until the fish is cooked to the desired doneness, turning to brown evenly and brushing frequently with the reserved orange juice mixture.

Stir the green onions and orange into the cooked rice. Spoon onto a deep serving platter. Arrange the kebabs over the rice.

"It's Greek to Me" Chicken

SERVES 4 | 3 OUNCES CHICKEN AND 3 TABLESPOONS SAUCE PER SERVING

Cooking spray

CHICKEN

1 pound chicken tenders, all visible fat discarded

1 teaspoon dried oregano, crumbled

1 teaspoon ground cumin

1 teaspoon onion powder

1/2 teaspoon paprika

1/8 teaspoon cayenne

1/8 teaspoon salt

3 tablespoons fresh lemon juice

2 teaspoons olive oil

2 medium garlic cloves, minced

TZATZIKI SAUCE

1/3 cup finely chopped peeled cucumber

1/3 cup fat-free plain yogurt

3 tablespoons fat-free sour cream

2 teaspoons snipped fresh dillweed

2 teaspoons fresh lemon juice

1 medium garlic clove, finely chopped

1/8 teaspoon salt

1/8 teaspoon pepper

Put the flavors of Greece on your family table: broiled chicken, lemon juice, olive oil, and spices balanced by the cool yogurt-based tzatziki sauce.

Preheat the broiler. Line a baking sheet with aluminum foil. Lightly spray with cooking spray.

Put the chicken in a medium nonmetallic bowl. In a small nonmetallic bowl, stir together the oregano, cumin, onion powder, paprika, cayenne, and 1/8 teaspoon salt. Sprinkle over the chicken. Using your fingertips, press the mixture so it adheres to the chicken.

In the same small bowl, combine the 3 tablespoons lemon juice, olive oil, and 2 minced garlic cloves. Pour over the chicken. Using your fingertips, rub into the chicken. Cover the bowl with plastic wrap and refrigerate for 10 minutes. Remove the chicken from the marinade, discarding the marinade. Transfer the chicken to the baking sheet.

Meanwhile, in a separate small bowl, stir together the sauce ingredients.

Broil the chicken 4 to 5 inches from the heat for 8 minutes. Turn over. Broil for 3 minutes, or until just firm to the touch and no longer pink in the center. Serve the sauce over the chicken.

PER SERVING

Calories	157
Total Fat	1.5 g
Saturated Fat	0.5 g
Trans Fat	0.0 g
Polyunsaturated Fat	0.5 g
Monounsaturated Fat	0.5 g
Cholesterol	68 mg
Sodium	246 mg
Carbohydrates	5 g
Fiber	1 g
Sugars	3 g
Protein	29 g

Dietary exchanges: 1/2 carbohydrate, 3 very lean meat

NUTRITION TIP:
Serve this low-cal, low-fat tzatziki sauce as a snacking dip with baked whole-wheat pita triangles or raw vegetables.

MAKE IT A MEAL
WITH whole-wheat couscous and broccoli.

Mini Chicken Pot Pies

SERVES 4 | 1 POT PIE PER SERVING

Cooking spray

1½ teaspoons olive oil and 1 teaspoon olive oil, divided use

1 cup chopped onion

1 cup baby carrots, cut crosswise into ½-inch pieces

1 large rib of celery, cut crosswise into ⅛-inch slices

12 ounces boneless, skinless chicken breasts, all visible fat discarded, cut into 1-inch cubes

2 medium red potatoes (about 8 ounces total), cut into ½-inch pieces, put in a medium bowl, and covered with 1¼ cups water (to keep them from discoloring)

1 10-ounce can low-fat condensed cream of mushroom soup (lowest sodium available)

1 cup fat-free, low-sodium chicken broth

1 teaspoon poultry seasoning

½ teaspoon dried thyme, crumbled

¼ teaspoon paprika

¼ teaspoon pepper

1 cup frozen petite green beans, cut into 1½-inch pieces, or frozen cut green beans

3 sheets phyllo dough, thawed if frozen

Everyone loves chicken pot pie! The phyllo dough in this easy, heart-healthy version gives you wonderful flakiness without the high fat of a typical pie crust.

Preheat the oven to 350°F. Line a baking sheet with aluminum foil. Lightly spray four 2-cup ramekins or 2-cup individual French onion soup tureens with cooking spray. Set aside.

In a 12-inch nonstick skillet or a Dutch oven, heat 1½ teaspoons oil over medium-high heat, swirling to coat the bottom. Add the onion, carrots, and celery. Reduce the heat to medium. Cook for 5 minutes, or until the onion and celery begin to soften, stirring frequently.

Meanwhile, put the chicken in a medium bowl. Drizzle with the remaining 1 teaspoon oil. Rub into the chicken. Stir into the cooked onion mixture. Cook for 3 minutes, or until golden, stirring frequently.

Drain the potatoes well. Pat dry. Stir the potatoes, soup, broth, poultry seasoning, thyme, paprika, and pepper into the chicken mixture. Bring to a simmer, still over medium heat. Remove from the heat.

Stir in the green beans. Spoon into the ramekins. Place on the baking sheet. Set aside to cool while you prepare the phyllo.

Cover a flat surface with wax paper. Unfold the phyllo onto a baking sheet. Keeping the unused phyllo covered with a damp towel or damp paper towels to prevent drying, carefully transfer one sheet of phyllo to the flat surface. Lightly spray the first sheet with cooking spray. Working quickly, uncover the unused phyllo. Peel off a second sheet and place it on the first. Re-cover the unused phyllo. Press the second sheet down so it adheres to the first. Lightly spray the second sheet with cooking spray. Repeat the process with the third sheet. Cut the stack into four 4½- × 5-inch rectangles, reserving the excess dough for another

use or discarding. With the sprayed side up, place the rectangles over the filling. Press down gently into the filling to form a short border. Press the dough against the side of the ramekin. Don't trim any excess; press any overhang up to seal the edges so the filling does not leak out. Lightly spray the edges of the phyllo with cooking spray.

Bake for 40 minutes, or until the phyllo is golden brown and the filling is bubbly. Serve immediately.

PER SERVING

Calories	294
Total Fat	6.0 g
Saturated Fat	1.0 g
Trans Fat	0.0 g
Polyunsaturated Fat	1.5 g
Monounsaturated Fat	3.0 g
Cholesterol	52 mg
Sodium	474 mg
Carbohydrates	35 g
Fiber	4 g
Sugars	7 g
Protein	25 g

Dietary exchanges: 2 starch, 1 vegetable, 3 lean meat

Turkey Surprise Meat Loaf

SERVES 4 | 2 1-INCH SLICES PER SERVING

Cooking spray

1/3 cup fat-free, low-sodium chicken broth

6 dry-packed sun-dried tomato halves

1 1/2 teaspoons canola or corn oil

3/4 cup chopped onion

8 ounces button mushrooms, sliced (about 2 1/2 cups)

1/4 teaspoon salt

1/4 teaspoon pepper

1/2 cup uncooked quick-cooking oatmeal

1/2 teaspoon dried thyme, crumbled

1/4 cup egg substitute

1 pound ground skinless turkey breast

1/2 cup low-fat sour cream

PER SERVING

Calories	262
Total Fat	6.0 g
Saturated Fat	1.5 g
Trans Fat	0.0 g
Polyunsaturated Fat	1.0 g
Monounsaturated Fat	2.0 g
Cholesterol	82 mg
Sodium	263 mg
Carbohydrates	18 g
Fiber	3 g
Sugars	6 g
Protein	34 g

Dietary exchanges: 1/2 starch, 1 vegetable, 3 lean meat

Kids will love it when you slice into this great-tasting meat loaf to find the surprise—a creamy center full of mushrooms! Heart-healthy oatmeal and lean turkey breast help keep down the saturated fat.

Preheat the oven to 375°F. Line an 8 1/2 × 4 1/2 × 2 1/2-inch loaf pan with aluminum foil, leaving some overhang. Lightly spray with cooking spray.

In a small saucepan, bring the broth to a boil over high heat. Remove from the heat. Add the tomatoes. Set aside.

In a large nonstick skillet, heat the oil over medium-high heat, swirling to coat the bottom. Cook the onion for 4 to 5 minutes, or until soft and beginning to brown.

Stir in the mushrooms, salt, and pepper. Cook for 6 to 8 minutes, or until soft, stirring occasionally. Transfer half the mixture to a food processor. Remove the other half from the heat.

Drain the rehydrated tomatoes, reserving the broth. Add the tomatoes, oatmeal, and thyme to the processor. Pulse 10 to 15 times, or until the mixture resembles granola.

Add the drained broth and egg substitute. Pulse 10 times.

Add the turkey. Pulse 5 to 10 times, or until blended. Spoon 2 cups mixture into the loaf pan. Using the back of a spoon, gently press the mixture from the center toward all 4 sides to form a depression with a sloping border about 1 inch high and about 3/4 inch thick.

Stir the sour cream into the reserved onion mixture. Spoon into the depression.

Add the remaining turkey mixture around the sides, then gently over the top (if you press too hard, the sour cream might ooze out the sides). Using the back of the spoon, smooth the

turkey mixture and press it down gently around the sides to seal. The meat loaf should be slightly mounded in the center, similar to a loaf of bread.

Bake for 1 hour to 1 hour 10 minutes, or until the internal temperature registers 165°F on an instant-read thermometer inserted in the center. Remove from the oven. Let stand for 5 minutes. Using the foil overhang, carefully transfer the meat loaf, still on the foil, from the pan to a flat surface. Using a spatula, transfer the meat loaf from the foil onto a platter. Slice and serve.

Spaghetti and Meatballs with Roasted Red Bell Pepper Sauce

SERVES 4 | 4 MEATBALLS, ½ CUP PASTA, AND ½ CUP SAUCE PER SERVING

MEATBALLS

1 pound extra-lean ground beef

1 slice light whole wheat bread, torn into small pieces

¼ cup egg substitute

¼ cup fat-free milk

1½ teaspoons dried Italian seasoning, crumbled

1 teaspoon Worcestershire sauce (lowest sodium available)

1 teaspoon onion powder

½ teaspoon garlic powder

¼ teaspoon pepper

4 ounces uncooked whole-wheat spaghetti

SAUCE

1 12-ounce jar roasted red bell peppers, drained

½ cup fat-free, low-sodium chicken broth

3 tablespoons all-purpose flour

1 medium garlic clove, minced

¼ teaspoon crushed red pepper flakes

½ cup fat-free half-and-half

¼ cup shredded or grated Parmesan cheese

2 tablespoons snipped fresh parsley

A popular Italian dish gets a modern update with extra-lean ground beef and whole-wheat bread and pasta.

Preheat the oven to 375°F. Line a baking sheet with foil.

In a medium bowl, using your hands or a spoon, combine the meatball ingredients. Shape into 16 meatballs about 2 inches in diameter. Transfer to the baking sheet.

Bake for 25 to 30 minutes, or until no longer pink in the center. Drain on paper towels.

Meanwhile, prepare the pasta using the package directions, omitting the salt and oil. Drain well in a colander.

While the meatballs bake and the pasta cooks, in a food processor or blender, process the roasted peppers, broth, flour, garlic, and red pepper flakes for 20 to 30 seconds, or until smooth. Pour the sauce into a medium saucepan. Bring to a simmer over medium-high heat, stirring occasionally.

Gradually add the half-and-half. Reduce the heat and simmer for 1 to 2 minutes, or until the mixture is thickened, stirring occasionally. Increase the heat to medium low.

Stir in the Parmesan. Cook for 1 minute, or until the cheese is melted, stirring occasionally. Reduce the heat to low and keep the mixture warm, stirring occasionally.

Spoon the pasta onto plates. Top with the meatballs. Pour the sauce over all. Garnish with the parsley.

PER SERVING	
Calories	362
Total Fat	7.5 g
Saturated Fat	3.0 g
Trans Fat	0.5 g
Polyunsaturated Fat	1.0 g
Monounsaturated Fat	3.0 g
Cholesterol	66 mg
Sodium	450 mg
Carbohydrates	40 g
Fiber	5 g
Sugars	5 g
Protein	36 g
Dietary exchanges: 2 starch, 1 vegetable, 4 lean meat	

Peach-Chutney Pork Roast

SERVES 4 | 3 OUNCES PORK AND 3 TABLESPOONS CHUTNEY PER SERVING

4½ ounces (about 1 cup) frozen unsweetened sliced peaches, partially thawed, chopped

2 teaspoons all-fruit orange marmalade and 2 tablespoons all-fruit orange marmalade, divided use

2 teaspoons finely chopped onion

1 teaspoon white wine vinegar

½ teaspoon minced peeled gingerroot

1 small garlic clove, minced

⅛ teaspoon salt

Cooking spray

1 1-pound boneless center-cut pork loin roast, all visible fat discarded

¼ teaspoon salt-free lemon pepper

PER SERVING

Calories	185
Total Fat	6.0 g
Saturated Fat	1.5 g
Trans Fat	0.0 g
Polyunsaturated Fat	0.5 g
Monounsaturated Fat	2.0 g
Cholesterol	66 mg
Sodium	117 mg
Carbohydrates	10 g
Fiber	1 g
Sugars	7 g
Protein	22 g

Dietary exchanges: ½ fruit, 3 lean meat

You can enjoy this tender pork roast at any time of year since the chutney features frozen fruit. The peaches here are flavored with orange marmalade and a hint of ginger.

In a small bowl, stir together the peaches, 2 teaspoons marmalade, onion, vinegar, gingerroot, garlic, and salt. Let stand at room temperature while roasting the pork.

Preheat the oven to 425°F. Line a small roasting pan with aluminum foil. Lightly spray with cooking spray.

Sprinkle the pork with the lemon pepper. Place in the pan.

Roast for 30 minutes. Brush the top of the pork with the remaining 2 tablespoons marmalade. Roast for 15 minutes, or until the pork is just slightly pink in the center and registers 155°F on an instant-read thermometer. Remove from the oven. Cover loosely with aluminum foil. Let stand for 10 minutes. Cut the pork into medium-thick slices. Serve with the chutney.

COOK'S TIP: Pork loin roasts are readily available but often are precut by the butcher into 2- or 3-pound pieces. Ask the butcher to cut a 1-pound roast for you, or purchase a 2-pound roast and cut in half. Freeze the half that you're not using right away for up to 12 months. When you're ready to use it, let the pork thaw in the refrigerator for about 24 hours.

NUTRITION TIP: Since food suppliers freeze fruit and vegetables within hours of their being picked, frozen peaches and other frozen fruits are just as vitamin-packed as fresh.

Easy Weeknight Chili

SERVES 4 | 1½ CUPS PER SERVING

8   ounces extra-lean ground beef

1   small green bell pepper, chopped

¾   cup chopped onion

2   medium garlic cloves, minced

1   tablespoon chili powder

2   teaspoons ground cumin

½   teaspoon dried oregano, crumbled

½   teaspoon salt

1   15-ounce can no-salt-added
    kidney beans or no-salt-added
    black beans, rinsed and drained

1   14.5-ounce can no-salt-added
    diced tomatoes, undrained

1   14-ounce can fat-free, no-salt-
    added beef broth

1   tablespoon yellow cornmeal
    Snipped fresh cilantro (optional)

Unlike most other chilis, this one doesn't require hours of cooking. Using extra-lean ground beef along with kidney beans or black beans gives you a robust mix that's low in unhealthy saturated fat but high in good nutrition.

I n a large saucepan, cook the beef, bell pepper, onion, and garlic over medium-high heat for 8 minutes, or until the beef is browned, stirring occasionally to turn and break up the beef.

Stir in the chili powder, cumin, oregano, and salt. Stir in the beans, tomatoes with liquid, and broth. Increase the heat to high and bring to a boil. Reduce the heat and simmer, covered, for 15 minutes, or until the bell pepper is tender.

Gradually add the cornmeal to the chili, stirring constantly. Cook for 2 minutes, or until thickened. Serve sprinkled with the cilantro.

PER SERVING

Calories	224
Total Fat	3.5 g
Saturated Fat	1.0 g
Trans Fat	0.0 g
Polyunsaturated Fat	0.5 g
Monounsaturated Fat	1.0 g
Cholesterol	31 mg
Sodium	452 mg
Carbohydrates	30 g
Fiber	8 g
Sugars	8 g
Protein	21 g

Dietary exchanges: 1½ starch,
  2 vegetable, 2 very lean meat

NUTRITION TIP:
For extra crunch and more vegetables, you can add familiar favorites such as chopped celery or carrots when you add the bell pepper. It's not authentic to the Old West, but it's a painless way to up your family's veggie intake.

NUTRITION TIP:
Tomatoes contain the antioxidant lycopene, which gives them their deep red color. Cooking tomatoes releases and concentrates the lycopene.

Bean and Potato Enchiladas Verde

Cooking spray

1 15-ounce can no-salt-added pinto beans, rinsed, drained, and mashed to desired texture

1 14.5-ounce can no-salt-added stewed tomatoes, undrained, divided use

1 tablespoon snipped fresh cilantro

1 tablespoon fresh lime juice

1 teaspoon chili powder

1 teaspoon salt-free Southwest chipotle seasoning blend; other salt-free smoky, spicy seasoning blend; or smoked paprika

1 teaspoon canola or corn oil

1½ cups frozen diced fat-free hash brown potatoes

¼ cup chopped onion

1 4-ounce can chopped green chiles, undrained

¾ cup green chile enchilada sauce

8 6-inch yellow corn tortillas

½ cup low-fat Cheddar cheese

PER SERVING

Calories	311
Total Fat	4.0 g
Saturated Fat	1.0 g
Trans Fat	0.0 g
Polyunsaturated Fat	1.0 g
Monounsaturated Fat	1.5 g
Cholesterol	3 mg
Sodium	520 mg
Carbohydrates	54 g
Fiber	10 g
Sugars	9 g
Protein	14 g

Dietary exchanges: 3 starch, 2 vegetable, 1 very lean meat

A hearty vegetarian spin on a Mexican classic, this dish is surprisingly easy to put together. We use low-fat cheese in this recipe and other baked dishes because it melts better than fat-free.

Preheat the oven to 350°F. Lightly spray a 9-inch square baking pan with cooking spray.

In a medium bowl, stir together the beans, ⅓ can stewed tomatoes (about ½ cup, including some liquid), cilantro, lime juice, chili powder, and seasoning blend.

In a medium nonstick skillet, heat the oil for 1 minute, swirling to coat the bottom. Cook the potatoes and onion for 12 minutes, or until golden brown, stirring frequently. Remove from the heat.

Stir the chiles with liquid into the potato mixture. Stir into the bean mixture.

In a separate medium bowl, stir together the remaining stewed tomatoes with liquid (about 1¼ cups) and enchilada sauce. Spread ½ cup mixture in the baking pan.

Put the tortillas on a microwaveable plate. Microwave on 100 percent power (high) for 45 seconds to soften. Put the tortillas in a single layer on a flat surface. Spread the bean mixture almost to the edge of each. Roll up jelly-roll style and place with the seam side down in the baking pan. Pour the remaining sauce mixture over the tortillas.

Bake for 15 to 20 minutes, or until heated through. Remove from the oven. Sprinkle with the Cheddar. Bake for 1 to 2 minutes, or until the Cheddar is melted.

Build-Your-Own Pizzas

SERVES 4 | 1 6-INCH PIZZA PER SERVING

1 cup all-purpose flour and ¼ cup all-purpose flour, divided use

½ cup whole-wheat flour

1 teaspoon fast-rise active dry yeast (about ½ of a ¼-ounce packet)

¼ teaspoon salt

½ cup warm water (110°F to 120°F)

2 teaspoons olive oil

1 teaspoon honey

1 tablespoon yellow cornmeal
Cooking spray

¼ cup plus 2 tablespoons no-salt-added tomato sauce

½ teaspoon dried Italian seasoning, crumbled

¼ teaspoon garlic powder

3 cups bite-size pieces red and yellow bell peppers, zucchini, and mushrooms (any combination)

¾ cup frozen soy-based sausage crumbles

1 cup shredded part-skim mozzarella cheese

PER SERVING

Calories	356
Total Fat	8.5 g
Saturated Fat	3.5 g
Trans Fat	0.0 g
Polyunsaturated Fat	1.0 g
Monounsaturated Fat	3.0 g
Cholesterol	18 mg
Sodium	454 mg
Carbohydrates	52 g
Fiber	5 g
Sugars	6 g
Protein	18 g

Dietary exchanges: 3 starch, 1½ vegetable, 1½ lean meat

Great-tasting pizza can be healthy, too, especially when you use whole-wheat flour, lots of fresh veggies, and cholesterol-free soy protein. To bring the family together, let the kids join in to roll and top their own pizzas.

In a medium bowl, stir together 1 cup all-purpose flour, whole-wheat flour, yeast, and salt.

In a small bowl, stir together the water, oil, and honey. Stir into the flour mixture until the dough begins to come together.

On a large flat surface, spread the remaining ¼ cup all-purpose flour in a circle about 12 inches in diameter, with the center only lightly dusted. Turn the dough out into the center of the circle. Knead for about 5 minutes, or until elastic but still soft, working in the remaining flour from the circle as necessary to prevent sticking. Let the dough rest for 15 minutes.

Meanwhile, preheat the oven to 450°F. Lightly spray two cookie sheets with cooking spray. Dust with the cornmeal.

In a small bowl, stir together the tomato sauce, Italian seasoning, and garlic powder.

Divide the dough into 4 pieces. Roll each into a 6-inch circle, using any remaining flour to keep the dough from sticking. Transfer 2 crusts to each cookie sheet. Spread 1½ tablespoons sauce over each crust. Top each with ¾ cup vegetables, 3 tablespoons sausage crumbles, and ¼ cup mozzarella.

Bake the pizzas for 12 to 14 minutes, or until the crusts are browned and crisp around the edges.

Popeye's Special Lasagna

SERVES 4 | 1½ CUPS PER SERVING

Cooking spray

2 teaspoons olive oil

⅓ cup chopped onion

2 medium garlic cloves, minced

1 14.5-ounce can no-salt-added diced tomatoes, undrained

1 8-ounce can no-salt-added tomato sauce

¼ teaspoon dried basil, crumbled

¼ teaspoon dried oregano, crumbled

¼ teaspoon salt

⅛ teaspoon pepper

1 10-ounce package frozen chopped spinach, thawed and squeezed dry

1 cup fat-free cottage cheese

4 ounces part-skim mozzarella cheese, shredded

6 oven-ready lasagna noodles

2 tablespoons shredded or grated Parmesan cheese

PER SERVING

Calories	326
Total Fat	8.5 g
Saturated Fat	3.5 g
Trans Fat	0.0 g
Polyunsaturated Fat	0.5 g
Monounsaturated Fat	3.0 g
Cholesterol	22 mg
Sodium	679 mg
Carbohydrates	41 g
Fiber	6 g
Sugars	11 g
Protein	23 g

Dietary exchanges: 2 starch, 2 vegetable, 2 lean meat

Oven-ready noodles streamline this spinach-enhanced classic.

Preheat the oven to 375°F. Lightly spray an 8-inch square glass baking dish with cooking spray.

In a large nonstick skillet, heat the oil over medium heat, swirling to coat the bottom. Cook the onion for 5 minutes, or until soft, stirring occasionally. Stir in the garlic. Cook for 1 minute. Stir in the tomatoes with liquid, tomato sauce, basil, and oregano. Bring to a boil. Cook for 5 minutes, or until slightly thickened, stirring occasionally. Stir in the salt and pepper.

In a medium bowl, stir together the spinach, cottage cheese, and mozzarella, breaking up any clumps of spinach.

Spread ¼ cup tomato sauce in the baking dish. Place 2 noodles on the sauce. Spread 1 cup spinach mixture over the noodles. Repeat. Place the remaining 2 noodles on the sauce. Spread the remaining sauce over the noodles to cover.

Bake, covered, for 30 minutes, or until the noodles are tender and the casserole is heated through. Sprinkle with the Parmesan. Bake, uncovered, for 5 minutes, or until the Parmesan melts. Let stand for 10 minutes before serving.

COOK'S TIP: Before adding dried herbs to a dish, rub them between your fingers to release their volatile oils. Add them early in the cooking process so their flavor has time to infuse the dish.

KIDS IN THE KITCHEN: Kids are more likely to appreciate mealtime when they take part in the preparation. Recipes that require assembly, like this lasagna, are great opportunities to get the family into the kitchen to help you.

Busy Nights

SEAFOOD

Citrus Tilapia 79

Crisp Catfish Fingers with
Chile-Lemon Dipping Sauce 81

Mustard-Lovers' Salmon 82

Almond-Crusted Sole 83

Bowtie Pasta and Salmon 84

Pistachio-Crusted Trout 86

No-Time Tuna Toss 87

Shrimp Tacos 89

Cracker-Coated Crab Cakes 90

POULTRY

Honey BBQ Chicken Nuggets 93

Hot Wing Chicken Fingers 94

Easy Stuffed Chicken 95

Chicken Parmesan 96

Chicken with Colored "Ribbons" 99

Better-Than-Takeout Chicken Stir-Fry 100

Chicken Tortilla Un-Wraps 102

Turkey Piccata 103

(continued on following page)

Chicken Tortilla Soup 105

Corkscrew Pasta with Turkey Sausage and Tomatoes 106

MEATS

Pesto Presto Sirloin 107

Ginger Beef Stir-Fry 108

Steak Soup 110

Meat Loaf "Mud Pies" 111

Meat "Loaf" with Hidden Vegetables 112

Tex-Mex Mac 'n' Cheese 113

Pita Joes 115

Pretzel Schnitzel 116

Simple, Savory Pork Chops 118

Green Noodles and Ham 119

VEGETARIAN

Portobello Pizzas 120

Pasta with No-Cook Tomato Sauce 122

Spring Ragù with Spiral Pasta 123

Good-for-You Fried Rice 125

Veggie Burgers with Kicked-Up Ketchup 126

White Bean and Spinach Soup 128

Fiesta Cobb Salad 129

Asian Vegetable Soup 131

Veggie Couscous Salad 132

Shepherd's Pie 133

Citrus Tilapia

SERVES 4 | 3 OUNCES FISH PER SERVING | START TO FINISH: 30 MINUTES

Cooking spray

$^1/_3$ to $^1/_2$ cup fresh orange juice

2 tablespoons fresh lime juice

$1^1/_2$ teaspoons ground cumin

1 teaspoon dried oregano, crumbled

$^1/_4$ teaspoon garlic powder

2 tilapia fillets (about 8 ounces each), rinsed and patted dry

$^1/_8$ teaspoon salt

$^1/_8$ teaspoon pepper

1 medium orange, cut into 4 wedges

8 fresh cilantro leaves

PER SERVING

Calories	109
Total Fat	2.0 g
Saturated Fat	1.0 g
Trans Fat	0.0 g
Polyunsaturated Fat	0.5 g
Monounsaturated Fat	0.5 g
Cholesterol	57 mg
Sodium	132 mg
Carbohydrates	0 g
Fiber	0 g
Sugars	0 g
Protein	23 g

Dietary exchanges: 3 very lean meat

A short marinating time is all that's needed to infuse thin, mild tilapia fillets with a duo of citrus juices and some seasonings.

Preheat the grill on medium high. Lightly spray a perforated flat grilling pan or a grilling basket designed for fish with cooking spray. (Tilapia may be too thin and delicate to grill directly on the rack.)

Meanwhile, in a shallow glass dish large enough to hold the fish in a single layer, stir together the orange juice, lime juice, cumin, oregano, and garlic powder. Add the fish, turning to coat. Cover and refrigerate for 10 minutes, turning once halfway through. Transfer the fish to a plate. Discard the marinade.

Sprinkle the fish on both sides with the salt and pepper. Transfer to the grilling pan or basket.

Grill for 5 minutes. Carefully turn over. Grill for 3 to 5 minutes, or until the fish flakes easily when tested with a fork. Cut each fillet in half. Serve garnished with the orange wedges and cilantro leaves.

NUTRITION TIP:
Brightly colored fruit garnishes make food more appetizing, especially to children. It's a simple way to dress up meals while adding a little more nutrition!

MAKE IT A MEAL
WITH grilled asparagus and grilled pineapple dusted with cinnamon.

Crisp Catfish Fingers with Chile-Lemon Dipping Sauce

SERVES 4 | 3 OUNCES FISH AND 1 HEAPING TABLESPOON SAUCE PER SERVING | START TO FINISH: 30 MINUTES

CATFISH FINGERS

1 large egg white

2 teaspoons water

1/2 cup yellow cornmeal

1 teaspoon chili powder

1/2 teaspoon finely chopped fresh thyme or scant 1/4 teaspoon dried, crumbled

1/4 teaspoon pepper

1/8 teaspoon salt

2 catfish fillets (about 8 ounces each), 1/4 to 1/2 inch thick, rinsed and patted dry, cut crosswise into 3/4-inch strips

DIPPING SAUCE

1/4 cup light mayonnaise

1 1/2 tablespoons fresh lemon juice

1 1/4 teaspoons very finely chopped fresh jalapeño, or to taste (optional)

1/2 medium garlic clove, very finely chopped

PER SERVING

Calories	229
Total Fat	8.5 g
Saturated Fat	2.0 g
Trans Fat	0.0 g
Polyunsaturated Fat	4.0 g
Monounsaturated Fat	2.5 g
Cholesterol	71 mg
Sodium	258 mg
Carbohydrates	17 g
Fiber	1 g
Sugars	0 g
Protein	21 g

Dietary exchanges: 1 starch, 3 lean meat

These kid-approved fish sticks are just as crisp and taste as satisfying as the deep-fried artery-cloggers you'll find in the frozen-food aisle. The dipping sauce adds a slightly sophisticated touch.

Preheat the oven to 450°F. Line a rimmed baking sheet with cooking parchment.

In a shallow bowl, whisk together the egg white and water until foamy. In another shallow bowl, using a fork, stir together the cornmeal, chili powder, thyme, pepper, and salt.

Set the bowl with the egg white, the bowl with the cornmeal mixture, and the baking sheet in a row, assembly-line fashion.

Dip some of the catfish strips in the egg white mixture, turning to coat. Put the strips in the cornmeal mixture, turning to coat. Repeat with the remaining strips. Place on the baking sheet in three rows with about 1/2 inch between the pieces.

Bake for 12 to 14 minutes, or until golden brown, turning once with tongs halfway through.

Meanwhile, in a small bowl, whisk together the dipping sauce ingredients until as smooth as possible. Serve with the fish.

COOK'S TIP ON COOKING PARCHMENT: This handy kitchen helper keeps baked goods, such as these fish fingers and cookies, from getting too brown on the bottom.

MAKE IT A MEAL *WITH* roasted sweet potato cubes and asparagus spears.

Mustard-Lovers' Salmon

SERVES 4 | 3 OUNCES FISH PER SERVING | START TO FINISH: 20 MINUTES

Cooking spray

4 salmon fillets with skin (about 5 ounces each), rinsed and patted dry

1/3 cup low-fat sour cream

2 1/2 tablespoons stone-ground mustard

1 1/2 teaspoons fresh lemon juice

2 small garlic cloves, minced

1/3 teaspoon salt-free lemon pepper

> **NUTRITION TIP:**
> Double the recipe and use the extra salmon on a green salad for a second serving of heart-healthy fish during the week.

> **MAKE IT A MEAL**
> *WITH* Veggie Swords (page 176) and boiled small red potatoes.

The mustard coating gives this broiled salmon a flavor boost and locks in moisture without adding the saturated fat and sodium of a rich sauce.

Preheat the broiler. Line a baking sheet with aluminum foil. Lightly spray with cooking spray.

Place the fish with the skin side down on the baking sheet.

In a small bowl, stir together the remaining ingredients. Spread over the top and sides of the fish.

Broil 5 to 6 inches from the heat for 10 to 12 minutes, or until the fish is cooked to the desired doneness.

PER SERVING

Calories	182
Total Fat	6.5 g
Saturated Fat	1.5 g
Trans Fat	0.0 g
Polyunsaturated Fat	1.5 g
Monounsaturated Fat	1.5 g
Cholesterol	68 mg
Sodium	292 mg
Carbohydrates	4 g
Fiber	0 g
Sugars	2 g
Protein	26 g

Dietary exchanges: 3 lean meat

Almond-Crusted Sole

SERVES 4 | 3 OUNCES FISH PER SERVING | START TO FINISH: 20 MINUTES

Cooking spray

4 sole fillets (about 4 ounces each), cut ½ inch thick, rinsed and patted dry

⅓ cup sliced almonds, coarsely chopped

2 tablespoons snipped fresh Italian (flat-leaf) parsley

⅛ teaspoon salt

⅛ teaspoon paprika

2 teaspoons grated lemon zest

2 teaspoons fresh lemon juice

PER SERVING

Calories	138
Total Fat	5.0 g
Saturated Fat	0.5 g
Trans Fat	0.0 g
Polyunsaturated Fat	1.5 g
Monounsaturated Fat	2.5 g
Cholesterol	53 mg
Sodium	156 mg
Carbohydrates	2 g
Fiber	1 g
Sugars	0 g
Protein	21 g

Dietary exchanges: 3 lean meat

COOK'S TIP: Because it involves no turning in the pan, baking is one of the easiest and most forgiving techniques for preparing fish. Try this recipe with other types of mild white fish, such as tilapia, that might tend to break apart if moved too much.

MAKE IT A MEAL *WITH*
Roasted Broccoli and Cauliflower (page 178) and tomato wedges.

A delicious combination, this simple dish of crunchy nuts and tender fish is rich in taste and good for your heart.

Preheat the oven to 425°F. Line a 13 × 9 × 2-inch baking pan with aluminum foil. Lightly spray the foil with cooking spray.

Arrange the fish in a single layer in the pan.

In a small bowl, stir together the remaining ingredients except the lemon juice. Sprinkle over the top of the fish. Using the back of a spoon, gently press the mixture so it adheres to the fish.

Bake for 5 minutes, or until the fish flakes easily when tested with a fork. Drizzle with the lemon juice.

Bowtie Pasta and Salmon

6 ounces uncooked bowtie pasta

2 teaspoons olive oil

2 medium garlic cloves, minced

¼ teaspoon crushed red pepper flakes

9 ounces broccoli florets (about 3 cups)

1 medium red bell pepper, thinly sliced

1 cup fat-free, low-sodium chicken broth

¼ teaspoon salt

1 7.1-ounce vacuum-sealed pouch pink salmon, flaked

2 tablespoons shredded or grated Parmesan cheese

Keep staple ingredients on hand for time-saver suppers like this one, with festive bowtie pasta, bright green broccoli, and heart-healthy salmon.

Prepare the pasta using the package directions, omitting the salt and oil. Drain well in a colander. Set aside.

Meanwhile, in a large nonstick skillet, heat the olive oil over medium-high heat, swirling to coat the bottom. Cook the garlic and crushed red pepper flakes for 5 to 10 seconds, stirring occasionally, being careful not to let the mixture burn.

Stir in the broccoli and bell pepper. Cook for 3 to 4 minutes, or until tender-crisp, stirring occasionally.

Add the broth and salt. Bring to a simmer and simmer until heated through, about 1 minute, stirring occasionally.

Stir in the pasta and salmon. Return to a simmer and simmer for 2 to 3 minutes, or until heated through, stirring occasionally. Serve sprinkled with the Parmesan.

PER SERVING

Calories	278
Total Fat	5.5 g
Saturated Fat	2.0 g
Trans Fat	0.0 g
Polyunsaturated Fat	1.0 g
Monounsaturated Fat	2.0 g
Cholesterol	20 mg
Sodium	480 mg
Carbohydrates	38 g
Fiber	3 g
Sugars	4 g
Protein	18 g

Dietary exchanges: 2 starch, 1 vegetable, 1½ lean meat

NUTRITION TIP: To be sure your family eats enough fruit and vegetables, make it your mantra to serve two vegetables or two fruits, or one of each, at every meal.

MAKE IT A MEAL *WITH* whole-wheat rolls and fresh strawberries with fat-free whipped topping.

Pistachio-Crusted Trout

SERVES 4 | 3 OUNCES FISH PER SERVING | START TO FINISH: 20 MINUTES

Cooking spray

⅓ cup raw shelled unsalted pistachios

1 tablespoon firmly packed snipped fresh parsley

⅛ teaspoon salt

Pinch of pepper

1½ tablespoons plain dry bread crumbs

2 to 3 teaspoons grated lemon zest

1 pound trout fillets with skin, rinsed and patted dry, cut into 4 servings

2 teaspoons olive oil

1 medium lemon, quartered

With a buttery flavor and lovely color from the pistachio crust, this fish entrée is on the table in about 20 minutes. Trout, like salmon, is a delicious source of heart-healthy fish oils.

Put the upper oven rack about 7 inches from the heating element. Put the lower rack in the lowest position. Preheat the broiler. Generously spray the rack of a broiler pan with cooking spray.

In a food processor, process the pistachios, parsley, salt, and pepper for 30 seconds, or until the nuts are finely ground and the mixture is bright green, like pesto. Transfer to a small bowl.

Stir in the bread crumbs and lemon zest.

Lay the fish on a large plate or cutting board. Brush the fish with the oil. Sprinkle with the pistachio mixture. Using your fingertips, press the mixture so it adheres to the fish. Using a spatula, carefully transfer to the broiler rack.

Broil on the upper oven rack for 1 minute, watching carefully until the nuts turn golden brown. Quickly move the fish to the lower rack. Broil for about 4 minutes, or until the fish flakes easily when tested with a fork, watching carefully so the nuts don't burn. Serve with the lemon wedges to squeeze over the fish.

PER SERVING

Calories	226
Total Fat	11.0 g
Saturated Fat	2.0 g
Trans Fat	0.0 g
Polyunsaturated Fat	3.0 g
Monounsaturated Fat	5.5 g
Cholesterol	67 mg
Sodium	128 mg
Carbohydrates	5 g
Fiber	1 g
Sugars	1 g
Protein	26 g

Dietary exchanges: ½ carbohydrate, 3 lean meat, ½ fat

NUTRITION TIP: Coating fish with nuts instead of deep-fried batters gives a satisfying crunch that's good for you, too!

COOK'S TIP: If you wish, you can quarter the zested lemon and use those wedges for squeezing over the fish. Otherwise, wrap the lemon in plastic wrap and refrigerate it for another use.

MAKE IT A MEAL *WITH* whole-wheat couscous and microwaved acorn squash.

No-Time Tuna Toss

SERVES 4 | 2 CUPS PER SERVING | START TO FINISH: 15 MINUTES

1 tablespoon red wine vinegar

1 small garlic clove, minced

¼ teaspoon Dijon mustard

⅛ teaspoon salt

⅛ teaspoon pepper

2 tablespoons olive oil (extra-virgin preferred)

4 cups torn romaine

2 medium tomatoes, cut into 1-inch pieces

2 6-ounce cans low-sodium chunk albacore tuna in water, drained and flaked

1 medium cucumber, peeled, halved lengthwise, and cut crosswise into ¼-inch slices

1 cup whole-grain Caesar croutons

¼ cup thinly sliced red onion

Remember those cans of tuna on the pantry shelf? Use them for this healthy spin on one of your family's favorite staples.

In a large bowl, whisk together the vinegar, garlic, mustard, salt, and pepper. Slowly whisk in the oil.

Add the remaining ingredients. Toss well. Serve immediately for the best texture.

NUTRITION TIP: If you are concerned about the mercury in fish, rest assured that in most cases, the health advantages of canned tuna outweigh the risk. However, if you are pregnant, nursing, or feeding young children, be sure to check the brand you buy to be sure the level of mercury is appropriate for your family. Instead of the tuna, you can use cubes of cooked chicken breast (cooked without salt) in this recipe, or you can omit the tuna or poultry and serve this as a side salad.

COOK'S TIP: If you have extra time, make your own croutons. Cut whole-wheat bread into ¾-inch cubes, arrange them in a single layer on a baking sheet, and bake at 375°F for 10 minutes, or until toasted.

MAKE IT A MEAL *WITH* raw carrot sticks and Strawberry-Orange Soup (page 36).

PER SERVING

Calories	229
Total Fat	9.5 g
Saturated Fat	1.5 g
Trans Fat	0.0 g
Polyunsaturated Fat	2.0 g
Monounsaturated Fat	5.5 g
Cholesterol	36 mg
Sodium	211 mg
Carbohydrates	11 g
Fiber	2 g
Sugars	4 g
Protein	23 g

Dietary exchanges: ½ starch, 1 vegetable, 3 lean meat

Shrimp Tacos

SERVES 4 | 2 TACOS PER SERVING | START TO FINISH: 25 MINUTES

½ cup fat-free sour cream

2 tablespoons snipped fresh cilantro

1 teaspoon canola or corn oil

13 to 14 ounces peeled raw shrimp, rinsed and patted dry

½ teaspoon chili powder

½ teaspoon ground cumin

2 medium garlic cloves, minced

8 6-inch corn tortillas

2 cups shredded lettuce, such as romaine or iceberg

1 small tomato, diced

2 tablespoons sliced black olives

PER SERVING

Calories	206
Total Fat	3.5 g
Saturated Fat	0.5 g
Trans Fat	0.0 g
Polyunsaturated Fat	1.0 g
Monounsaturated Fat	1.5 g
Cholesterol	173 mg
Sodium	308 mg
Carbohydrates	21 g
Fiber	2 g
Sugars	4 g
Protein	22 g
Dietary exchanges: 1½ starch, 3 very lean meat	

Tasty seafood tacos are all the rage, and since you can buy peeled and deveined shrimp either fresh or frozen, these are super-easy to prepare.

In a small bowl, stir together the sour cream and cilantro. Cover and refrigerate until ready to use.

In a large nonstick skillet, heat the oil over medium-high heat, swirling to coat the bottom. Add the shrimp to the pan.

Sprinkle the chili powder and cumin on the shrimp. Sprinkle with the garlic. Cook for 3 to 4 minutes if using large shrimp, or 2 to 3 minutes if using small, or until the shrimp are pink on the outside, stirring occasionally. Remove from the heat.

Using the package directions, warm the tortillas.

Put the tortillas on a flat surface. Sprinkle with the lettuce, tomato, and olives. Spoon the sour cream mixture on each. Top with the shrimp. Fold 2 opposite sides of the tortilla toward the center. If you prefer a dramatic presentation instead, place 2 unfolded tacos side by side on a dinner plate. Fold each in half. Push a 6-inch wooden skewer through both tacos near the tops to hold them together. Repeat with the remaining tacos. Your family will be able to remove the skewers easily before eating the tacos.

NUTRITION TIP:
Shrimp are relatively high in cholesterol, but they are also very low in harmful saturated fat. Even if you're watching your cholesterol, you can still occasionally enjoy shellfish, including shrimp, as part of a balanced diet.

MAKE IT A MEAL
WITH bottled salsa (lowest sodium available) with raw veggie dippers and instant brown rice seasoned with turmeric.

Cracker-Coated Crab Cakes

SERVES 4 | 2 CRAB CAKES PER SERVING | START TO FINISH: 25 MINUTES

½ teaspoon canola or corn oil and 1 teaspoon canola or corn oil, divided use

½ medium red bell pepper, finely chopped

8 ounces fresh crab claw meat, picked over to discard bits of shell

12 saltine-style crackers with unsalted tops, finely crushed

2 large egg whites

2 tablespoons light mayonnaise

2 tablespoons fat-free milk

1 tablespoon Dijon mustard

¼ teaspoon seafood seasoning (lowest sodium available)

⅛ teaspoon cayenne (optional)

⅛ teaspoon salt

1 medium lemon, quartered (optional)

Regular crackers instead of bread crumbs are the secret ingredient that helps bind these mild and tender cakes. Look for crackers that don't contain trans fat.

In a large nonstick skillet, heat ½ teaspoon oil over medium heat, swirling to coat the bottom. Cook the bell pepper for 4 minutes, or until tender, stirring frequently. Remove from the heat. Transfer to a small plate to let cool quickly.

Meanwhile, in a medium bowl, stir together the crabmeat, cracker crumbs, egg whites, mayonnaise, milk, mustard, seafood seasoning, and cayenne. Stir in the cooled bell pepper. Shape into 8 small patties about 2½ inches in diameter.

In the same skillet, heat the remaining 1 teaspoon oil over medium heat, swirling to coat the bottom. Cook the crab cakes for 2 to 3 minutes on each side, or until golden brown and cooked through. Serve sprinkled with the salt and garnished with the lemon wedges

PER SERVING

Calories	159
Total Fat	6.0 g
Saturated Fat	1.0 g
Trans Fat	0.5 g
Polyunsaturated Fat	2.0 g
Monounsaturated Fat	2.0 g
Cholesterol	46 mg
Sodium	513 mg
Carbohydrates	10 g
Fiber	1 g
Sugars	1 g
Protein	16 g

Dietary exchanges: ½ starch, 2 lean meat

COOK'S TIP: For a quick sauce to top the crab cakes, stir together ½ cup light sour cream and 1 teaspoon Louisiana hot sauce. (This is a Cajun-style sauce made from aged cayenne peppers and is not what we use when we call for red hot-pepper sauce.)

COOK'S TIP: For a more colorful dish, reserve 2 tablespoons of the cooked bell peppers to use for garnish.

MAKE IT A MEAL *WITH* broccoli and Island Fruit Salad (page 48).

Honey BBQ Chicken Nuggets

SERVES 4 | 3 OUNCES CHICKEN AND 2 TABLESPOONS SAUCE PER SERVING | START TO FINISH: 30 MINUTES

Cooking spray

3 tablespoons all-purpose flour

1 teaspoon onion powder

½ teaspoon garlic powder

⅛ teaspoon pepper

1 pound boneless, skinless chicken breasts, all visible fat discarded, cut into 1-inch cubes

3 tablespoons fat-free milk

½ cup plain dried bread crumbs

¼ cup plus 2 tablespoons barbecue sauce (lowest sodium available)

1 tablespoon cider vinegar

1 tablespoon honey

1 teaspoon grated orange zest

PER SERVING

Calories	269
Total Fat	2.0 g
Saturated Fat	0.5 g
Trans Fat	0.0 g
Polyunsaturated Fat	0.5 g
Monounsaturated Fat	0.5 g
Cholesterol	66 mg
Sodium	336 mg
Carbohydrates	30 g
Fiber	1 g
Sugars	15 g
Protein	29 g

Dietary exchanges: 1 starch, 1 carbohydrate, 3 very lean meat

Baked instead of fried, these finger-friendly nuggets are great when served with a zesty barbecue sauce for delicious dipping.

Preheat the oven to 400°F. Lightly spray a baking sheet with cooking spray.

In a medium bowl, stir together the flour, onion powder, garlic powder, and pepper. Add the chicken pieces, stirring to coat.

Add the milk, stirring again to coat.

Put the bread crumbs in a medium shallow bowl or pie pan. Using a slotted spoon, transfer the chicken in batches (about 6 pieces at a time) to the bread crumbs. Roll to coat. Transfer to the baking sheet. Repeat with the remaining chicken. Lightly spray the tops and sides of the chicken with cooking spray.

Bake for 20 minutes, or until the chicken is golden brown on the outside and no longer pink in the center.

Meanwhile, in a small saucepan, stir together the remaining ingredients. Bring to a simmer over medium-high heat, stirring occasionally. Reduce the heat and simmer for 5 minutes, or until the flavors have blended, stirring occasionally. Serve as a dipping sauce for the chicken.

KIDS IN THE KITCHEN: If your little cooks are old enough, let them help you make this modern version of a classic by assembling the ingredients, stirring, and coating the chicken. The more involved kids are in the preparation, the more they appreciate the meal.

MAKE IT A MEAL *WITH* packaged coleslaw mix and green beans.

Hot Wing Chicken Fingers

SERVES 4 | 3 OUNCES CHICKEN PER SERVING | START TO FINISH: 30 MINUTES

Cooking spray

1 6-ounce container fat-free plain yogurt

1 tablespoon hot wing sauce (lowest sodium available)

¾ cup panko

2 tablespoons all-purpose flour

¼ teaspoon paprika

8 chicken breast tenders (about 1 pound total), all visible fat discarded

SPICY SAUCE (OPTIONAL)

1 teaspoon light tub margarine

1 tablespoon hot wing sauce

Satisfy your family's cravings for hot wings with this healthy dish. Bake tender chicken in a yogurt-panko crust for low-fat crunch, then heat things up with a spicy sauce if you wish.

Preheat the oven to 450°F. Lightly spray a baking sheet with cooking spray.

In a shallow dish or pie pan, whisk together the yogurt and hot wing sauce until blended. In a separate shallow dish or pie pan, stir together the panko, flour, and paprika. Set the dish with the yogurt mixture, the dish with the panko mixture, and the baking sheet in a row, assembly-line fashion.

Dip 1 chicken tender in the yogurt mixture, turning to coat. Dip the tender in the panko mixture, turning to coat. Place on the baking sheet. Repeat with the remaining tenders, placing them in a single layer. Lightly spray the tops with cooking spray.

Bake for 10 minutes. Turn over. Lightly spray the tops with cooking spray. Bake for 10 minutes, or until the chicken is no longer pink in the center.

In a small microwaveable bowl, microwave the margarine on 100 percent power (high) for 15 to 20 seconds. Stir in the hot wing sauce. Drizzle over the cooked chicken.

PER SERVING (without sauce)

Calories	202
Total Fat	1.5 g
Saturated Fat	0.5 g
Trans Fat	0.0 g
Polyunsaturated Fat	0.5 g
Monounsaturated Fat	0.5 g
Cholesterol	67 mg
Sodium	217 mg
Carbohydrates	14 g
Fiber	1 g
Sugars	3 g
Protein	30 g

Dietary exchanges: 1 starch, 3 very lean meat

PER SERVING (with sauce)

Calories	206
Total Fat	2.0 g
Saturated Fat	0.5 g
Trans Fat	0.0 g
Polyunsaturated Fat	0.5 g
Monounsaturated Fat	0.5 g
Cholesterol	67 mg
Sodium	318 mg
Carbohydrates	14 g
Fiber	1 g
Sugars	3 g
Protein	30 g

Dietary exchanges: 1 starch, 3 very lean meat

COOK'S TIP: Bottled sauces, such as hot wing sauce, can be high in sodium. Be sure to check the labels and choose sauces with the lowest sodium available.

MAKE IT A MEAL *WITH* corn and Creamy Chop-Chop Salad (page 45).

Easy Stuffed Chicken

SERVES 4 | 3 OUNCES CHICKEN AND 1 TABLESPOON CHEESE-TOMATO MIXTURE PER SERVING | START TO FINISH: 30 MINUTES

4 boneless, skinless chicken breast halves (about 4 ounces each), all visible fat discarded

1/4 cup low-fat garden vegetable tub cream cheese

2 ounces grape tomatoes (about 1/4 cup), halved

1 medium green onion, chopped

These quick chicken pockets hold a creamy and guilt-free cheese surprise inside.

Put a chicken breast half on a cutting board. Using a boning knife or other long, thin knife, make a pocket by cutting a slit along a long side in the thickest part of the chicken. Gradually work the knife into the breast, making a pocket about 3 inches long and being careful not to cut all the way through the breast. Try to keep the knife blade parallel to the cutting board. Repeat with the remaining chicken.

In a small bowl, stir together the cream cheese, tomatoes, and green onion until blended. Spoon into each chicken pocket. Press the edges of the opening together to form a seal. Secure with wooden toothpicks.

Heat a large nonstick skillet over medium heat. Cook the chicken for 4 minutes. Turn over. Cook, covered, for 5 minutes, or until the chicken is no longer pink in the center. Transfer the chicken to a cutting board. Discard the toothpicks. Cut the chicken crosswise into the desired number of slices.

PER SERVING

Calories	159
Total Fat	3.5 g
Saturated Fat	1.5 g
Trans Fat	0.0 g
Polyunsaturated Fat	0.5 g
Monounsaturated Fat	0.5 g
Cholesterol	73 mg
Sodium	171 mg
Carbohydrates	2 g
Fiber	0 g
Sugars	2 g
Protein	28 g
Dietary exchanges: 3 very lean meat	

NUTRITION TIP: Put extra grape tomatoes in a bowl and offer them to kids while you're making dinner. These tiny treats are ideal finger food, and kids loves popping them into their mouths as they do homework or help you in the kitchen.

MAKE IT A MEAL *WITH* Strawberry Patch Salad (page 44) and microwaved sweet potatoes.

Chicken Parmesan

SERVES 4 | 3 OUNCES CHICKEN PER SERVING | START TO FINISH: 30 MINUTES

¼ cup egg substitute

½ cup plain dry bread crumbs

1 teaspoon dried Italian seasoning, crumbled

1 teaspoon garlic powder

½ teaspoon onion powder

¼ teaspoon pepper

4 boneless, skinless chicken breast halves (about 4 ounces each), all visible fat discarded

2 teaspoons olive oil

Olive oil spray

¾ cup spaghetti sauce (lowest sodium available)

⅓ cup finely shredded or shredded part-skim mozzarella cheese

PER SERVING

Calories	249
Total Fat	6.0 g
Saturated Fat	2.0 g
Trans Fat	0.0 g
Polyunsaturated Fat	1.0 g
Monounsaturated Fat	2.5 g
Cholesterol	72 mg
Sodium	409 mg
Carbohydrates	14 g
Fiber	2 g
Sugars	4 g
Protein	33 g

Dietary exchanges: 1 starch, 3½ lean meat

This quick and healthy dish has all the gooey goodness of the Italian classic but less saturated fat and sodium.

Pour the egg substitute into a shallow dish. In a separate shallow dish, stir together the bread crumbs, Italian seasoning, garlic and onion powders, and pepper.

Set the dish with the egg substitute, the dish with the bread crumb mixture, and a large plate in a row, assembly-line fashion.

Dip 1 piece of chicken in the egg substitute, turning to coat. Dip in the bread crumb mixture, shaking off any excess, then pressing so the mixture adheres to the chicken. Put the chicken on the plate. Repeat with the remaining chicken. Let stand for 5 minutes.

In a large nonstick skillet, heat the oil over medium-high heat for 2 minutes, swirling to coat the bottom.

Lightly spray the smooth side of the chicken with olive oil spray. Put the chicken with the sprayed side down in the skillet. Reduce the heat to medium. Cook for 6 minutes, or until deep brown. Turn over. Cook for 3 minutes, or until golden. Push the chicken toward the center of the skillet.

Pour the spaghetti sauce over the chicken. Sprinkle with the mozzarella. Cook, covered, for 3 minutes, or until the chicken is cooked through, the sauce is bubbly, and the mozzarella is melted.

COOK'S TIP: Grated mozzarella is too powdery for this recipe. You can use regular shredded instead of finely shredded cheese, but you may not get quite so much coverage.

MAKE IT A MEAL *WITH* spinach salad and whole-wheat spaghetti.

Chicken with Colored "Ribbons"

SERVES 4 | 3 OUNCES CHICKEN AND ½ CUP VEGETABLES PER SERVING | START TO FINISH: 30 MINUTES

Cooking spray

1 medium red bell pepper, cut lengthwise into strips about ½ inch wide

½ medium yellow bell pepper, cut lengthwise into strips about ½ inch wide

½ medium orange bell pepper, cut lengthwise into strips about ½ inch wide

1 cup onion slices (about ¼ inch thick)

1 teaspoon olive oil and 2 teaspoons olive oil, divided use

¼ teaspoon salt and ¼ teaspoon salt, divided use

¼ teaspoon white pepper and ¼ teaspoon white pepper, divided use

3 medium garlic cloves, minced

4 boneless, skinless chicken breast halves (about 4 ounces each), all visible fat discarded

⅔ cup fat-free, low-sodium chicken broth

1 teaspoon dried Italian seasoning, crumbled

Searing lean chicken breasts in a skillet while cooking colorful strips of bell pepper separately lets you assemble a dish with layers of flavors in almost no time.

Lightly spray a Dutch oven with cooking spray. Heat over medium-high heat. Add the bell peppers and onion. Stir in 1 teaspoon oil. Cook for 8 minutes, or until the onion is golden and the bell peppers begin to soften, stirring frequently.

Reduce the heat to low. Sprinkle ¼ teaspoon salt and ¼ teaspoon pepper over the bell peppers and onion. Cook for 8 minutes, or until the bell peppers begin to brown or blister, stirring frequently.

Meanwhile, in a small bowl, stir together the garlic, remaining 2 teaspoons oil, remaining ¼ teaspoon salt, and remaining ¼ teaspoon pepper. Using your fingertips, rub the mixture all over the chicken.

Heat a small nonstick skillet over medium-high heat for 2 minutes. Cook the chicken with the smooth side down for 4 minutes, or until golden brown. Turn over. Cook for 2 minutes.

Push the bell pepper mixture toward the center of the Dutch oven. Place the chicken pieces close together on top.

In a small bowl, stir together the broth and Italian seasoning. Pour over all. Increase the heat to medium-high and bring to a simmer. Spoon some of the broth and bell pepper mixture over the chicken. Reduce the heat and simmer for 5 minutes.

Spoon the bell pepper mixture and chicken onto plates. Spoon the sauce over all.

PER SERVING

Calories	189
Total Fat	5.0 g
Saturated Fat	1.0 g
Trans Fat	0.0 g
Polyunsaturated Fat	0.5 g
Monounsaturated Fat	3.0 g
Cholesterol	66 mg
Sodium	378 mg
Carbohydrates	8 g
Fiber	2 g
Sugars	4 g
Protein	28 g

Dietary exchanges: 2 vegetable, 3 lean meat

MAKE IT A MEAL *WITH* a garden salad and pineapple canned in its own juice.

Better-Than-Takeout Chicken Stir-Fry

SERVES 4 | 1 CUP CHICKEN AND VEGETABLES PER SERVING | START TO FINISH: 30 MINUTES

1 teaspoon canola or corn oil and 1 teaspoon canola or corn oil, divided use

½ cup diced onion

1½ teaspoons minced peeled gingerroot

2 medium garlic cloves, finely chopped

8 ounces chicken tenders, all visible fat discarded, cut crosswise into ¾-inch strips

1 cup snow peas or sugar snap peas, trimmed

1 medium zucchini, cut in matchstick-size pieces

½ medium red bell pepper, cut into ¼-inch strips

¼ cup sliced water chestnuts, drained, rinsed, and patted dry

2½ teaspoons soy sauce (lowest sodium available)

1½ tablespoons finely chopped walnuts

1 teaspoon toasted sesame oil

Here's a healthy, homemade stir-fry to put on the table in 30 minutes—quicker than waiting for the delivery person!

Heat a nonstick wok or large nonstick skillet over medium-high heat for 2 minutes. Add 1 teaspoon oil, swirling to coat the bottom. Add the onion, gingerroot, and garlic. Reduce the heat to medium. Cook for 3 to 5 minutes, or until the onion begins to brown, stirring constantly. Push the onion mixture slightly up the side.

Add the remaining oil, swirling to coat the bottom. Increase the heat to medium high. Cook the chicken for 3 minutes, stirring constantly without disturbing the onion mixture.

Add the peas, zucchini, and bell pepper. Stir together all the vegetables, including the onion mixture, and the chicken. Cook for 3 to 5 minutes, or until the chicken is cooked through and the vegetables are bright and tender-crisp, stirring constantly.

Stir in the water chestnuts and soy sauce. Cook for 1 minute, or until the ingredients are heated through, stirring as needed. Serve sprinkled with the walnuts and drizzled with the oil.

PER SERVING

Calories	146
Total Fat	6.0 g
Saturated Fat	0.5 g
Trans Fat	0.0 g
Polyunsaturated Fat	2.5 g
Monounsaturated Fat	2.5 g
Cholesterol	33 mg
Sodium	127 mg
Carbohydrates	8 g
Fiber	2 g
Sugars	4 g
Protein	15 g

Dietary exchanges: 2 vegetable, 2 lean meat

NUTRITION TIP:
Some people douse their food with soy sauce without thinking—even before they taste for saltiness. Soy sauce (even the low-sodium variety) is very high in sodium, so remind your family to add it only sparingly as a condiment—or not at all.

MAKE IT A MEAL
WITH instant brown rice and light canned pears sprinkled with crystallized ginger.

Chicken Tortilla Un-Wraps

SERVES 4 | 1 TORTILLA, 2½ OUNCES CHICKEN, ½ CUP SALAD, AND ⅓ CUP TOPPING PER SERVING | START TO FINISH: 25 MINUTES

12 ounces boneless, skinless chicken breasts, all visible fat discarded

1 teaspoon salt-free steak seasoning blend

1 teaspoon olive oil

4 6-inch corn tortillas

2 cups shredded lettuce (romaine preferred)

½ cup picante sauce (lowest sodium available)

½ cup fat-free sour cream

¼ cup shredded fat-free sharp Cheddar cheese

8 medium pitted black olives, sliced (about ¼ cup)

¼ cup snipped fresh cilantro

This is an open-face wrap, so you eat it with a knife and fork and get to savor the individual ingredients.

Sprinkle both sides of the chicken with the seasoning blend. Using your fingertips, press the seasoning blend so it adheres to the chicken.

In a large nonstick skillet, heat the oil over medium-high heat, swirling to coat the bottom. Cook the chicken for 4 minutes on each side, or until no longer pink in the center. Transfer to a cutting board and thinly slice.

Using the package directions, warm the tortillas. Transfer to plates.

Top in order with the lettuce, picante sauce, sour cream, Cheddar, olives, chicken, and cilantro.

PER SERVING

Calories	200
Total Fat	3.5 g
Saturated Fat	0.5 g
Trans Fat	0.0 g
Polyunsaturated Fat	0.5 g
Monounsaturated Fat	2.0 g
Cholesterol	56 mg
Sodium	458 mg
Carbohydrates	15 g
Fiber	2 g
Sugars	3 g
Protein	25 g

Dietary exchanges: 1 starch, 3 very lean meat

KIDS IN THE KITCHEN: Serve family style and have everyone make his or her own un-wrap at the table.

MAKE IT A MEAL *WITH* mango slices and no-salt-added canned black beans seasoned with cumin.

Turkey Piccata

¼ cup all-purpose flour

1 teaspoon dried thyme, crumbled

½ teaspoon onion powder

¼ teaspoon pepper

⅛ teaspoon salt

4 turkey breast cutlets (about
    3 ounces each), all visible fat
    discarded

1½ teaspoons olive oil and 1½
    teaspoons olive oil, divided use

¾ cup thinly sliced onion

¾ cup fat-free, low-sodium chicken
    broth

2 medium garlic cloves, finely
    chopped

¼ cup fresh lemon juice

2 tablespoons capers, drained

PER SERVING

Calories	155
Total Fat	2.0 g
Saturated Fat	0.5 g
Trans Fat	0.0 g
Polyunsaturated Fat	0.5 g
Monounsaturated Fat	1.0 g
Cholesterol	58 mg
Sodium	251 mg
Carbohydrates	11 g
Fiber	1 g
Sugars	2
Protein	22 g

Dietary exchanges: ½ carbohydrate,
    3 very lean meat

MAKE IT A MEAL
WITH whole-wheat
fettuccine and Asparagus
Parmesan (page 190).

Lean turkey cutlets, already cut in individual portions, help streamline the preparation of this simple yet sophisticated dish. In just a half-hour from when you enter the kitchen, you can put an Italian restaurant classic on your table.

In a pie pan or shallow bowl, stir together the flour, thyme, onion powder, pepper, and salt. Add 1 turkey cutlet, turning to coat. Shake off the excess. Transfer to a large plate. Repeat with the remaining cutlets.

Heat a large nonstick skillet for 2 minutes over medium-high heat. Add 1½ teaspoons oil, swirling to coat the bottom. Put the turkey in the skillet. (Don't overcrowd. If necessary, cook the cutlets in batches.) Cook for 3 minutes, or until browned. Turn over. Carefully add the remaining 1½ teaspoons oil, swirling to coat the bottom as much as possible. Cook for 2 minutes, or until light brown. Transfer the turkey to a separate large plate. Cover loosely with aluminum foil.

Put the onion, broth, and garlic in the skillet, scraping to dislodge any browned bits. Stir well. Bring to a boil over medium-high heat. Reduce the heat to medium. Cook for 3 minutes, or until the onion begins to soften and the broth is reduced by almost half, stirring frequently.

Stir in the lemon juice and capers. Return the turkey and any accumulated juices to the skillet. Spoon the sauce over the turkey. Bring just to a boil, still over medium heat. Reduce the heat and simmer, covered, for 5 minutes, or until the sauce is bubbly. Serve the sauce over the turkey.

NUTRITION TIP: Meats and poultry tend to lose weight as they cook. You'll usually start with about 4 ounces raw to get the 3 ounces recommended as the limit per serving. Skinless turkey breast cutlets are naturally so lean, however, that they lose very little weight while cooking.

Chicken Tortilla Soup

Cooking spray

1 pound chicken tenders, all visible fat discarded, cut into bite-size pieces

1 medium green bell pepper

1 medium rib of celery

½ medium onion (about 4 ounces)

2 medium garlic cloves

1 medium fresh jalapeño pepper (optional)

2 medium Italian plum (Roma) tomatoes

2 14.5-ounce cans fat-free, low-sodium chicken broth

½ cup frozen whole-kernel corn

½ cup fresh cilantro, snipped

Juice of 1 medium lime

1 teaspoon chili powder

1 teaspoon ground cumin

½ cup baked tortilla chips

½ medium avocado

¼ cup low-fat Mexican blend shredded cheese

This appealing Mexican-inspired soup is a terrific example of how to enjoy a variety of vegetables. The baked chips and low-fat cheese add crunch and body.

Lightly spray a large saucepan or Dutch oven with cooking spray. Cook the chicken over medium-high heat for 5 minutes, or until browned, stirring occasionally.

Meanwhile, chop the bell pepper, celery, and onion. Mince the garlic. Wearing disposable gloves, chop the jalapeño, discarding the ribs and seeds for less heat. Stir into the chicken and cook for 3 to 5 minutes, or until tender, stirring frequently.

While the vegetables cook with the chicken, seed and chop the tomatoes. Stir into the chicken mixture with the broth, corn, cilantro, lime juice, chili powder, and cumin. Bring to a boil, still over medium-high heat. Reduce the heat and simmer for 10 minutes.

Meanwhile, crush the tortilla chips and thinly slice the avocado.

When the soup is ready, sprinkle with the chips and Mexican blend cheese. Garnish with the avocado.

PER SERVING

Calories	260
Total Fat	7.5 g
Saturated Fat	2.0 g
Trans Fat	0.0 g
Polyunsaturated Fat	1.0 g
Monounsaturated Fat	3.5 g
Cholesterol	70 mg
Sodium	241 mg
Carbohydrates	17 g
Fiber	4 g
Sugars	4 g
Protein	32 g

Dietary exchanges: ½ starch, 1 vegetable, 3½ lean meat

MAKE IT A MEAL *WITH* spinach salad and whole-wheat breadsticks.

Corkscrew Pasta with Turkey Sausage and Tomatoes

SERVES 4 | 1½ CUPS PER SERVING | START TO FINISH: 30 MINUTES

8 ounces whole-wheat fusilli

1 teaspoon olive oil and 1 teaspoon olive oil, divided use

8 ounces (about 2 links) uncooked mild Italian turkey sausage

½ cup diced onion (yellow preferred)

2 medium garlic gloves, chopped

1 pound tomatoes, finely chopped

1 teaspoon chopped fresh oregano

¼ teaspoon pepper

⅛ teaspoon crushed red pepper flakes, or to taste

1 tablespoon plus 1 teaspoon shredded or grated Parmesan cheese

1 teaspoon whole fresh oregano leaves

PER SERVING

Calories	345
Total Fat	9.0 g
Saturated Fat	2.5 g
Trans Fat	0.0 g
Polyunsaturated Fat	2.0 g
Monounsaturated Fat	4.0 g
Cholesterol	49 mg
Sodium	443 mg
Carbohydrates	49 g
Fiber	9 g
Sugars	6 g
Protein	18 g

Dietary exchanges: 3 starch,
1 vegetable, 1 medium-fat meat

Fresh tomatoes and low-fat turkey sausage pair in this hearty, but not heavy, whole-wheat pasta dish. Dial the heat up or down by varying the amount of crushed red pepper flakes you use.

Cook the pasta using the package directions, omitting the salt and oil. Drain well in a colander.

Meanwhile, in a large nonstick skillet, heat 1 teaspoon oil over medium-high heat, swirling to coat the bottom. Squeeze the sausage from the casing directly into the skillet, breaking up any large pieces with a spoon. Cook for about 7 minutes, or until browned, stirring frequently and continuing to break up any large pieces. Transfer to a plate.

Add the remaining oil to the same skillet, swirling to coat the bottom. Reduce the heat to medium low. Cook the onion and garlic for 3 minutes, stirring constantly.

Stir in the tomatoes, chopped oregano, pepper, red pepper flakes, and sausage. Increase the heat to medium and bring to a simmer. Reduce the heat and cook at a steady simmer for 5 minutes.

Transfer the pasta to a serving bowl. Stir the sausage mixture into the pasta. Serve sprinkled with the Parmesan and garnished with the oregano leaves.

NUTRITION TIP: Turkey sausage is a more heart healthy alternative to regular beef or pork sausages because turkey is leaner and much lower in saturated fat.

MAKE IT A MEAL *WITH* garden salad and fat-free or low-fat vanilla frozen yogurt with fresh raspberries.

Pesto Presto Sirloin

SERVES 4 | 3 OUNCES BEEF AND 2 TABLESPOONS SAUCE PER SERVING | START TO FINISH: 30 MINUTES

Cooking spray

1 tablespoon fresh lemon juice

1 teaspoon dried oregano, crumbled

½ teaspoon garlic powder

¼ teaspoon pepper

1 1-pound boneless sirloin steak, ¾ to 1 inch thick, all visible fat discarded, quartered

PESTO

1 cup loosely packed fresh basil (about 1 ounce)

½ cup fat-free, low-sodium chicken broth

2 tablespoon shredded or grated Parmesan cheese

1 teaspoon cornstarch

1 teaspoon olive oil

1 medium garlic clove

½ teaspoon grated lemon zest

1 tablespoon plus 1 teaspoon pine nuts, dry-roasted

There's plenty of flavor in this dish, including lemon, garlic, oregano, and basil. Cooking the low-fat pesto sauce for only a few minutes lets it retain the fresh taste of a traditional pesto and thickens it without adding calories.

Preheat the broiler. Lightly spray a broiler pan and rack with cooking spray.

In a shallow glass dish, stir together the lemon juice, oregano, garlic powder, and pepper. Add the steaks, turning several times to coat. Let stand for 5 minutes.

Meanwhile, in a food processor or blender, process the pesto ingredients for 20 to 30 seconds, or until smooth. Pour into a small saucepan. Bring to a simmer over medium-high heat. Simmer for 1 to 2 minutes, or until thickened, stirring occasionally. Remove from the heat.

Broil the steaks about 4 inches from the heat for 4 to 6 minutes on each side, or to the desired doneness. Serve topped with the pesto and pine nuts.

PER SERVING

Calories	190
Total Fat	8.0 g
Saturated Fat	2.5 g
Trans Fat	0.0 g
Polyunsaturated Fat	1.0 g
Monounsaturated Fat	3.5 g
Cholesterol	48 mg
Sodium	102 mg
Carbohydrates	3 g
Fiber	1 g
Sugars	1 g
Protein	27 g

Dietary exchanges: 3 lean meat

NUTRITION TIP:
Pine nuts add heart-healthy omega-3 oil as well as flavor. When you prepare this recipe, make a double batch of pesto so you'll have plenty left over for other uses. Drizzle it over other broiled meats, spoon it over whole-grain pasta, or use it as a spread or dip.

MAKE IT A MEAL
WITH Orange-Kissed Broccoli (page 190) and bow-shape pasta.

Ginger Beef Stir-Fry

SERVES 4 | 1 CUP BEEF AND VEGETABLES AND ½ CUP RICE PER SERVING | START TO FINISH: 30 MINUTES

1 pound flank steak, all visible fat and silver skin discarded, cut across the grain into ¼-inch strips

2 medium garlic cloves, minced

1 teaspoon grated peeled gingerroot

½ cup uncooked instant brown rice

¾ cup fat-free, no-salt-added beef broth

¼ cup hoisin sauce

3 tablespoons soy sauce (lowest sodium available)

1 tablespoon cornstarch

1 teaspoon canola or corn oil

¼ teaspoon crushed red pepper flakes (optional)

3 ounces broccoli florets

½ medium yellow, red, or green bell pepper, cut into thin strips

1 medium carrot, cut crosswise into ¼-inch slices

2 medium stalks of bok choy, stems and leaves cut crosswise into ½-inch slices

1 8-ounce can sliced water chestnuts, drained

PER SERVING

Calories	288
Total Fat	8.5 g
Saturated Fat	3.0 g
Trans Fat	0.0 g
Polyunsaturated Fat	1.0 g
Monounsaturated Fat	4.0 g
Cholesterol	48 mg
Sodium	466 mg
Carbohydrates	25 g
Fiber	4 g
Sugars	6 g
Protein	27 g

Dietary exchanges: 1 starch, 2 vegetable, 3 lean meat

This colorful stir-fry is full of fiber from the brown rice and veggies. Prep the ingredients first so the fast-paced cooking process goes like clockwork.

In a medium bowl, stir together the steak, garlic, and ginger. Set aside.

Prepare the rice using the package directions, omitting the salt and margarine.

Meanwhile, in another medium bowl, combine the broth, hoisin sauce, soy sauce, and cornstarch, stirring until the cornstarch is dissolved. Set aside.

In a wok or large nonstick skillet, heat the oil and red pepper flakes over medium-high heat, swirling to coat the bottom. Cook the steak mixture for 4 to 5 minutes, or until the steak is browned (it may be slightly pink in the center), stirring constantly. Transfer to a plate. Set aside.

Put the broccoli, bell pepper, and carrot in the pan. Cook, still over medium-high heat, for 2 to 3 minutes, or until tender-crisp, stirring constantly. If the mixture becomes too dry, add 1 to 2 tablespoons water.

Stir in the bok choy and water chestnuts. Cook for 1 to 2 minutes, or until the bok choy is tender-crisp and warmed through, stirring constantly. Make a well in the center.

Pour the broth mixture into the well. Cook for 1 to 2 minutes, or until the broth mixture thickens, occasionally stirring just the broth mixture.

Stir in the beef. Cook for 1 to 2 minutes, or until warmed through, stirring occasionally. Serve over the rice.

Steak Soup

SERVES 4 | 1½ CUPS PER SERVING | START TO FINISH: 30 MINUTES

1 teaspoon olive oil

2 medium ribs of celery, cut crosswise into ½-inch pieces

2 medium carrots, cut crosswise into ½-inch pieces

½ cup coarsely chopped onion

2 medium garlic cloves, minced
    Cooking spray

4 large red potatoes (about 1 pound total), cut into ¾-inch cubes

3 cups fat-free, no-salt-added beef broth

2 tablespoons steak sauce (lowest sodium available)

1 teaspoon dried thyme, crumbled

½ teaspoon pepper

1 1-pound boneless sirloin steak, all visible fat discarded, quartered

PER SERVING

Calories	283
Total Fat	6.0 g
Saturated Fat	2.0 g
Trans Fat	0.0 g
Polyunsaturated Fat	0.5 g
Monounsaturated Fat	2.5 g
Cholesterol	46 mg
Sodium	235 mg
Carbohydrates	28 g
Fiber	4 g
Sugars	6 g
Protein	29 g

Dietary exchanges: 1½ starch, 1 vegetable, 3 lean meat

When you're rushed for dinner, let chunky vegetables simmer in broth while you quickly broil a steak. Pair them for a satisfying meal in a bowl for your meat-and-potato lovers. (See photograph on page 76.)

In a large saucepan, heat the oil over medium-high heat, swirling to coat the bottom. Cook the celery, carrots, onion, and garlic for 2 to 3 minutes, or until tender, stirring occasionally.

Meanwhile, preheat the broiler. Lightly spray a broiler pan and rack with cooking spray.

Stir the potatoes, broth, steak sauce, and thyme into the celery mixture. Increase the heat to high and bring to a simmer, 1 to 2 minutes, stirring occasionally. Reduce the heat and simmer, covered, for 15 minutes, or until the potatoes are tender.

While the soup simmers, sprinkle the pepper on both sides of the steaks.

Broil the steaks about 4 inches from the heat for 4 to 6 minutes on each side, or to the desired doneness. Transfer to a cutting board. Cut into ¾-inch pieces. Stir into the soup. Simmer for 1 minute so the flavors blend.

NUTRITION TIP:
When you prepare meat-based soups like this one, bump up the veggies by adding the favorites you have on hand.

MAKE IT A MEAL
WITH cucumber, tomato, and red onion salad and Chocolate-Berry Yogurt Parfaits (page 224).

Meat Loaf "Mud Pies"

SERVES 4 | 1 PATTY AND ¼ CUP SAUCE PER SERVING | START TO FINISH: 30 MINUTES

1 pound extra-lean ground beef

1 tablespoon Dijon mustard

1 tablespoon Worcestershire sauce (lowest sodium available)

½ teaspoon garlic powder

⅛ teaspoon salt and ⅛ teaspoon salt, divided use

½ teaspoon canola or corn oil and ½ teaspoon canola or corn oil, divided use

1 6-ounce onion, thinly sliced

½ cup fat-free bottled beef gravy (lowest sodium available)

¼ cup snipped fresh parsley

¼ cup water

½ teaspoon sugar

¼ teaspoon instant coffee granules

Worcestershire sauce, browned onion, and rich beef gravy create the deeply flavored sauce for these lean beef patties.

In a medium bowl, stir together the beef, mustard, Worcestershire sauce, garlic powder, and ⅛ teaspoon salt. Shape into 4 patties about ½ inch thick and 4 inches in diameter.

In a large nonstick skillet, heat ½ teaspoon oil over medium-high heat, swirling to coat the bottom. Cook the patties, covered, for 5 minutes on each side, or until no longer pink in the center. Transfer to a large plate. Cover with aluminum foil to keep warm.

Pour the remaining ½ teaspoon oil into the skillet, swirling to coat the bottom. Cook the onion for 8 minutes, or until richly browned, stirring frequently.

Stir in the gravy, parsley, water, sugar, coffee granules, and remaining ⅛ teaspoon salt. Cook for 15 seconds, stirring constantly. Spoon over the patties.

PER SERVING

Calories	197
Total Fat	7.0 g
Saturated Fat	2.5 g
Trans Fat	0.5 g
Polyunsaturated Fat	1.0 g
Monounsaturated Fat	3.0 g
Cholesterol	62 mg
Sodium	467 mg
Carbohydrates	8 g
Fiber	1 g
Sugars	4 g
Protein	26 g

Dietary exchanges: ½ carbohydrate, 3 lean meat

KIDS IN THE KITCHEN: Kids love to make mud pies, so put those talents to work in your kitchen! Ask children to assemble and stir together the ingredients and then shape the patties for dinner.

MAKE IT A MEAL *WITH* sugar snap peas and In-a-Hurry Curry Couscous (page 179).

Meat "Loaf" with Hidden Vegetables

SERVES 4 | 1 PATTY PER SERVING | START TO FINISH: 25 MINUTES

1 pound extra-lean ground beef

1/2 cup uncooked quick-cooking oatmeal

1/2 medium zucchini, shredded

1/4 cup spaghetti sauce (lowest sodium available) and 1/2 cup spaghetti sauce (lowest sodium available), divided use

2 large egg whites

1/4 teaspoon salt

1 teaspoon canola or corn oil

2 tablespoons water

1 tablespoon plus 1 teaspoon shredded or grated Parmesan cheese

PER SERVING

Calories	231
Total Fat	8.0 g
Saturated Fat	3.0 g
Trans Fat	0.5 g
Polyunsaturated Fat	1.0 g
Monounsaturated Fat	3.5 g
Cholesterol	64 mg
Sodium	436 mg
Carbohydrates	11 g
Fiber	2 g
Sugars	3 g
Protein	29 g

Dietary exchanges: 1 starch, 3 lean meat

Substituting patties for the traditional loaf will shorten the cooking time of this favorite comfort food. This healthy version includes oats and zucchini, plus spaghetti sauce inside and out.

In a medium bowl, stir together the beef, oatmeal, zucchini, 1/4 cup spaghetti sauce, egg whites, and salt. Shape into 4 patties about 1/2 inch thick and about 4 inches in diameter.

In a large nonstick skillet, heat the oil over medium heat, swirling to coat the bottom. Cook the patties, covered, for 5 minutes. Turn over. Reduce the heat to medium low.

Add the water, lifting the patties slightly to allow the water to cover the bottom of the pan.

Spoon the remaining 1/2 cup spaghetti sauce onto the patties. Cook, covered, for 10 minutes, or until the patties are no longer pink in the center. Serve sprinkled with the Parmesan.

NUTRITION TIP: The use of shredded zucchini in this recipe is a great example of how to add more vegetables to your meals. Try the same technique with other recipes your family loves.

MAKE IT A MEAL WITH green beans and Lighten-Up Mashed Potatoes (page 182).

COOK'S TIP: Adding the water keeps the patties from overbrowning and helps them stay moist.

Tex-Mex Mac 'n' Cheese

SERVES 4 | 1¼ CUPS PER SERVING | START TO FINISH: 25 MINUTES

4 ounces dried whole-wheat elbow macaroni

Cooking spray (if using Dutch oven)

12 ounces extra-lean ground beef

1 cup chopped onion

1 small green bell pepper, chopped (about 1 cup)

1 tablespoon chili powder

3 medium garlic cloves, finely chopped

1 teaspoon dried oregano, crumbled

⅛ teaspoon cayenne

⅛ teaspoon salt

⅓ cup salsa (lowest sodium available)

2 tablespoons no-salt-added tomato paste

¾ cup fat-free evaporated milk

½ cup shredded low-fat sharp Cheddar cheese

2 medium green onions, sliced (optional)

This wholesome skillet supper is just what you need on a busy night. It's easy to prepare, and the whole family will love it.

Prepare the pasta using the package directions, omitting the salt and oil. Drain well in a colander.

Meanwhile, if using a Dutch oven, lightly spray with cooking spray. In the Dutch oven or a 12-inch nonstick skillet, stir together the beef, onion, bell pepper, chili powder, garlic, oregano, cayenne, and salt. Cook over medium-high heat for 8 minutes, or until the beef is browned and the onion and bell pepper are soft, stirring frequently to turn and break up the beef.

Stir in the salsa and tomato paste. Cook for 2 minutes, stirring constantly. Remove from the heat.

Stir in the evaporated milk and Cheddar. Cover and set aside if the pasta isn't ready.

When the pasta is cooked, stir into the beef mixture. Cook over medium heat for about 4 minutes, or until heated through, stirring frequently. Serve topped with the green onions.

PER SERVING

Calories	308
Total Fat	6.0 g
Saturated Fat	2.5 g
Trans Fat	0.5 g
Polyunsaturated Fat	1.0 g
Monounsaturated Fat	2.0 g
Cholesterol	52 mg
Sodium	388 mg
Carbohydrates	35 g
Fiber	4 g
Sugars	11 g
Protein	31 g

Dietary exchanges: 2 starch, 1 vegetable, 3½ lean meat

NUTRITION TIP: Keep portions appropriate to the age of your children. A heaping plate of food can be intimidating instead of inviting to a small child. Let your child's hunger be your guide—you can always offer seconds if appropriate!

MAKE IT A MEAL *WITH* steamed carrots and green peas.

Pita Joes

SERVES 4 | 2 STUFFED PITA HALVES PER SERVING | START TO FINISH: 30 MINUTES

1 pound extra-lean ground beef

²/₃ cup chopped onion

1 medium carrot, chopped

2 ounces zucchini, finely chopped

1 medium garlic clove, minced

1 14.5-ounce can no-salt-added whole tomatoes, drained and chopped

1 8-ounce can no-salt-added tomato sauce

1 tablespoon firmly packed light brown sugar

2 teaspoons chili powder

2 teaspoons Worcestershire sauce (lowest sodium available)

1 teaspoon dry mustard

¹/₈ teaspoon salt

¹/₈ teaspoon pepper

4 7-inch whole-wheat pita pockets

PER SERVING

Calories	409
Total Fat	8.0 g
Saturated Fat	2.5 g
Trans Fat	0.5 g
Polyunsaturated Fat	1.5 g
Monounsaturated Fat	2.5 g
Cholesterol	62 mg
Sodium	636 mg
Carbohydrates	54 g
Fiber	8 g
Sugars	12 g
Protein	34 g

Dietary exchanges: 3 starch, 2 vegetable, 3 lean meat

These great-tasting "Joes" are packed with vegetables and are lower in fat than most sloppy Joes—plus the pitas make them neater to eat.

In a large nonstick skillet, cook the beef, onion, carrot, zucchini, and garlic over medium-high heat for 10 minutes, or until the beef is no longer pink, stirring frequently to turn and break up the beef. Drain and discard any liquid.

Stir in the remaining ingredients except the pitas. Reduce the heat to medium and cook for 10 minutes, stirring occasionally.

Just before serving, cut each pita in half, wrap all in paper towels, and microwave on 100 percent power (high) for 45 to 60 seconds, or until warm. Or preheat the oven to 350°F, wrap the pitas in aluminum foil, and warm in the oven for about 10 minutes.

Spoon ¹/₂ cup beef mixture into the pocket of each pita half.

COOK'S TIP ON PITA BREAD: Look for pita bread made with whole-wheat flour for added nutrition and fiber. Use the leftover pitas to make Pick-Your-Own Pita Chips (page 26) for after-school snacks.

MAKE IT A MEAL *WITH* corn on the cob and mixed fruit.

Pretzel Schnitzel

SERVES 4 | 3 OUNCES PORK PER SERVING | START TO FINISH: 20 MINUTES

½ cup fat-free milk

½ cup egg substitute

1 cup crushed unsalted pretzels
(about 3 ounces)

½ teaspoon pepper (coarsely ground
preferred)

¼ teaspoon salt
Cooking spray

2 teaspoons olive oil and
2 teaspoons olive oil, divided use

1 1-pound pork tenderloin, all
visible fat discarded, quartered,
pounded into 7 × 4-inch pieces

2 medium lemons, halved

PER SERVING

Calories	258
Total Fat	8.0 g
Saturated Fat	1.5 g
Trans Fat	0.0 g
Polyunsaturated Fat	1.0 g
Monounsaturated Fat	4.5 g
Cholesterol	59 mg
Sodium	246 mg
Carbohydrates	21 g
Fiber	1 g
Sugars	2 g
Protein	25 g

Dietary exchanges: 1½ starch,
3 lean meat

No-salt pretzels make a terrific crisp coating for this succulent pork dish with the fun-to-say name.

Preheat the oven to 250°F.

Pour the milk into a shallow dish or pie pan. Pour the egg substitute into a separate shallow dish or pie pan. Put the pretzel crumbs on a large plate. Stir the pepper and salt into the crumbs. Set the dishes and the plate in a row, assembly-line fashion.

Lightly spray a large skillet with cooking spray. Pour in 2 teaspoons oil, swirling to coat the bottom. Heat over medium-high heat.

Meanwhile, dip 1 piece of pork in the milk, turning to coat. Let any excess drip off. Dip in the egg substitute, turning to coat. Let any excess drip off. Dip in the crumbs, turning to coat. Gently shake off any excess crumbs. Place the pork in the skillet. Repeat with the second piece of pork. Cook for 2 minutes, or until the coating is crisp. Turn over. Cook for 2 to 3 minutes, or until the coating is crisp and the pork is no longer pink in the center. Transfer to an oven-safe platter. Put in the oven to keep warm. Repeat the process with the remaining 2 pieces of pork.

Just before serving, squeeze the lemon over the pork.

NUTRITION TIP: Try using salt-free pretzel crumbs for coatings in other favorite recipes, too—they're much lower in sodium than seasoned bread crumbs.

MAKE IT A MEAL *WITH* Sweet-and-Sour Red Cabbage (page 179) and boiled gold-skin potatoes.

Simple, Savory Pork Chops

SERVES 4 | 1 PORK CHOP AND 1½ TEASPOONS SAUCE PER SERVING | START TO FINISH: 15 MINUTES

4 bone-in pork loin chops (about 5 ounces each), all visible fat discarded

1 medium garlic clove, halved crosswise

2 teaspoons salt-free garlic-and-herb seasoning blend

1 teaspoon olive oil and 2 teaspoons olive oil, divided use

¼ cup water

2 teaspoons Worcestershire sauce (lowest sodium available)

¼ teaspoon salt

PER SERVING

Calories	192
Total Fat	10.5 g
Saturated Fat	3.0 g
Trans Fat	0.0 g
Polyunsaturated Fat	1.0 g
Monounsaturated Fat	6.0 g
Cholesterol	62 mg
Sodium	194 mg
Carbohydrates	0 g
Fiber	0 g
Sugars	0 g
Protein	22 g

Dietary exchanges: 3 lean meat, ½ fat

There are many ways to serve food with tons of flavor but without fatty frying or heavy sauces. In this case, it just takes the simple addition of a secret ingredient—water!

Rub both sides of the pork with the garlic. Sprinkle both sides with the seasoning blend.

In a large nonstick skillet, heat 1 teaspoon oil over medium-high heat, swirling to coat the bottom. Cook the pork for 4 minutes on each side, or until no longer pink in the center. Transfer to a large plate.

Add the water, Worcestershire sauce, salt, and remaining 2 teaspoons oil to the skillet, scraping to dislodge any browned bits. Stir. Cook for 1 minute, or until reduced to 2 tablespoons liquid. Spoon over the pork.

COOK'S TIP: To remove the garlic odor from your fingertips, rub them on anything made of stainless steel or chrome—your kitchen faucet, for example.

MAKE IT A MEAL WITH Creamy, Cheesy Spinach (page 187) and microwaved apple slices dusted with cinnamon.

Green Noodles and Ham

SERVES 4 | 1 CUP PER SERVING | START TO FINISH: 20 MINUTES

8 ounces dried spinach fettuccine

Cooking spray

5 ounces lower-sodium, low-fat ham, all visible fat discarded, diced (about 1 cup)

1 cup fat-free milk

1 tablespoon all-purpose flour

2 tablespoons low-fat tub cream cheese

¾ cup frozen peas, partially thawed

¼ cup shredded or grated Parmesan cheese

PER SERVING

Calories	320
Total Fat	5.5 g
Saturated Fat	2.5 g
Trans Fat	0.0 g
Polyunsaturated Fat	1.0 g
Monounsaturated Fat	1.5 g
Cholesterol	25 mg
Sodium	489 mg
Carbohydrates	49 g
Fiber	4 g
Sugars	8 g
Protein	20 g

Dietary exchanges: 3½ starch, 1½ lean meat

> **NUTRITION TIP:** Try pastas in delicious vegetable flavors: tomato, garlic, artichoke, red bell pepper, mushroom, and spinach.

> **MAKE IT A MEAL** *WITH* garden salad and warmed peach halves sprinkled with brown sugar.

Green eggs aren't the only green things to eat with ham!

Prepare the pasta using the package directions, omitting the salt and oil. Drain well in a colander. Set aside.

Meanwhile, spray a large skillet with cooking spray. Cook the ham over medium heat for 2 minutes, or until heated through.

In a small bowl, whisk together the milk and flour until smooth. Pour over the ham. Heat for 2 to 3 minutes, or until thickened, stirring frequently.

Stir in the cream cheese. Cook for 1 to 2 minutes, or until melted, stirring constantly.

Stir in the peas. Cook for 2 to 3 minutes, or until heated through. Stir in the pasta and Parmesan.

Portobello Pizzas

SERVES 4 | 1 PIZZA PER SERVING | START TO FINISH: 30 MINUTES

4 portobello mushrooms (about
    4 ounces each), stems discarded

Cooking spray

2 medium Italian plum (Roma)
    tomatoes, diced

4 ounces frozen artichoke hearts,
    thawed and quartered

¼ cup shredded or grated Parmesan
    cheese

1 tablespoon balsamic vinegar

1 medium garlic clove, minced

½ teaspoon dried oregano, crumbled

½ cup shredded part-skim mozzarella
    cheese

1 ounce crumbled soft goat cheese
    (about ¼ cup)

¼ cup sliced black olives

PER SERVING

Calories	124
Total Fat	6.5 g
Saturated Fat	3.5 g
Trans Fat	0.0 g
Polyunsaturated Fat	0.5 g
Monounsaturated Fat	2.0 g
Cholesterol	16 mg
Sodium	292 mg
Carbohydrates	9 g
Fiber	4 g
Sugars	3 g
Protein	9 g

Dietary exchanges: 2 vegetable,
    1 medium-fat meat

MAKE IT A MEAL
WITH tossed salad.

Hearty portobello mushrooms make an unusual and satisfying base for these savory three-cheese pizzas.

Preheat the oven to 400°F.

Lightly spray both sides of the mushrooms with cooking spray. Place with the smooth side down on a nonstick baking sheet.

Bake for 10 minutes, or until tender. Leave the oven on. Transfer the baking sheet to a cooling rack. If needed, blot the gill side of the cooked mushrooms with paper towels to remove any excess liquid.

Meanwhile, in a small bowl, stir together the tomatoes, artichokes, Parmesan, vinegar, garlic, and oregano. Spoon the tomato mixture onto the baked mushrooms. Sprinkle with the mozzarella and goat cheese. Top with the olives.

Bake for 10 minutes, or until the cheeses are melted and the topping is heated through.

COOK'S TIP ON THAWING ARTICHOKES: If you didn't remember to thaw the artichokes you need for this dish, no problem. While the mushrooms are baking, put the artichokes in a microwaveable bowl and microwave at 50 percent power (defrost) for about 5 minutes, or until thawed. The start-to-finish time will remain the same.

COOK'S TIP ON PORTOBELLO MUSHROOMS: The gills on the underside of portobello mushrooms tend to release a dark gray liquid when the mushrooms are cooked. You can easily remove the gills by scraping them with a spoon before you cook the mushrooms. You can skip that step for this recipe since the ingredients are placed on top of the mushrooms and there is no stirring; thus, the "gill liquid" won't be a factor.

Pasta with No-Cook Tomato Sauce

SERVES 4 | 1½ CUPS PER SERVING | START TO FINISH: 20 MINUTES

8 ounces dried whole-wheat linguini, spaghetti, or vermicelli

3 large tomatoes, chopped and drained

¼ cup chopped fresh basil

2 tablespoons olive oil (extra-virgin preferred)

1 small garlic clove, minced

½ teaspoon salt

⅛ teaspoon pepper

¼ cup finely shredded or grated Parmesan cheese

Crushed red pepper flakes to taste (optional)

This super-fast, super-easy entrée is perfect for using the season's best tomatoes and fragrant fresh basil.

Prepare the pasta using the package directions, omitting the salt and oil. Drain well in a colander.

Meanwhile, in a large bowl, stir together the remaining ingredients except the Parmesan.

Stir in the hot pasta. Serve sprinkled with the Parmesan and red pepper flakes.

> MAKE IT A MEAL
> *WITH* garden salad and Squash with Carrot Matchsticks (page 192).

PER SERVING

Calories	304
Total Fat	9.0 g
Saturated Fat	2.0 g
Trans Fat	0.0 g
Polyunsaturated Fat	1.0 g
Monounsaturated Fat	5.5 g
Cholesterol	4 mg
Sodium	387 mg
Carbohydrates	48 g
Fiber	9 g
Sugars	6 g
Protein	12 g

Dietary exchanges: 3 starch, 1 vegetable, 1 fat

Spring Ragù with Spiral Pasta

SERVES 4 | 1 CUP PASTA AND ¾ CUP SAUCE PER SERVING | START TO FINISH: 30 MINUTES

8 ounces dried whole-wheat fusilli or other novelty pasta

1 tablespoon olive oil

2 medium carrots, diced

¾ cup chopped onion

½ medium yellow bell pepper, diced

4 ounces baby portobello (cremini) mushrooms, coarsely chopped

1 large garlic clove, minced

1 15-ounce can tomato puree

1 small tomato, diced

½ teaspoon crushed fennel seeds

½ teaspoon honey

⅛ teaspoon salt

⅛ teaspoon crushed red pepper flakes, or to taste

PER SERVING

Calories	316
Total Fat	4.5 g
Saturated Fat	0.5 g
Trans Fat	0.0 g
Polyunsaturated Fat	1.0 g
Monounsaturated Fat	2.5 g
Cholesterol	0 mg
Sodium	132 mg
Carbohydrates	62 g
Fiber	12 g
Sugars	13 g
Protein	12 g

Dietary exchanges: 3 starch, 3 vegetable

> MAKE IT A MEAL
> *WITH* whole-wheat rolls, and honeydew melon wedges with blueberries sprinkled on top.

The combination of fennel seeds and red pepper flakes duplicates the flavors of traditional Italian sausage, but without the high levels of sodium and saturated fat.

Prepare the pasta using the package directions, omitting the salt and oil. Drain well in a colander. Cover to keep warm.

Meanwhile, in a large nonstick skillet, heat the oil over medium heat, swirling to coat the bottom. Cook the carrots and onion for 4 to 5 minutes, or until the onion is soft, stirring occasionally.

Stir in the bell pepper. Cook for 1 minute.

Stir in the mushrooms and garlic. Cook for 5 minutes, or until the mushrooms begin to soften, stirring occasionally.

Stir in the remaining ingredients except the pasta. Reduce the heat and simmer for 5 to 8 minutes, or until slightly reduced and thickened, stirring occasionally. Serve over the pasta.

Good-for-You Fried Rice

SERVES 4 | 1½ CUPS PER SERVING | START TO FINISH: 30 MINUTES

½ cup frozen shelled edamame
    (green soybeans)

1 cup hot water

1 cup uncooked instant brown rice

1 teaspoon canola or corn oil and
    1 teaspoon canola or corn oil,
    divided use

½ cup egg substitute

3 medium carrots, chopped

1½ cups sliced mushrooms, any kind
    or combination

4 ounces snow peas, trimmed

1 teaspoon minced peeled
    gingerroot

1 medium garlic clove, minced

¼ teaspoon pepper

8 ears canned baby corn, rinsed

2 teaspoons soy sauce (lowest
    sodium available)

1 medium green onion, sliced

PER SERVING

Calories	202
Total Fat	4.5 g
Saturated Fat	0.5 g
Trans Fat	0.0 g
Polyunsaturated Fat	1.5 g
Monounsaturated Fat	2.0 g
Cholesterol	0 mg
Sodium	229 mg
Carbohydrates	30 g
Fiber	6 g
Sugars	5 g
Protein	10 g

Dietary exchanges: 1½ starch,
  2 vegetable, ½ fat

Packed with veggies, this fried rice entrée is ready in just minutes.

Put the edamame in a small bowl. Pour the water over the edamame. Let stand for 1 minute. Drain well and set aside.

Prepare the rice using the package directions, omitting the salt and margarine. Pour the cooked rice onto a large pan, such as a 10 × 15 × 2-inch jelly-roll pan, to cool slightly.

Meanwhile, in a small nonstick skillet, heat 1 teaspoon oil over medium-low heat, swirling to coat the bottom. Pour in the egg substitute. As it cooks, lift the edge of the egg substitute with a spatula and tilt the skillet so the uncooked portion flows under the edge. Cook for 1 to 2 minutes, or until set. Transfer to a large plate. Cover with aluminum foil to keep warm.

In a large nonstick skillet, heat the remaining 1 teaspoon oil over medium-high heat, swirling to coat the bottom. Cook the carrots, mushrooms, snow peas, gingerroot, garlic, and pepper for 4 minutes, or until the carrots and snow peas are tender-crisp, stirring frequently.

Stir in the corn. Cook for 1 minute, stirring frequently.

Stir in the cooked rice and soy sauce.

Cut the cooked egg substitute into small pieces. Gently fold into the rice mixture. Cook for 1 minute, or until the rice is hot, stirring gently. Remove from the heat. Serve sprinkled with the green onions.

MAKE IT A MEAL *WITH*
a mixture of cucumbers and tomatoes
sprinkled with plain rice wine vinegar.

Veggie Burgers with Kicked-Up Ketchup

SERVES 4 | 1 PATTY AND 2 TABLESPOONS KETCHUP PER SERVING | START TO FINISH: 30 MINUTES

Cooking spray

1 15-ounce can no-salt-added chickpeas, rinsed and drained

1 cup canned sweet potatoes (packed without liquid or in light syrup), drained if needed

1/2 cup shredded carrot

1/2 cup shredded zucchini (about 1/2 small)

1/2 cup chopped spinach (about 1/2 ounce)

1/2 cup frozen whole-kernel corn

1/4 cup all-purpose flour

1 tablespoon toasted wheat germ

1/2 teaspoon garlic powder

1/2 teaspoon onion powder

1/2 teaspoon ground cumin

1/4 teaspoon pepper

1 tablespoon olive oil

1/4 cup plus 1 tablespoon no-salt-added ketchup

1 tablespoon Dijon mustard

1 tablespoon honey

1 tablespoon fresh lemon juice

Kids know that ketchup makes everything better, especially when it's been jazzed up with lemon, honey, and Dijon mustard.

Preheat the oven to 375°F. Lightly spray a baking sheet with cooking spray.

In a food processor, process the chickpeas and sweet potatoes for 20 to 30 seconds, or until slightly chunky to almost smooth, scraping the side occasionally. Transfer to a medium bowl.

Stir the carrot, zucchini, spinach, corn, flour, wheat germ, garlic powder, onion powder, cumin, and pepper into the chickpea mixture. Shape into 4 patties about 4 inches in diameter. Lightly spray both sides with cooking spray.

In a large nonstick skillet, heat the oil over medium-high heat. Cook the patties for 2 to 3 minutes on each side, or until browned. Transfer to the baking sheet.

Bake for 10 minutes, or until heated through.

Meanwhile, in a small bowl, stir together the remaining ingredients. Spoon over the cooked patties.

PER SERVING

Calories	299
Total Fat	5.0 g
Saturated Fat	0.5 g
Trans Fat	0.0 g
Polyunsaturated Fat	0.5 g
Monounsaturated Fat	2.5 g
Cholesterol	0 mg
Sodium	154 mg
Carbohydrates	56 g
Fiber	7 g
Sugars	15 g
Protein	9 g
Dietary exchanges: 4 starch	

COOK'S TIP: By browning the patties, then finishing them in the oven, you'll have perfectly cooked patties that are golden brown on the outside and completely cooked in the center.

MAKE IT A MEAL WITH whole-wheat couscous and Strawberry-Mango Smoothies (page 33).

White Bean and Spinach Soup

SERVES 4 | 1¾ CUPS PER SERVING | START TO FINISH: 30 MINUTES

2 teaspoons olive oil

1 large carrot, chopped

¾ cup chopped onion

1 medium rib of celery, chopped

2 medium garlic cloves, minced

2 15-ounce cans no-salt-added cannellini beans, rinsed and drained

2 cups low-sodium vegetable broth

1 cup water

½ teaspoon dried thyme, crumbled

2 medium tomatoes, chopped

2 ounces spinach, chopped

¼ teaspoon salt

¼ teaspoon pepper

This super-simple recipe tastes as if it simmered all day, but actually it takes only minutes. Adding fresh spinach and chopped tomatoes toward the end of cooking brightens the flavor and boosts the nutrients.

In a large saucepan, heat the oil over medium-high heat, swirling to coat the bottom. Cook the carrot, onion, celery, and garlic for 5 minutes, or until the onion is soft, stirring occasionally.

Increase the heat to high. Stir in the beans, broth, water, and thyme. Bring to a boil. Reduce the heat and simmer, covered, for 10 minutes, or until the carrot is tender.

Increase the heat to high. Stir in the remaining ingredients. Cook for 2 minutes, or just until heated through.

PER SERVING

Calories	229
Total Fat	4.0 g
Saturated Fat	0.5 g
Trans Fat	0.0 g
Polyunsaturated Fat	2.0 g
Monounsaturated Fat	1.5 g
Cholesterol	0 mg
Sodium	272 mg
Carbohydrates	37 g
Fiber	11 g
Sugars	7 g
Protein	12 g

Dietary exchanges: 2 starch, 2 vegetable, 1 lean meat

NUTRITION TIP:
Beans are super-nutritious and a good alternative to meat: They're low in fat and high in protein, fiber, and beneficial complex carbs. Try all the different bean varieties in this and other bean-based recipes. When you buy canned beans, look for brands that have no added salt.

MAKE IT A MEAL
WITH Italian Pita Chips (page 26) and cantaloupe wedges with fat-free or low-fat vanilla frozen yogurt.

Fiesta Cobb Salad

SERVES 4 | 1½ CUPS SALAD AND 2 TABLESPOONS DRESSING PER SERVING | START TO FINISH: 15 MINUTES

SALAD

5 cups torn romaine (about 7½ ounces)

1 cup canned no-salt-added black beans, rinsed and drained

½ cup frozen whole-kernel corn, thawed

1 medium Italian plum (Roma) tomato, diced

2 medium green onions, chopped

1 small avocado, chopped

DRESSING

3 tablespoons fat-free sour cream

3 tablespoons low-fat buttermilk

2 teaspoons cider vinegar

1 medium garlic clove, minced

½ teaspoon chili powder

¼ teaspoon ground cumin

½ cup shredded low-fat Mexican cheese blend

¼ cup crushed baked tortilla chips (about ½ cup whole)

Corn, tomatoes, black beans, and avocado provide a fabulous combination of color, taste, and nutrition in one easy salad.

In a large salad bowl, toss the salad ingredients.

In a small bowl, whisk together the dressing ingredients. Drizzle over the salad. Toss to combine. Sprinkle with the cheese blend and tortilla chips.

NUTRITION TIP: The more well-chosen add-ons in your salad, the better! It's easy to serve a really healthy salad if you incorporate a wide variety of dark leafy greens and deeply colored vegetables, such as carrots and beets. Don't be hesitant to add fruit and nuts as well. The avocado in this recipe is another great choice: It's rich in helpful monounsaturated fat, the same kind that's found in olive oil.

MAKE IT A MEAL *WITH* whole-wheat breadsticks, and bananas combined with unsweetened frozen peaches.

PER SERVING

Calories	228
Total Fat	9.0 g
Saturated Fat	3.0 g
Trans Fat	0.0 g
Polyunsaturated Fat	1.5 g
Monounsaturated Fat	4.5 g
Cholesterol	10 mg
Sodium	195 mg
Carbohydrates	27 g
Fiber	8 g
Sugars	6 g
Protein	11 g

Dietary exchanges: 1½ starch, 1 vegetable, 1 lean meat, 1 fat

Asian Vegetable Soup

SERVES 4 | 1½ CUPS PER SERVING | START TO FINISH: 25 MINUTES

1 teaspoon canola or corn oil

3 tablespoons minced peeled gingerroot

2 medium garlic cloves, minced

4 cups water

2 tablespoons soy sauce (lowest sodium available)

8 ounces frozen shelled edamame (green soybeans)

4 ounces snow peas, trimmed and thinly sliced

2 ounces shiitake mushrooms, stems discarded, or button mushrooms, sliced

1 medium carrot, cut in half lengthwise and thinly sliced crosswise

⅛ teaspoon crushed red pepper flakes

6 ounces light firm tofu, drained if needed, cut into ½ inch cubes

½ teaspoon toasted sesame oil

⅛ teaspoon salt

2 medium green onions, thinly sliced (optional)

Ginger-soy broth is the base for this veggie-packed entrée soup. Vary the vegetables depending on what you have on hand: Try thinly sliced bell pepper, zucchini, asparagus, cabbage, or any other family favorites.

In a large saucepan, heat the oil over medium heat, swirling to coat the bottom. Cook the gingerroot and garlic for 1 minute, stirring constantly.

Pour in the water and soy sauce. Increase the heat to high and bring to a boil.

Stir in the edamame, snow peas, mushrooms, carrot, and red pepper flakes. Return to a boil. Reduce the heat to medium and cook for 5 minutes, or until the carrot is tender.

Stir in the tofu, sesame oil, and salt. Top each serving with the green onions.

PER SERVING

Calories	154
Total Fat	6.0 g
Saturated Fat	1.0 g
Trans Fat	0.0 g
Polyunsaturated Fat	2.5 g
Monounsaturated Fat	2.0 g
Cholesterol	0 mg
Sodium	334 mg
Carbohydrates	13 g
Fiber	5 g
Sugars	3 g
Protein	12 g

Dietary exchanges: 1 starch, 1½ lean meat

NUTRITION TIP:
Edamame are green (immature) soybeans that are available both fresh and frozen, shelled or still in their pods. They provide protein with no saturated fat and have a sweetly nutty flavor. Steam them to eat by themselves or add them to soups, salads, casseroles, and side dishes. Edamame still in the pods make great snack food: Kids (and most adults) love to pop the soybeans right into their mouths! Just remember to discard the pods—they are too tough to eat.

MAKE IT A MEAL *WITH* spinach salad and whole-wheat rolls.

Veggie Couscous Salad

SERVES 4 | 1½ CUPS PER SERVING | START TO FINISH: 30 MINUTES

⅔ cup uncooked whole-wheat couscous

½ cup frozen green peas

¾ cup low-sodium vegetable broth
   Cooking spray

¼ cup pineapple juice

2 tablespoons cider vinegar

1 tablespoon light brown sugar

2 teaspoons olive oil (extra-virgin preferred)

1 teaspoon dried oregano, crumbled

⅛ teaspoon pepper

4 ounces eggplant, cut crosswise in ½-inch slices

1 4-ounce zucchini, cut crosswise in ½-inch slices

1 4-ounce yellow summer squash, cut crosswise in ½-inch slices

1 medium red bell pepper, halved lengthwise, ribs and seeds discarded

¼ cup sliced almonds, dry-roasted

Mild-flavored couscous is a perfect foil for a medley of quickly grilled vegetables. A sweet-tart dressing and a sprinkling of almonds add healthy omega-3 oils and round out this light but nutritious entrée.

Prepare the couscous using the package directions, adding the peas, substituting the vegetable broth for the water, and omitting the salt and oil. Fluff with a fork. Cover to keep warm.

Meanwhile, lightly spray the grill rack with cooking spray. Preheat the grill on medium high.

In a large bowl, whisk together the pineapple juice, vinegar, brown sugar, oil, oregano, and pepper. Set aside.

Lightly spray both sides of the eggplant, zucchini, and yellow squash with cooking spray (the bell pepper doesn't need to be sprayed). Grill the vegetables, including the bell pepper, for 2 to 3 minutes on each side, or until tender.

Transfer the zucchini and yellow squash to a large bowl. Transfer the bell pepper and eggplant to a cutting board. Cut the bell pepper and eggplant into 1-inch pieces. Add with the couscous to the squash mixture, stirring to combine.

Stir in the pineapple juice mixture. Serve garnished with the almonds.

PER SERVING

Calories	260
Total Fat	6.0 g
Saturated Fat	0.5 g
Trans Fat	0.0 g
Polyunsaturated Fat	1.5 g
Monounsaturated Fat	3.5 g
Cholesterol	0 mg
Sodium	36 mg
Carbohydrates	45 g
Fiber	9 g
Sugars	9 g
Protein	9 g

Dietary exchanges: 2½ starch, 1 vegetable, 1 fat

NUTRITION TIP:
Whole-wheat couscous cooks as quickly as the regular kind and has lots more fiber. Bump up the nutritional value of the staples in your pantry by using whole-wheat or whole-grain versions when possible.

MAKE IT A MEAL
WITH grilled bananas dusted with cinnamon.

Shepherd's Pie

SERVES 4 | 1½ CUPS PER SERVING | START TO FINISH: 20 MINUTES

1 teaspoon canola or corn oil

¾ cup finely chopped onion

6 ounces zucchini, diced

1⅓ cups water

1 tablespoon light tub margarine

1¼ cups fat-free milk

1⅓ cups uncooked instant potatoes

⅛ teaspoon garlic powder

2 cups frozen soy protein crumbles

1½ teaspoons ground cumin

¼ teaspoon salt

½ cup shredded fat-free sharp
   Cheddar cheese

2 tablespoons snipped fresh parsley

Even if you're not a vegetarian, it's good to add some meat-free dishes, such as this easy version of the British staple, to your menu planning. (Shh . . . If you don't tell them, your family will never know there's no meat.)

In a medium nonstick skillet, heat the oil over medium heat, swirling to coat the bottom. Cook the onion for about 3 minutes, or until beginning to brown on the edges, stirring frequently.

Stir in the zucchini. Cook for 4 minutes, or until the zucchini is just tender, stirring frequently. Remove from the heat. Cover to keep warm.

In a medium saucepan, bring the water and margarine to a boil over high heat. Pour in the milk. Stir in the instant potatoes and garlic powder. Remove from the heat. Cover to keep warm.

Stir the frozen crumbles and cumin into the onion mixture. Cook over medium heat for 2 to 3 minutes, or until heated through, stirring frequently. Remove from the heat.

Sprinkle with the salt. Spoon the potatoes over the onion mixture. Using the back of a spoon, spread evenly. Sprinkle the Cheddar, then the parsley, over all.

PER SERVING

Calories	233
Total Fat	2.5 g
Saturated Fat	0.0 g
Trans Fat	0.0 g
Polyunsaturated Fat	0.5 g
Monounsaturated Fat	1.5 g
Cholesterol	4 mg
Sodium	560 mg
Carbohydrates	31 g
Fiber	5 g
Sugars	6 g
Protein	22 g

Dietary exchanges: 2 starch,
   2½ very lean meat

COOK'S TIP: Frozen soy crumbles are precooked. You should heat them, not cook them, so they retain their "ground beef" texture and don't begin to break down.

MAKE IT A MEAL *WITH* cooked carrots, and fresh strawberries with kiwifruit.

Plan-Aheads

Tandoori-Style Chicken

SERVES 4 | 3 OUNCES CHICKEN PER SERVING

SPICE BLEND

- 1 tablespoon curry powder
- 1 teaspoon ground ginger
- 1/2 teaspoon ground cinnamon
- 1/2 teaspoon cayenne
- 1/4 teaspoon ground nutmeg
- 1/8 teaspoon salt

- 1/2 cup fat-free plain yogurt
- 4 ounces onion, coarsely grated (about 1/3 cup)
- 1 teaspoon olive oil
- 2 medium garlic cloves, finely chopped
- 1 pound chicken tenders, all visible fat discarded
- Cooking spray

PER SERVING

Calories	147
Total Fat	2.5 g
Saturated Fat	0.5 g
Trans Fat	0.0 g
Polyunsaturated Fat	0.5 g
Monounsaturated Fat	1.0 g
Cholesterol	66 mg
Sodium	159 mg
Carbohydrates	3 g
Fiber	1 g
Sugars	1 g
Protein	27 g
Dietary exchanges: 3 very lean meat	

In a pinch, you can marinate the tenders for this richly spiced dish for just one hour, but for the fullest flavor, marinate them overnight.

In a small nonstick skillet, stir together the spice blend ingredients. Warm over medium heat for 4 minutes, or until fragrant, stirring constantly. Pour into a medium bowl.

Stir in the yogurt, onion, oil, and garlic. Spoon over the chicken. Gently rub into the chicken. Cover and refrigerate for 12 to 24 hours, turning occasionally.

Preheat the broiler. Lightly spray the broiler pan and rack with cooking spray.

Remove the chicken from the marinade. Let any excess drip off. Discard the leftover marinade. Put the chicken on the rack, leaving space between the pieces.

Broil the chicken about 6 inches from the heat for 7 minutes. Turn over. Broil for 5 minutes, or until just firm to the touch and no longer pink in the center.

> **NUTRITION TIP:**
> Cooking with a variety of spices adds flavor and complexity so foods don't need lots of added salt or fat.

> **MAKE IT A MEAL**
> *WITH* instant brown rice, microwaved green beans, and whole-wheat pita bread.

Italian Chicken Noodle Soup

SERVES 4 | 1½ CUPS PER SERVING

1 teaspoon olive oil

1 pound boneless, skinless chicken breasts, all visible fat discarded, diced

2 14.5-ounce cans fat-free, low-sodium chicken broth

1½ cups water

1 medium rib of celery, chopped

1 medium carrot, chopped

½ cup chopped onion

¼ medium zucchini, chopped

1 tablespoon dried minced garlic

1 teaspoon dried basil, crumbled

1 teaspoon dried oregano, crumbled

¼ teaspoon pepper

⅛ teaspoon crushed red pepper flakes

2 ounces dried whole-wheat fettuccine, broken into 1-inch pieces

2 tablespoons snipped fresh Italian (flat-leaf) parsley

Three classic Italian flavorings—garlic, basil, and oregano—add an interesting twist to this wholesome chicken soup.

In a large nonstick skillet, heat the oil over medium-high heat, swirling to coat the bottom. Cook the chicken for 5 minutes, or until it is just barely done and the edges are light golden brown, stirring frequently. Drain. Transfer to a 3- to 4-quart slow cooker.

Stir in the broth, water, celery, carrot, onion, zucchini, garlic, basil, oregano, pepper, and red pepper flakes. Cook, covered, on low for 7 to 8 hours or on high for 3 to 4 hours.

If using the low setting, turn the slow cooker to high about 30 minutes before serving time. Cook, covered, on high for 15 minutes.

Stir in the pasta. Cook, covered, on high for 15 minutes, or until the pasta is tender. Stir in the parsley.

PER SERVING

Calories	218
Total Fat	3.0 g
Saturated Fat	0.5 g
Trans Fat	0.0 g
Polyunsaturated Fat	0.5 g
Monounsaturated Fat	1.0 g
Cholesterol	66 mg
Sodium	152 mg
Carbohydrates	17 g
Fiber	4 g
Sugars	3 g
Protein	31 g

Dietary exchanges: 1 starch, 3 very lean meat

COOK'S TIP ON SLOW COOKERS: The exact timing is not critical when using slow cookers, so times usually are given in a range. For best results, fill a slow cooker about half full, and use the cover. For 4 servings, it's generally best to use a 3- to 4-quart slow cooker. Save the 5- to 6-quart slow cookers for larger amounts.

NUTRITION TIP: Your grandmother was right! Research indicates that chicken soup contains anti-inflammatory ingredients that slow the movement of white cells and therefore ease the symptoms of upper respiratory infections.

Three-Bean Turkey Chili

SERVES 4 | 1½ CUPS PER SERVING

2 ounces dried red kidney beans (about ⅓ cup), sorted for stones and shriveled beans and rinsed

2 ounces dried Great Northern beans (about ⅓ cup), sorted for stones and shriveled beans and rinsed

2 ounces dried black beans (about ⅓ cup), sorted for stones and shriveled beans and rinsed

Cooking spray

1 pound ground skinless turkey breast

1 14.5-ounce can no-salt-added tomatoes, undrained

1¾ cups no-salt-added tomato juice

2 cups chopped onion

2 tablespoons chili powder

1 tablespoon dried minced garlic

1 teaspoon ground cumin

¼ teaspoon crushed red pepper flakes

¼ teaspoon pepper

⅛ teaspoon salt

Soaking the dried beans overnight in cold water softens them so they can go in the slow cooker with the rest of the hearty ingredients for this great-tasting chili. (See photograph on page 134.)

In a large bowl, soak the beans overnight in cold water to cover by at least 3 inches. Drain and rinse the beans. Transfer to a 3- to 4-quart slow cooker.

Lightly spray a large skillet with cooking spray. Cook the turkey over medium heat for 5 minutes, or until browned, stirring frequently to turn and break up the turkey. Drain well. Transfer to the slow cooker.

Stir in the remaining ingredients. Cook, covered, on low for 8 to 9 hours or on high for 3 to 4 hours.

> **KIDS IN THE KITCHEN:** Organize older kids around the table to help sort dried beans for stones. Sharing a repetitive task fosters conversation or storytelling.

PER SERVING

Calories	339
Total Fat	2.0 g
Saturated Fat	0.5 g
Trans Fat	0.0 g
Polyunsaturated Fat	0.5 g
Monounsaturated Fat	0.5 g
Cholesterol	77 mg
Sodium	259 mg
Carbohydrates	41 g
Fiber	11 g
Sugars	13 g
Protein	40 g

Dietary exchanges: 2 starch, 2 vegetable, 4 very lean meat

Peppered Pot Roast

SERVES 6 | 2½ OUNCES BEEF AND ⅔ CUP VEGETABLES PER SERVING

6 medium red potatoes (about 9 ounces total), halved

2 4-ounce onions, cut into ½-inch wedges

3 medium carrots, cut crosswise into 1-inch pieces

2 medium ribs of celery, cut crosswise into 1-inch pieces

1 medium bay leaf

2 teaspoons salt-free steak seasoning blend

1½ pounds boneless beef chuck shoulder roast, all visible fat discarded

1 teaspoon canola or corn oil

¼ cup water

1 teaspoon instant coffee granules

¾ teaspoon dried oregano, crumbled

½ teaspoon salt

PER SERVING

Calories	233
Total Fat	8.0 g
Saturated Fat	2.5 g
Trans Fat	0.0 g
Polyunsaturated Fat	0.5 g
Monounsaturated Fat	3.0 g
Cholesterol	65 mg
Sodium	300 mg
Carbohydrates	15 g
Fiber	3 g
Sugars	5 g
Protein	25 g

Dietary exchanges: ½ starch, 1 vegetable, 3 lean meat

COOK'S TIP: Adding the coffee granules gives the dish a deeper beef flavor.

This slow-cooker roast needs no attention during the day, yet rewards you with down-home flavor at night.

Put the potatoes, onions, carrots, celery, and bay leaf in a 3- to 4-quart slow cooker.

Sprinkle the seasoning blend over the roast. Using your fingertips, press the seasoning blend so it adheres to the roast. In a medium nonstick skillet, heat the oil over medium-high heat, swirling to coat the bottom. Cook the roast for 3 minutes on each side, or until richly browned. Transfer to the slow cooker.

Put the remaining ingredients in the skillet. Stir, scraping to dislodge any browned bits. Pour over the roast. Cook, covered, on low for 8 hours or on high for 4 hours, or until the roast is tender. Discard the bay leaf. Transfer the roast and vegetables to a serving platter.

Steak-on-a-Stick

SERVES 4 | 1 KEBAB PER SERVING

1 pound boneless sirloin steak, all visible fat discarded, cut into 20 cubes

¼ cup light balsamic salad dressing and ¼ cup light balsamic salad dressing, divided use

2 teaspoons Worcestershire sauce (lowest sodium available)

1 teaspoon dried oregano, crumbled
  Cooking spray

¾ cup uncooked instant brown rice

1¼ cups water

1 medium zucchini, halved lengthwise, each half cut crosswise into 8 pieces

½ medium red bell pepper, cut into 16 squares

¼ cup snipped fresh parsley

PER SERVING

Calories	247
Total Fat	7.0 g
Saturated Fat	2.0 g
Trans Fat	0.0 g
Polyunsaturated Fat	1.0 g
Monounsaturated Fat	3.0 g
Cholesterol	46 mg
Sodium	373 mg
Carbohydrates	17 g
Fiber	2 g
Sugars	3 g
Protein	27 g
Dietary exchanges: 1 starch, 3 lean meat	

COOK'S TIP: Be careful not to overcook the kebabs, or the steak will be tough.

Kebabs are popular with every age, and they're super-easy to put together when you have extra hands—big or little—to help thread the ingredients on the skewers.

Put the steak and ¼ cup salad dressing in an 8-inch square glass baking dish. Turn to coat. Cover and refrigerate for 8 to 24 hours, turning occasionally if desired.

In a small bowl, stir together the Worcestershire sauce, oregano, and remaining ¼ cup salad dressing. Cover and refrigerate.

About 20 minutes before you want to serve the steak, remove the dressing mixture from the refrigerator. Set aside.

Meanwhile, soak four 10-inch wooden skewers for at least 10 minutes in cold water to keep them from charring, or use metal skewers.

Preheat the broiler. Lightly spray a broiler pan and rack with cooking spray.

Prepare the rice using the package directions but using 1¼ cups water and omitting the salt and margarine. Remove from the heat. Keep covered to stay warm.

Meanwhile, drain the steak, discarding the marinade. Transfer to a large plate. For each kebab, alternate 5 pieces of steak, 4 pieces of zucchini, and 4 pieces of bell pepper on a skewer, starting and ending with the steak.

Broil the kebabs at least 4 inches from the heat for 4 minutes. Turn over. Broil for 3 minutes, or to the desired doneness.

Spoon the rice onto a platter. Place the kebabs on the rice. Spoon the reserved salad dressing mixture over all. Sprinkle with the parsley.

Southwestern Beef Stew

SERVES 4 | 1¼ CUPS PER SERVING

1½ cups chopped onions

1 large red bell pepper, cut into ½-inch dice

1 large garlic clove, chopped

1 9-ounce package frozen whole-kernel corn, thawed

1 pound extra-lean beef stew meat, all visible fat discarded, patted dry

¼ teaspoon salt

⅛ teaspoon pepper

2 teaspoons canola or corn oil

1 14.5-ounce can no-salt-added diced tomatoes, undrained

1 4-ounce can diced mild green chiles, drained

½ cup medium salsa (lowest sodium available)

1 teaspoon ground cumin

½ teaspoon grated orange zest

¼ teaspoon dried oregano, crumbled

¼ cup fresh orange juice

2 tablespoons yellow cornmeal

2 tablespoons water

PER SERVING

Calories	340
Total Fat	11.0 g
Saturated Fat	3.0 g
Trans Fat	0.0 g
Polyunsaturated Fat	1.0 g
Monounsaturated Fat	5.0 g
Cholesterol	71 mg
Sodium	459 mg
Carbohydrates	36 g
Fiber	7 g
Sugars	13 g
Protein	26 g
Dietary exchanges: 1½ starch, 2 vegetable, 3 lean meat	

What could be more comforting than a slow-cooker stew ready and waiting at dinnertime? Just dish it out, turn off the TV, and gather the family to talk over the day's events as you eat.

In a 3- to 4-quart slow cooker, stir together the onions and bell pepper. Scatter the garlic on top. Add the corn. (Don't stir.)

Put the meat on a plate. Sprinkle with the salt and pepper.

In a large skillet, heat the oil over medium-high heat, swirling to coat the bottom. Cook the meat for 7 to 9 minutes, or until browned on all sides. Remove the skillet from the heat. Spoon the meat into the slow cooker.

In the same skillet, stir together the tomatoes with liquid, green chiles, salsa, cumin, orange zest, and oregano, scraping up any browned bits from the bottom. Stir in the orange juice. Pour the mixture into the slow cooker.

Cook, covered, on low for 8 to 9 hours, or until the meat is tender. About 10 minutes before serving, increase the heat to high. (Cooking only on the high setting is not recommended for this recipe.)

In a small bowl, stir together the cornmeal and water. Gently stir into the stew. Let cook for 10 minutes to thicken.

COOK'S TIP: You can make this more or less spicy, depending on personal taste. For more zip, use hotter canned green chiles. For less heat, go with mild instead of medium salsa.

NUTRITION TIP: Salsas vary widely in the amount of sodium they contain. Take a look at the nutritional information for several brands to pick the lowest you can find.

Squash and Wild Rice Medley

SERVES 4 | 1½ CUPS PER SERVING

2 cups low-sodium vegetable broth

2 cups ¾-inch cubes butternut squash

¾ cup uncooked wild rice

¼ cup chopped onion

½ teaspoon poultry seasoning

1 3.5-ounce package (about ⅔ cup) low-fat feta crumbles

½ cup unsweetened dried fruit, such as berry medley, blueberries, cranberries, or cherries

¼ cup slivered almonds

PER SERVING

Calories	285
Total Fat	6.5 g
Saturated Fat	2.0 g
Trans Fat	0.0 g
Polyunsaturated Fat	1.5 g
Monounsaturated Fat	2.5 g
Cholesterol	9 mg
Sodium	357 mg
Carbohydrates	47 g
Fiber	6 g
Sugars	12 g
Protein	13 g
Dietary exchanges: 2 starch, 1 fruit, 1 lean meat	

Wild rice lends visual appeal, texture, and the nutritional benefits of grain to this vegetarian meal in a pot. Dried berries, slivered almonds, and crumbles of sharp feta add interest.

In a 3- to 4-quart slow cooker, stir together the broth, squash, wild rice, onion, and poultry seasoning. Cook, covered, on low for 3 hours to 3 hours 30 minutes, or until the wild rice kernels have partially split open. (The high setting is not recommended for this recipe.)

Before serving, gently stir in the feta, dried fruit, and almonds. Cook, covered, for 5 minutes, to warm through.

COOK'S TIP: Look in the produce department for bags of butternut squash cubes. So much quicker and easier than starting from scratch!

COOK'S TIP ON WILD RICE: Wild rice has a pleasantly nutty taste. When cooking wild rice, remember that it's considered done when the kernel separates a bit (the rice will still be slightly chewy). Hand-harvested wild rice will take a little more time to cook than cultivated wild rice. The package should indicate which method was used.

Lots of Lentils Chili

SERVES 4 | 1½ CUPS PER SERVING

4 cups water

1 14.5-ounce can no-salt-added crushed tomatoes, undrained

1¼ cups dried brown lentils, sorted for stones and shriveled lentils and rinsed

1 small green bell pepper, chopped

⅓ cup chopped onion

2 tablespoons chili powder

1 tablespoon ground cumin

2 medium garlic cloves, minced

½ teaspoon dried oregano, crumbled

½ teaspoon salt

¼ teaspoon pepper

1 tablespoon fresh lime juice

¼ cup shredded fat-free Cheddar cheese

2 medium green onions, thinly sliced

After just a few minutes of prep time, you can let the slow cooker do the work for this heart-healthy entrée. The tiny lentils are packed with big nutrition, especially protein and fiber.

In a 3- to 4-quart slow cooker, stir together the water, tomatoes with liquid, lentils, bell pepper, onion, chili powder, cumin, garlic, oregano, salt, and pepper. Cook, covered, on low for 8 to 10 hours or on high for 5 hours.

Stir in the lime juice. Serve sprinkled with the Cheddar and green onions.

> NUTRITION TIP: When you prepare chilis and stews, try doubling the recipe to fill your freezer with emergency entrées for busy nights. Spoon individual portions into separate containers, mark with the date, and freeze so they'll be ready for family members on the go—and so the food will thaw and reheat faster. This recipe will keep for up to three months in the freezer.

PER SERVING

Calories	304
Total Fat	1.0 g
Saturated Fat	0.0 g
Trans Fat	0.0 g
Polyunsaturated Fat	0.5 g
Monounsaturated Fat	0.0 g
Cholesterol	1 mg
Sodium	430 mg
Carbohydrates	55 g
Fiber	12 g
Sugars	10 g
Protein	24 g

Dietary exchanges: 3 starch, 2 vegetable, 2 very lean meat

Make-Ahead Minestrone

Cooking spray

3 cups low-sodium vegetable broth

1 14.5-ounce can no-salt-added diced tomatoes, undrained

1 cup chopped onion

1 cup baby carrots, cut crosswise into ¼-inch pieces

⅔ cup no-salt-added kidney beans, rinsed and drained

⅔ cup no-salt-added chickpeas, rinsed and drained

2 tablespoons no-salt-added tomato paste

2 teaspoons dried Italian seasoning, crumbled

3 medium garlic cloves, finely chopped

1 medium bay leaf

½ teaspoon pepper

⅛ teaspoon salt

1 medium zucchini, ends trimmed, halved lengthwise and halves cut crosswise into ½-inch wedges

3 cups coarsely chopped kale (about 3 ounces)

2 ounces dried whole-wheat elbow macaroni

2 tablespoons shredded or grated Parmesan cheese

Chockful of vegetables and beans, this delicious, comforting soup simmers while you go about your day. Stirring in the pasta just before serving time keeps it nice and firm to the bite.

Lightly spray a 3- to 4-quart slow cooker with cooking spray. Put in the broth, tomatoes with liquid, onion, carrots, beans, chickpeas, tomato paste, Italian seasoning, garlic, bay leaf, pepper, and salt, stirring to combine.

Gently stir the zucchini into the broth mixture. Cook, covered, on low for 7 hours or on high for 4 hours.

Stir in the kale and pasta. Cook, covered, on high for 30 minutes. Discard the bay leaf. Serve the soup sprinkled with the Parmesan.

NUTRITION TIP:

Refrigerate leftover beans in a covered plastic bowl or resealable plastic bag. Sprinkle them over salads later in the week or mash them to use in a quick dip to enjoy with fresh veggies or whole-grain crackers.

PER SERVING

Calories	222
Total Fat	1.5 g
Saturated Fat	0.5 g
Trans Fat	0.0 g
Polyunsaturated Fat	0.5 g
Monounsaturated Fat	0.5 g
Cholesterol	2 mg
Sodium	240 mg
Carbohydrates	43 g
Fiber	9 g
Sugars	10 g
Protein	13 g

Dietary exchanges: 1½ starch, 4 vegetable, ½ very lean meat

Cook Once, Eat Twice

SEAFOOD

Roasted Salmon with Cucumber-Lime Sauce 148/
Salmon Cakes with Lemon-Caper Sauce 149

Tropical Shrimp-on-a-Stick 150/Grilled Shrimp and
Pineapple Salad with Ginger-Sesame Dressing 153

POULTRY

Mediterranean Grilled Chicken with Red Bell Pepper
Salsa 154/Italian Chicken and Penne Salad 157

Gobble-It-Up Roasted Turkey with Gravy 158/
Turkey Tetrazzini 161

MEATS

South of the Border Beef 162/Beef Tortilla Casserole 165

Roasted Pork Tenderloin and Vegetables 166/
Pork and Veggie Lettuce Wraps 167

VEGETARIAN

Zucchini Boats 168/Three-Cheese Manicotti 171

Grilled Vegetable and Bulgur Salad 172/
Grilled-Vegetable Paninis 173

Roasted Salmon with Cucumber-Lime Sauce

SERVES 4 | 3 OUNCES FISH AND 2 TABLESPOONS SAUCE PER SERVING (PLUS 12 OUNCES FISH RESERVED)

Cooking spray

8 salmon fillets (about 4 ounces each), rinsed and patted dry

½ teaspoon salt and ⅛ teaspoon salt, divided use

¼ teaspoon pepper

1 medium cucumber, peeled, seeded, and coarsely shredded (about ½ cup)

¼ cup fat-free plain yogurt

1 tablespoon snipped fresh Italian (flat-leaf) parsley

¼ teaspoon grated lime zest

2 teaspoons fresh lime juice

PER SERVING

Calories	159
Total Fat	4.5 g
Saturated Fat	0.5 g
Trans Fat	0.0 g
Polyunsaturated Fat	1.5 g
Monounsaturated Fat	1.0 g
Cholesterol	65 mg
Sodium	314 mg
Carbohydrates	3 g
Fiber	0 g
Sugars	2 g
Protein	26 g

Dietary exchanges: 3 lean meat

Yogurt spiked with cucumber and lime is a cool and delicate counterpoint for heart-healthy salmon. The extra salmon will give you a head start on Salmon Cakes with Lemon-Caper Sauce (page 149) later in the week.

Preheat the oven to 350°F. Line a rimmed baking sheet with aluminum foil. Lightly spray with cooking spray. Arrange the fish on the baking sheet. Sprinkle the fish with ½ teaspoon salt and the pepper.

Bake for 10 to 12 minutes, or until the fish is cooked to the desired doneness.

Meanwhile, in a small bowl, stir together the cucumber, yogurt, parsley, lime zest, lime juice, and remaining ⅛ teaspoon salt.

Transfer 4 fillets to plates. Serve with the sauce. Refrigerate the remaining fillets in an airtight container for use within three to four days in Salmon Cakes with Lemon-Caper Sauce.

COOK'S TIP: Sometimes it's less expensive to buy a larger piece of salmon instead of small fillets or steaks. If you opt to use a 2-pound piece of salmon for this recipe, roasting will probably take 16 to 18 minutes. Before you cook salmon, press the flesh to locate any thin bones remaining in the fish. Keep a clean pair of tweezers in your kitchen to use for pulling out the bones.

Salmon Cakes with Lemon-Caper Sauce

SERVES 4 | 1 PATTY AND 2 TABLESPOONS SAUCE PER SERVING

SALMON PATTIES

4 cooked salmon fillets (about 3 ounces each) from Roasted Salmon with Cucumber-Lime Sauce, flaked, crumbled, or broken into chunks

¼ cup plain dry bread crumbs and ¼ cup plain dry bread crumbs, divided use

2 medium green onions, chopped

2 tablespoons snipped fresh Italian (flat-leaf) parsley

1 large egg white

1 teaspoon grated lemon zest

2 teaspoons olive oil

LEMON-CAPER SAUCE

¼ cup light mayonnaise

¼ cup fat-free plain yogurt

1 tablespoon snipped fresh Italian (flat-leaf) parsley

1 tablespoon capers, drained and finely chopped

1 teaspoon fresh lemon juice

¼ teaspoon red hot-pepper sauce

❖

1 medium lemon, quartered

If your family likes salmon cakes made with canned salmon, they'll love this version, which uses fresh salmon pieces left over from Roasted Salmon with Cucumber-Lime Sauce (page 148).

In a medium bowl, stir together the fish, ¼ cup bread crumbs, green onions, parsley, egg white, and lemon zest. Divide the mixture into 4 balls. Lightly flatten each to about 3 inches in diameter. Cover and refrigerate for 20 minutes.

Sprinkle the remaining ¼ cup bread crumbs on a large plate. Put the cakes on the plate and turn to coat both sides.

In a large nonstick skillet, heat the oil over medium heat, swirling to coat the bottom. Cook the patties for 2 to 3 minutes on each side, or until heated through and browned.

Meanwhile, in a small bowl, stir together the sauce ingredients. Spoon over the cakes. Serve with the lemon wedges.

COOK'S TIP: If your supermarket carries fat-free Greek-style yogurt, give it a try in this sauce. Thicker and creamier than regular yogurt, Greek-style yogurt provides a richer flavor, too.

NUTRITION TIP: To get in extra vegetables, serve the cakes on mixed spring greens.

PER SERVING

Calories	284
Total Fat	12.5 g
Saturated Fat	2.0 g
Trans Fat	0.0 g
Polyunsaturated Fat	5.0 g
Monounsaturated Fat	4.0 g
Cholesterol	70 mg
Sodium	536 mg
Carbohydrates	13 g
Fiber	1 g
Sugars	2 g
Protein	29 g

Dietary exchanges: 1 starch, 3 lean meat, ½ fat

Tropical Shrimp-on-a-Stick

SERVES 4 | 1 KEBAB PER SERVING (PLUS 12 OUNCES SHRIMP AND ¼ PINEAPPLE RESERVED)

Cooking spray

½ pineapple

2 pounds raw shrimp in shells
(16 to 20 count), peeled, rinsed,
and patted dry (about 1 pound
8 ounces peeled)

8 mango cubes, about ¾ inch each

½ small red onion, cut into 4 wedges
(about ½ inch each), separated
into layers

½ cup fresh lime juice

⅓ cup plain rice vinegar

1 tablespoon honey

2 teaspoons minced peeled
gingerroot

½ teaspoon toasted sesame oil

PER SERVING

Calories	155
Total Fat	1.5 g
Saturated Fat	0.5 g
Trans Fat	0.0 g
Polyunsaturated Fat	0.5 g
Monounsaturated Fat	0.5 g
Cholesterol	147 mg
Sodium	172 mg
Carbohydrates	20 g
Fiber	2 g
Sugars	15 g
Protein	17 g

Dietary exchanges: 1 fruit,
½ carbohydrate, 2½ very lean meat

Jimmy Buffett would love this dish! Succulent shrimp sizzles on the grill, then is skewered with tropical fruit for a sweet and tangy meal. This recipe allows you to cook enough shrimp and pineapple so you'll have plenty to make Grilled Shrimp and Pineapple Salad with Ginger-Sesame Dressing (page 153) another evening.

Lightly spray the grill rack with cooking spray. Preheat the grill on medium high. Soak six 12-inch wooden skewers for at least 10 minutes in cold water to keep them from charring, or use metal skewers.

Peel and core the pineapple half. Cut in half lengthwise. Cut one of the pieces into 12 cubes, each about 1 inch. Cut the other piece into 2 wedges. Set the wedges aside.

Alternately skewer half the shrimp with the pineapple cubes, mango cubes, and red onion pieces on four of the skewers. Skewer the remaining shrimp (for use in Grilled Shrimp and Pineapple Salad with Ginger-Sesame Dressing) on two of the skewers.

In a small bowl, stir together the remaining ingredients.

Grill the kebabs, skewered shrimp, and reserved pineapple wedges for 4 to 6 minutes, or until the shrimp turns pink and is cooked through and the fruit is hot, turning to grill evenly and brushing generously with the lime juice mixture.

Transfer the kebabs to a serving platter. Remove the shrimp for Grilled Shrimp and Pineapple Salad with Ginger-Sesame Dressing from the skewers. Refrigerate those shrimp and the pineapple wedges in an airtight container or wrap them tightly in plastic wrap for use within three to four days.

Grilled Shrimp and Pineapple Salad with Ginger-Sesame Dressing

SERVES 4 | 3 OUNCES SHRIMP, 1½ CUPS SALAD, AND 2 TABLESPOONS DRESSING PER SERVING

SALAD

12 ounces grilled shrimp from Tropical Shrimp-on-a-Stick

2 cups torn romaine

2 wedges grilled pineapple from Tropical Shrimp-on-a-Stick, cut into ½-inch pieces

12 grape tomatoes

¼ small jícama, peeled and chopped (about ¼ cup)

¼ cup chopped mango

DRESSING

¼ cup plain rice vinegar

3 tablespoons fat-free, low-sodium chicken broth

2 teaspoons minced peeled gingerroot

1½ teaspoons toasted sesame oil

1 medium garlic clove, minced

1 tablespoon sesame seeds, dry-roasted

PER SERVING

Calories	157
Total Fat	4.0 g
Saturated Fat	0.5 g
Trans Fat	0.0 g
Polyunsaturated Fat	1.5 g
Monounsaturated Fat	1.5 g
Cholesterol	147 mg
Sodium	179 mg
Carbohydrates	13 g
Fiber	3 g
Sugars	8 g
Protein	17 g

Dietary exchanges: 1 fruit, 3 lean meat

Using the shrimp and pineapple you grilled when you made the Tropical Shrimp-on-a-Stick (page 150), you can serve this tropical island salad in just minutes.

In a salad bowl, toss together the salad ingredients.

In a small bowl, whisk together the dressing ingredients. Drizzle over the salad. Toss to combine. Serve sprinkled with the sesame seeds.

> **COOK'S TIP ON JÍCAMA:** This unique root vegetable has a thick brown skin and refreshingly crunchy flesh. When buying, look for jícama that feels firm and has no blemishes or mold on the surface. Use a sharp knife or vegetable peeler to remove the skin. Cut the flesh into slices or sticks to use with dips, as a snack, or in salads or stir-fries, or add cubes of jícama to soup near the end of the cooking time.

Mediterranean Grilled Chicken with Red Bell Pepper Salsa

SERVES 4 | 3 OUNCES CHICKEN AND 2½ TABLESPOONS SALSA PER SERVING
(PLUS 12 OUNCES CHICKEN RESERVED)

2 tablespoons fresh lemon juice

2 tablespoons white wine vinegar
  and 1 teaspoon white wine
  vinegar, divided use

1 tablespoon olive oil and 1 teaspoon olive oil, divided use

2 medium garlic cloves, minced,
  and 1 medium garlic clove,
  minced, divided use

½ teaspoon dried oregano, crumbled

½ teaspoon dried basil, crumbled

2 pounds boneless, skinless chicken
  breasts, all visible fat discarded,
  pounded to ½-inch thickness

½ large red bell pepper, cut into
  1-inch strips

  Cooking spray

2 tablespoons chopped fresh basil

1 tablespoon minced shallot

PER SERVING

Calories	145
Total Fat	2.5 g
Saturated Fat	0.5 g
Trans Fat	0.0 g
Polyunsaturated Fat	0.5 g
Monounsaturated Fat	1.0 g
Cholesterol	66 mg
Sodium	75 mg
Carbohydrates	2 g
Fiber	1 g
Sugars	1 g
Protein	27 g

Dietary exchanges: 3 very lean meat

> NUTRITION TIP: Cut
> leftover bell peppers into strips
> for lunchbox treats.

*Top this tasty and versatile grilled chicken with colorful red bell
pepper on one night, then use the rest in Italian Chicken and Penne
Salad (page 157) a few days later.*

In a small bowl, stir together the lemon juice, 2 tablespoons vinegar, 1 tablespoon oil, 2 garlic cloves, oregano, and dried basil.
Put the chicken in a large glass dish. Pour the marinade over the
chicken, turning to coat. Cover and refrigerate for 30 minutes,
turning over after 15 minutes.

Meanwhile, lightly brush both sides of each bell pepper strip
with the remaining 1 teaspoon oil.

Lightly spray a grill rack with cooking spray. Preheat the grill
on medium high.

Drain the chicken. Discard the marinade. Arrange the chicken
and bell pepper strips on different sides of the grill. Grill the
chicken for 7 to 9 minutes on each side, or until no longer pink
in the center. Transfer to a cutting board. Cover with aluminum foil. Let stand for 10 minutes. At the same time, grill the
bell pepper strips with the skin side down for 10 to 12 minutes,
or until the skin is blistered and slightly charred. Transfer to a
small bowl. Cover loosely with a towel. Let stand for 10 minutes.

With the tip of a sharp knife, remove the charred skin from the
bell peppers. Chop the bell peppers. Return to the small bowl.
Stir in the fresh basil, shallot, remaining 1 teaspoon vinegar,
and remaining garlic clove.

Cut half the chicken crosswise into pieces about ½ inch wide.
Arrange on a serving plate. Top with the bell pepper salsa.
Refrigerate the remaining cooked chicken in an airtight
container and use within three to four days to make the Italian
Chicken and Penne Salad.

Italian Chicken and Penne Salad

SERVES 4 | 3 OUNCES CHICKEN AND 1½ CUPS SALAD MIXTURE PER SERVING

6 ounces dried whole-wheat penne

12 ounces grilled chicken from Mediterranean Grilled Chicken with Red Bell Pepper Salsa, cut into bite-size pieces (about 2 cups)

5 ounces grape tomatoes, halved (about ¾ cup)

3 ounces button mushrooms, sliced (about ¾ cup)

2½ ounces frozen artichoke hearts, thawed, drained, and chopped (about ½ cup)

1 small green onion, sliced

DRESSING

3 tablespoons white wine vinegar

3 tablespoons fat-free, low-sodium chicken broth

1 tablespoon olive oil (extra-virgin preferred)

1 large garlic clove, minced

½ teaspoon dried oregano, crumbled

⅛ teaspoon salt

⅛ teaspoon pepper

2 tablespoons pine nuts, dry-roasted

2 tablespoons snipped fresh Italian (flat-leaf) parsley

1 tablespoon shredded or grated Parmesan cheese

4 large lettuce leaves, such as romaine or red leaf

The classic Italian flavors of artichokes, mushrooms, tomatoes, pine nuts, and oregano quickly blend together in this wonderful chicken and pasta salad, which uses reserved chicken from Mediterranean Grilled Chicken with Red Bell Pepper Salsa (page 154).

Prepare the pasta using the package directions, omitting the salt and oil.

Meanwhile, in a large bowl, stir together the chicken, tomatoes, mushrooms, artichoke hearts, and green onion.

In a small bowl, whisk together the dressing ingredients.

Stir the cooked pasta into the chicken mixture. Pour the dressing over all. Toss to combine. Sprinkle with the pine nuts, parsley, and Parmesan. Toss.

Place a lettuce leaf on each plate. Spoon the salad mixture onto or beside each leaf.

COOK'S TIP ON PINE NUTS: Look for pine nuts, the nuts of pinecones, in the Italian, ethnic food, or nuts section of the grocery store. You may also find them labeled with their Italian name, pignoli. To dry-roast these ivory-colored nuts, spread them in a single layer on a baking pan. Bake at 350°F for 5 to 7 minutes, or until lightly roasted. Watch carefully so the nuts do not burn.

PER SERVING

Calories	358
Total Fat	8.0 g
Saturated Fat	1.5 g
Trans Fat	0.0 g
Polyunsaturated Fat	2.0 g
Monounsaturated Fat	3.5 g
Cholesterol	67 mg
Sodium	198 mg
Carbohydrates	38 g
Fiber	8 g
Sugars	4 g
Protein	36 g

Dietary exchanges: 2 starch, 1 vegetable, 3 lean meat

Gobble-It-Up Roasted Turkey with Gravy

SERVES 4 | 3 OUNCES TURKEY AND 2 TABLESPOONS GRAVY PER SERVING (PLUS 12 OUNCES TURKEY RESERVED)

Cooking spray

1 cup fat-free, low-sodium chicken broth and ¼ cup fat-free, low-sodium chicken broth, divided use

¼ teaspoon salt

⅛ teaspoon pepper and ¼ teaspoon pepper, divided use

1 2½-pound bone-in turkey breast, skin and all visible fat discarded

1 tablespoon olive oil

3 medium garlic cloves, finely chopped

½ teaspoon dried rosemary, crushed

1 tablespoon all-purpose flour

½ teaspoon garlic powder

½ teaspoon onion powder

PER SERVING

Calories	156
Total Fat	3.0 g
Saturated Fat	0.5 g
Trans Fat	0.0 g
Polyunsaturated Fat	0.5 g
Monounsaturated Fat	1.5 g
Cholesterol	78 mg
Sodium	143 mg
Carbohydrates	2 g
Fiber	0 g
Sugars	0 g
Protein	28 g
Dietary exchanges: 4 very lean meat	

Browning the turkey breast before roasting creates a beautiful golden color and adding broth to the pan guarantees moist white meat. Wrap half the turkey and refrigerate it for Turkey Tetrazzini (page 161) later in the week.

Preheat the oven to 325°F. Put a cooling rack in a 13 × 9 × 2-inch baking pan. Lightly spray both with cooking spray. Pour 1 cup broth into the pan.

Sprinkle the salt and ⅛ teaspoon pepper all over the turkey. Rub the top of the turkey with the oil.

Heat a large nonstick skillet over medium-high heat for 2 minutes. Put the turkey with the meatier side down in the skillet. Cook for 4 minutes, or until golden brown. Transfer to the rack in the baking pan.

Sprinkle the garlic over the turkey. Rub the garlic in. Sprinkle with the rosemary.

Cut a piece of aluminum foil large enough to cover the turkey. Lightly spray the foil with cooking spray. Cover the pan tightly with the foil with the sprayed side down.

Roast, covered with the foil, for 20 minutes. Baste with the remaining ¼ cup broth. Roast, uncovered, for 35 minutes, or until the turkey registers 165°F on an instant-read thermometer inserted in the thickest part of the breast. Transfer the turkey to a platter, reserving ¾ cup pan drippings and discarding any remaining. Let the turkey cool for 15 minutes.

Meanwhile, pour the drippings into a microwaveable cup. Microwave on 100 percent power (high) for about 2 minutes, or until the drippings boil.

In a small skillet, stir together the flour, garlic powder, and onion powder. Cook over medium heat for 5 minutes, or until warmed and light golden brown, stirring constantly. Slowly whisk the drippings into the skillet, whisking constantly to dissolve the flour. Bring to a boil, still over medium heat. Reduce the heat and simmer for 3 minutes, or until the desired consistency, whisking constantly. Stir in the remaining ¼ teaspoon pepper.

Put half the turkey in an airtight container. Refrigerate for use within three to four days in Turkey Tetrazzini. Thinly slice the other half on the diagonal. Serve the sliced turkey with the gravy.

NUTRITION TIP:
Eating the skin with roasted poultry can triple the amount of total fat in your meal! Roast a whole bird with its skin on to retain moisture, but discard the fatty skin before serving the poultry.

Turkey Tetrazzini

SERVES 4 | 1½ CUPS PER SERVING

Cooking spray

4 ounces dried whole-wheat
   spaghetti

2 teaspoons olive oil

½ cup chopped onion

8 ounces zucchini, cut crosswise
   into ¼-inch slices (about 2 cups)

2 medium garlic cloves, finely
   chopped

¼ teaspoon ground nutmeg

¼ teaspoon white pepper

1 10.75-ounce can low-fat
   condensed cream of mushroom
   soup (lowest sodium available)

⅔ cup fat-free milk

12 ounces turkey from Gobble-It-Up
   Roasted Turkey with Gravy, cut
   into ½-inch cubes

¼ cup panko

1 tablespoon shredded or grated
   Parmesan cheese

PER SERVING

Calories	357
Total Fat	7.0 g
Saturated Fat	1.5 g
Trans Fat	0.0 g
Polyunsaturated Fat	1.5 g
Monounsaturated Fat	3.5 g
Cholesterol	83 mg
Sodium	466 mg
Carbohydrates	37 g
Fiber	6 g
Sugars	6 g
Protein	36 g

Dietary exchanges: 2 starch,
   1 vegetable, 4 lean meat

This favorite uses turkey breast from Gobble-It-Up Roasted Turkey (page 158) and adds sliced zucchini. Whole-wheat spaghetti and low-sodium, low-fat cream soup make this version as heart-healthy as it is delicious. Try adding carrots, green beans, broccoli, or other veggies to this casserole to expand your family's palate.

Preheat the oven to 350°F. Lightly spray an 8-inch square baking pan with cooking spray.

Prepare the pasta using the package directions, omitting the salt and oil and cooking until almost tender, 3 to 4 minutes less than directed. Drain well in a colander. Set aside.

Meanwhile, heat a large nonstick skillet over medium heat for 2 minutes. Add the oil, swirling to coat the bottom. Cook the onion for 3 minutes, or until it begins to soften, stirring frequently. Reduce the heat to low.

Stir in the zucchini. Cook for 3 minutes, or until it begins to soften and turns light brown, stirring constantly.

Sprinkle with the garlic, nutmeg, and pepper. Cook for 2 minutes, stirring constantly.

Stir in the soup and milk. Increase the heat to medium and bring to a simmer. Simmer for 3 minutes, or until the mixture begins to thicken. Remove from the heat.

Stir in the turkey, then the pasta. Spoon into the pan, lightly smoothing the top.

In a small bowl, stir together the panko and Parmesan. Sprinkle over the casserole. Lightly spray with cooking spray.

Bake for 25 minutes, or until the pasta is bubbly and the top is browned.

South of the Border Beef

SERVES 4 | ¾ CUP BEEF MIXTURE AND ¾ CUP NOODLES PER SERVING
(PLUS 2½ CUPS BEEF MIXTURE RESERVED)

Cooking spray

½ cup water

3 tablespoons all-purpose flour and ⅓ cup all-purpose flour, divided use

3 medium garlic cloves, minced

1 teaspoon chili powder

¾ teaspoon ground cumin

¼ teaspoon dried oregano, crumbled

¼ teaspoon salt

1 tablespoon salt-free Southwest chipotle seasoning blend, other salt-free smoky, spicy seasoning blend, or smoked paprika

2 pounds extra-lean beef stew cubes, all visible fat discarded

2 teaspoons olive oil

¾ cup chopped onion

1 14.5-ounce can no-salt-added diced tomatoes, undrained

1 4-ounce can chopped green chiles, undrained

4 ounces dried whole-wheat noodles

1 tablespoon salt-free all-purpose seasoning blend

1 tablespoon plus 1 teaspoon shredded or grated Parmesan cheese

¼ cup snipped fresh cilantro

1 tablespoon plus 1 teaspoon finely chopped green onions

This hearty slow-cooker stew features traditional Southwestern ingredients and spices for lots of low-sodium flavor. Although the ingredients list is long, the preparation steps aren't difficult, and you will have the base for Beef Tortilla Casserole (page 165) to serve later in the week.

Lightly spray a 3- to 4-quart slow cooker with cooking spray.

In a small bowl, combine the water, 3 tablespoons flour, garlic, chili powder, cumin, oregano, and salt. Set aside.

In a large resealable plastic bag, combine the Southwest chipotle seasoning blend and remaining ⅓ cup flour. Add the beef cubes. Seal the bag and shake to coat the beef.

In a large nonstick skillet, heat the oil over medium-high heat, swirling to coat the bottom. Add the onion and beef cubes, reserving any remaining flour mixture. Cook for 8 to 10 minutes, or until the meat is browned, stirring frequently. Transfer the mixture to the slow cooker.

Stir in the tomatoes with liquid, green chiles with liquid, and reserved flour mixture. Cook, covered, on low for 6 to 8 hours or on high for 4 hours, or until the beef is tender.

Shortly before serving time, prepare the noodles using the package directions, adding the all-purpose seasoning blend and omitting the salt and oil. Drain well in a colander.

Stir the Parmesan into the noodles.

Transfer 2½ cups beef mixture to an airtight container and refrigerate for use within three to four days in the Beef Tortilla Casserole. Serve the remaining 3 cups beef mixture over the noodle mixture. Garnish with the cilantro and green onions.

PER SERVING

Calories	354
Total Fat	11.0 g
Saturated Fat	4.0 g
Trans Fat	0.0 g
Polyunsaturated Fat	0.5 g
Monounsaturated Fat	5.0 g
Cholesterol	79 mg
Sodium	248 mg
Carbohydrates	34 g
Fiber	6 g
Sugars	4 g
Protein	30 g

Dietary exchanges: 2 starch,
  1 vegetable, 3 lean meat

COOK'S TIP ON SLOW COOKERS:

For fast and easy cleanup, try using a disposable plastic liner made for slow cookers. You can skip the step of spraying the slow cooker with cooking spray.

NUTRITION TIP: If

you can't find extra-lean stew meat—some packaged stew meat comes from leftover trimmings and may be high in saturated fat—buy a lean cut such as sirloin or top round and cut it into bite-size cubes yourself. You'll know what you're getting, and you may actually save time since you won't have small bits of fat to trim from a number of small cubes of meat.

Beef Tortilla Casserole

Cooking spray

2½ cups reserved South of the Border Beef

8 6-inch yellow corn tortillas

½ cup low-fat Cheddar cheese

½ cup chopped romaine

2 medium Italian plum (Roma) tomatoes, chopped

½ cup fat-free sour cream

PER SERVING

Calories	326
Total Fat	10.0 g
Saturated Fat	3.5 g
Trans Fat	0.0 g
Polyunsaturated Fat	1.0 g
Monounsaturated Fat	4.5 g
Cholesterol	71 mg
Sodium	335 mg
Carbohydrates	30 g
Fiber	4 g
Sugars	5 g
Protein	28 g

Dietary exchanges: 2 starch, 3 lean meat

NUTRITION TIP: Buy extra corn tortillas to make baked tortilla chips as a healthy after-school snack. When the tortilla casserole is done, increase the oven temperature to 475°F. Cut the extra tortillas into quarters and place on a baking sheet. Bake for 3 minutes. Serve with Mango and Black Bean Salsa (page 21).

Enjoy this delicious Mexican favorite with a healthy twist. Use corn tortillas for half the calories and half the fat of flour tortillas—plus they contain about five times less sodium! The filling is the mixture you reserved from South of the Border Beef (page 162).

Preheat the oven to 350°F. Lightly spray a 9-inch square baking pan with cooking spray.

In a medium saucepan, heat the reserved beef mixture over medium-high heat for 8 to 10 minutes, or until heated through, stirring frequently. If the sauce part of the mixture is too thick, gradually stir in a little water, 1 tablespoon at a time, until the consistency of thick gravy.

Stack the tortillas on a microwaveable plate. Microwave on 100 percent power (high) for about 45 seconds to soften.

Put the tortillas in a single layer on a flat surface. Using a slotted spoon, remove the beef cubes from the saucepan. Spoon down the center of each tortilla. Roll the tortillas jelly-roll style and place with the seam side down in the baking pan. Pour the remaining sauce over the tortillas.

Bake for 15 to 20 minutes, or until heated through. Sprinkle with the Cheddar. Bake for 1 to 2 minutes, or until the cheese is melted.

To serve, sprinkle with the romaine and tomatoes. Spoon a dollop of sour cream on each enchilada.

Roasted Pork Tenderloin and Vegetables

SERVES 4: 3 OUNCES PORK, ½ CUP POTATOES, AND ½ CUP VEGETABLES PER SERVING (PLUS 12 OUNCES PORK CUBES RESERVED)

Cooking spray

1 teaspoon onion powder

1 teaspoon garlic powder

1 teaspoon dried oregano, crumbled

1 teaspoon light brown sugar

1 teaspoon paprika

½ teaspoon pepper

2 1-pound pork tenderloins, all visible fat discarded

4 medium red potatoes, cut into ¾-inch cubes

4 ounces medium button or cremini mushrooms, quartered

1 medium bell pepper (any color), cut into ¾-inch pieces

2 medium parsnips, cut crosswise into ½-inch slices

½ medium red onion (about 2½ to 3 ounces), chopped into ¾-inch squares

2 tablespoons Dijon mustard

1 tablespoon fresh chopped rosemary

1 teaspoon olive oil

Fill your home with the "what's for dinner—something smells good" aromas of roasting pork and vegetables. The second cooked tenderloin goes into the savory Pork and Veggie Lettuce Wraps (page 167).

Preheat the oven to 375°F. Lightly spray two 13 × 9 × 2-inch baking pans with cooking spray. Set aside.

In a small bowl, stir together the onion powder, garlic powder, oregano, brown sugar, paprika, and pepper. Put the tenderloins in one of the baking pans. Rub the entire amount of the spice mixture over all. Using your fingertips, gently press the rub so it adheres to the pork.

In a medium bowl, stir together the remaining ingredients. Transfer to the second baking pan. Lightly spray the vegetables and pork with cooking spray.

Bake for 30 to 35 minutes, or until the pork registers 160°F on an instant-read thermometer and the vegetables are tender. Transfer the pans to cooling racks. Let the pork rest for 10 minutes. Cover the vegetables with aluminum foil to keep warm.

Slice one of the tenderloins and arrange the slices on a platter. Arrange the vegetables around the tenderloin. Refrigerate the remaining tenderloin in an airtight container for use in the Pork and Veggie Lettuce Wraps within four days.

PER SERVING

Calories	261
Total Fat	5.0 g
Saturated Fat	1.0 g
Trans Fat	0.0 g
Polyunsaturated Fat	0.5 g
Monounsaturated Fat	2.0 g
Cholesterol	58 mg
Sodium	214 mg
Carbohydrates	30 g
Fiber	6 g
Sugars	7 g
Protein	25 g

Dietary exchanges: 2 starch, 3 very lean meat

Pork and Veggie Lettuce Wraps

SERVES 4 | 4 LETTUCE WRAPS PER SERVING

1 teaspoon olive oil

1 cup shredded carrots

1 cup shredded cabbage (green, red, or a combination)

12 ounces cooked pork from Roasted Pork Tenderloin and Vegetables, cut into ½-inch cubes

¼ cup barbecue sauce (lowest sodium available)

3 tablespoons all-fruit strawberry spread

1 tablespoon balsamic vinegar or cider vinegar

16 large leaves Bibb lettuce

1 medium apple, diced (Granny Smith, Fuji, or Gala preferred)

Wraps are an easy way to have your meat and veggies in one delicious package. Foods you can eat with your hands are usually a big hit with little kids—and lots of big kids, too! Because you cooked the pork cubes when you made Roasted Pork Tenderloin and Vegetables (page 166), this recipe is terrific for nights when you don't have much time to prepare dinner.

In a medium saucepan, heat the oil over medium heat, swirling to coat the bottom. Cook the carrots and cabbage for 1 to 2 minutes, or until tender-crisp, stirring occasionally.

Stir in the pork cubes, barbecue sauce, strawberry spread, and vinegar. Cook over medium heat for about 5 minutes, or until heated through, stirring occasionally.

Arrange 4 lettuce leaves on each plate. Spoon about 2 tablespoons pork mixture onto each leaf. Sprinkle with the apple. Roll up as desired.

PER SERVING

Calories	237
Total Fat	4.0 g
Saturated Fat	1.0 g
Trans Fat	0.0 g
Polyunsaturated Fat	0.5 g
Monounsaturated Fat	2.0 g
Cholesterol	58 mg
Sodium	177 mg
Carbohydrates	27 g
Fiber	4 g
Sugars	20 g
Protein	22 g

Dietary exchanges: 1 fruit, 1 vegetable, ½ carbohydrate, 3 very lean meat

NUTRITION TIP: For variety, try these wraps with any cooked meat or poultry, such as shredded lean beef or grilled chicken.

Zucchini Boats

SERVES 4 | 2 ZUCCHINI BOATS PER SERVING (PLUS 1 CUP MUSHROOM MIXTURE RESERVED)

1 teaspoon olive oil

6 ounces button mushrooms, coarsely chopped (about 2 cups)

1 cup chopped onion

1 medium red bell pepper, chopped

2 medium garlic cloves, minced

1 cup low-sodium vegetable broth

⅓ cup uncooked quick-cooking barley

1 12-ounce package refrigerated soy crumbles

½ teaspoon ground cumin

½ teaspoon chili powder

¼ teaspoon salt

Cooking spray

4 medium zucchini

1 cup water

1 cup shredded low-fat Cheddar cheese

PER SERVING

Calories	277
Total Fat	7.0 g
Saturated Fat	2.0 g
Trans Fat	0.0 g
Polyunsaturated Fat	2.5 g
Monounsaturated Fat	2.0 g
Cholesterol	6 mg
Sodium	723 mg
Carbohydrates	28 g
Fiber	8 g
Sugars	6 g
Protein	29 g

Dietary exchanges: 1 starch, 2 vegetable, 3 lean meat

> **KIDS IN THE KITCHEN**: Children will love hollowing out and filling the zucchini as they help you get ready for the "launch."

Ahoy, soy! The whole family will enjoy this fiber-packed, Southwestern-influenced dish—on land or by sea! Once prepared, this recipe leaves enough mushroom mixture to serve double-duty in an Italian-inspired pasta dish, Three-Cheese Manicotti (page 171), in a few days.

In a large nonstick skillet, heat the oil over medium-high heat, swirling to coat the bottom. Cook the mushrooms, onion, bell pepper, and garlic for 5 to 6 minutes, or until soft, stirring occasionally. Spoon 1 cup mixture into a small airtight container and refrigerate for use in Three-Cheese Manicotti within five days.

Pour the broth into the skillet with the remaining mushroom mixture. Bring to a simmer over medium-high heat. Stir in the barley. Reduce the heat and simmer, covered, for 10 to 15 minutes, or until the barley is tender.

Stir in the soy crumbles, cumin, chili powder, and salt. Remove from the heat. Set aside.

Preheat the oven to 350°F. Lightly spray a 13 × 9 × 2-inch baking pan with cooking spray.

Cut each zucchini in half lengthwise. With a spoon or melon baller, scrape out the seeds and just enough flesh to make a cavity for stuffing. (You can either freeze the seeds and flesh in an airtight container for up to 6 months for another use, such as in vegetable soup, as stuffing for pasta shells, or combined with cooked rice, or discard them.) Spoon the mushroom mixture into the cavities. Place the zucchini in the baking pan. Carefully pour the water around—not on—the zucchini. Cover the pan tightly with aluminum foil.

Bake for 30 minutes, or until the zucchini is tender when tested with a fork inserted all the way through the zucchini in the center. Sprinkle the Cheddar cheese over the filling. Bake, uncovered, for 5 minutes, or until the cheese is melted.

Three-Cheese Manicotti

Cooking spray

8 uncooked manicotti tubes

1 cup mushroom mixture from Zucchini Boats

1 15-ounce container fat-free ricotta cheese

½ cup shredded part-skim mozzarella cheese

¼ cup egg substitute

1 teaspoon dried oregano, crumbled

¼ teaspoon salt

¼ teaspoon pepper

½ cup fat-free, low-sodium chicken broth

½ cup fat-free half-and-half

1½ tablespoons all-purpose flour

¼ cup shredded or grated Parmesan cheese

2 tablespoons bottled basil pesto

2 medium Italian plum (Roma) tomatoes, each cut into 6 or 8 wedges

An unusually pretty way to serve manicotti, these pasta tubes are stuffed with the mushroom mixture from Zucchini Boats (page 168), presented with vibrant red tomatoes, and drizzled with creamy sauce and with green pesto.

Preheat the oven to 350°F. Lightly spray a 13 × 9 × 2-inch baking pan with cooking spray.

Meanwhile, cook the manicotti tubes using the package directions, omitting the salt and oil. Drain well in a colander. Transfer to the baking pan.

In a medium bowl, stir together the reserved mushroom mixture, ricotta cheese, mozzarella cheese, egg substitute, oregano, salt, and pepper. With a small spoon, gently stuff the tubes. Cover the pan tightly with aluminum foil.

Bake for 25 to 30 minutes, or until heated through.

Meanwhile, in a small saucepan, whisk together the broth, half-and-half, and flour. Bring to a simmer over medium-high heat, whisking constantly. Reduce the heat and simmer for 1 to 2 minutes, or until the mixture thickens. Stir in the Parmesan cheese. Remove from the heat.

Put 2 manicotti tubes on each plate. Pour the sauce onto each serving. Drizzle with the pesto. Garnish with the tomato wedges.

PER SERVING

Calories	395
Total Fat	8.5 g
Saturated Fat	3.5 g
Trans Fat	0.0 g
Polyunsaturated Fat	0.5 g
Monounsaturated Fat	3.5 g
Cholesterol	24 mg
Sodium	658 mg
Carbohydrates	48 g
Fiber	3 g
Sugars	11 g
Protein	32 g

Dietary exchanges: 3 starch, 3 lean meat

COOK'S TIP: You also can try different pastas that can be stuffed, such as jumbo shells and cannelloni, in this recipe. You'll need about 4½ ounces of dried pasta.

Grilled Vegetable and Bulgur Salad

SERVES 4 | 1¼ CUPS PER SERVING (PLUS 2 CUPS VEGETABLES AND 2 TABLESPOONS PLUS 2 TEASPOONS VINAIGRETTE RESERVED)

Cooking spray

10 cups vegetable pieces, such as any combination of ¼-inch carrot rounds or ¾-inch diced zucchini, portobello mushroom caps, eggplant, red onion, or red bell pepper

1 tablespoon olive oil and ¼ cup olive oil, divided use

1 15-ounce can no-salt-added chickpeas, rinsed and drained

1½ cups water

1 cup uncooked bulgur

¼ teaspoon salt and ⅛ teaspoon salt, divided use

¼ cup balsamic vinegar

⅛ teaspoon pepper

2 tablespoons finely chopped fresh basil

8 leaves of leafy lettuce, such as red-leaf lettuce

PER SERVING

Calories	284
Total Fat	12.5 g
Saturated Fat	2.0 g
Trans Fat	0.0 g
Polyunsaturated Fat	1.5 g
Monounsaturated Fat	8.5 g
Cholesterol	0 mg
Sodium	270 mg
Carbohydrates	40 g
Fiber	10 g
Sugars	7 g
Protein	7 g
Dietary exchanges: 2 starch, 2 vegetable, 2 fat	

Wonder why this recipe calls for so many vegetables? As they grill, most veggies shrink a lot, and you're also cooking enough for a quick supper of Grilled-Vegetable Paninis (page 173) later in the week.

Lightly spray a perforated grilling pan or grilling basket with cooking spray. Preheat the grill on medium low.

In a large bowl, toss the vegetable pieces with 1 tablespoon oil.

Grill the vegetables in the grilling pan or basket for 15 to 20 minutes, or until browned and tender-crisp, turning every 5 minutes (with tongs if cooking on the grilling pan). Transfer 2 cups vegetables to an airtight container and refrigerate for use within two days in Grilled-Vegetable Paninis. Return the remaining vegetables to the large bowl. Stir in the chickpeas.

Meanwhile, in a medium saucepan, bring the water to a boil over high heat. Stir in the bulgur and ¼ teaspoon salt. Reduce the heat to low. Cook, covered, for 10 minutes, or until all the water is absorbed.

While the bulgur cooks, in a small bowl, whisk together the vinegar, pepper, and remaining ⅛ teaspoon salt. Whisk in the remaining ¼ cup oil and basil. Pour 2 tablespoons plus 2 teaspoons vinaigrette into a bottle or other airtight container and refrigerate for use within two days in Grilled-Vegetable Paninis.

Stir the bulgur into the grilled vegetables.

Pour the remaining vinaigrette into the salad, tossing well. Let cool at room temperature for at least 30 minutes; for peak flavor, cover and refrigerate for several hours. Then spoon the salad onto the leaves.

Grilled-Vegetable Paninis

SERVES 4 | 1 PANINI PER SERVING

4 whole-grain ciabatta rolls or 2 whole-grain hoagie rolls, halved lengthwise

2 tablespoons plus 2 teaspoons vinaigrette from Grilled Vegetable and Bulgur Salad

2 cups grilled vegetables from Grilled Vegetable and Bulgur Salad

¾ cup shredded part-skim mozzarella

PER SERVING

Calories	255
Total Fat	10.5 g
Saturated Fat	3.5 g
Trans Fat	0.0 g
Polyunsaturated Fat	1.0 g
Monounsaturated Fat	5.5 g
Cholesterol	14 mg
Sodium	412 mg
Carbohydrates	31 g
Fiber	4 g
Sugars	5 g
Protein	10 g

Dietary exchanges: 1½ starch, 2 vegetable, 1 lean meat, 1 fat

This takeoff on the popular panini is broiled, not cooked using a panini-maker. Use the vegetables and vinaigrette from Grilled Vegetable and Bulgur Salad (page 172) for super-speedy preparation.

Preheat the broiler. Line a broiler pan with aluminum foil.

Place the rolls side by side with the cut sides up on the broiler pan. (If using ciabatta rolls, place so the 2 halves of each roll are touching.) Drizzle with the vinaigrette. Spoon the vegetables on the rolls.

Broil 8 to 10 inches from the heat for 2 minutes to warm the vegetables. Top with the mozzarella. Broil for 1 to 2 minutes, or until the mozzarella is melted. Serve open-face.

> **NUTRITION TIP:**
> Almost everyone loves sandwiches, but you should be aware that most bread is high in sodium. Open-face sandwiches are an ideal way to cut the sodium and still enjoy an American favorite. Also, instead of buying white bread with refined flour, choose a whole-grain product. It provides more flavor as well as more nutrients.

Vegetables and Side Dishes

Veggie Swords

SERVES 4 | 1 KEBAB PER SERVING

8 cherry tomatoes

1 medium zucchini, halved lengthwise, each half cut crosswise into 8 pieces

½ 4-ounce onion (cut lengthwise), layers separated to get 16 pieces (plus more onion if needed for enough pieces)

1½ tablespoons olive oil

1½ tablespoons fresh lemon juice

¾ teaspoon chopped fresh rosemary or ¼ teaspoon dried rosemary, crushed

½ medium garlic clove, minced

⅛ teaspoon salt

PER SERVING

Calories	67
Total Fat	5.0 g
Saturated Fat	0.5 g
Trans Fat	0.0 g
Polyunsaturated Fat	0.5 g
Monounsaturated Fat	3.5 g
Cholesterol	0 mg
Sodium	80 mg
Carbohydrates	5 g
Fiber	1 g
Sugars	3 g
Protein	1 g
Dietary exchanges: 1 vegetable, 1 fat	

Because of the dramatic presentation, kebabs are great for easy entertaining—or just for fun for dinner at home. (See photograph on page 174.)

Preheat the broiler. Line a baking sheet with aluminum foil. Soak four 10-inch wooden skewers for at least 10 minutes in cold water to keep them from charring, or use metal skewers.

Put a tomato on each skewer. Alternating, thread the zucchini and onion on the skewers. End with the remaining tomatoes (or see the Kids in the Kitchen tip in the left-hand column). Put the kebabs on the baking sheet.

In a small bowl, whisk together the remaining ingredients. Using a pastry brush, lightly brush the kebabs with the mixture, reserving what you don't use.

Broil the vegetables at least 4 inches from the heat for 3 minutes on each side, basting with the oil mixture halfway through. Transfer the kebabs to a platter. Spoon the remaining oil mixture over all.

KIDS IN THE KITCHEN: Whenever you make kebabs, make a game of threading the skewers to involve the kids. Let them decide how they want to order the ingredients and see if they can recognize their own "creation" after it's been broiled.

Pasta with Veggie Confetti

SERVES 4 | ½ CUP PER SERVING

- 2 ounces dried whole-wheat, whole-grain, or high-fiber pasta, such as whole-wheat penne
- ⅔ cup fat-free, low-sodium chicken broth
- 2 large garlic cloves, minced
- 9 medium asparagus spears, trimmed and cut into 1-inch pieces (about 1 cup)
- ¼ large red bell pepper, chopped
- ¼ cup coarsely shredded carrot
- 2 tablespoons chopped fresh basil
- 1 tablespoon shredded or grated Parmesan cheese

PER SERVING

Calories	74
Total Fat	0.5 g
Saturated Fat	0.5 g
Trans Fat	0.0 g
Polyunsaturated Fat	0.0 g
Monounsaturated Fat	0.0 g
Cholesterol	1 mg
Sodium	37 mg
Carbohydrates	14 g
Fiber	3 g
Sugars	2 g
Protein	4 g
Dietary exchanges: 1 starch	

> **NUTRITION TIP:**
> Adding vegetables to pasta can make it easier for picky eaters to enjoy new tastes. Try different combinations of flavor and color!

Use your favorite pasta shape, such as farfalle (bowties), penne, or rotini, in this simple dish. For more nutrients, choose whole-wheat, whole-grain, or high-fiber pasta.

Prepare the pasta using the package directions, omitting the salt and oil. Drain well in a colander.

Meanwhile, in a medium saucepan, cook the broth and garlic over high heat for 3 minutes.

Stir in the asparagus. Reduce the heat to medium and cook, covered, for 3 minutes.

Stir in the cooked pasta and bell pepper. Cook, covered, for 2 minutes.

Stir in the carrot and basil. Cook, covered, for 1 minute. Remove from the heat. Sprinkle with the Parmesan before serving.

Roasted Broccoli and Cauliflower

SERVES 4 | ½ CUP PER SERVING

3 cups cauliflower florets (2-inch pieces) (10 to 11 ounces)

2 cups broccoli florets (2-inch pieces) (about 5 ounces)

2 teaspoons olive oil and 1 teaspoon olive oil, divided use

3 tablespoons shredded or grated Parmesan cheese

⅛ teaspoon salt

⅛ teaspoon pepper

Roasting intensifies the flavor of broccoli and cauliflower.

Preheat the oven to 425°F.

Stir the cauliflower, broccoli, and 2 teaspoons oil to coat. Place in one layer on a baking sheet.

Roast for 15 minutes. Stir. Roast for 5 minutes, or until beginning to brown on the edges. Put in a bowl and stir in the remaining ingredients.

PER SERVING

Calories	80
Total Fat	4.5 g
Saturated Fat	1.0 g
Trans Fat	0.0 g
Polyunsaturated Fat	0.5 g
Monounsaturated Fat	3.0 g
Cholesterol	3 mg
Sodium	174 mg
Carbohydrates	7 g
Fiber	3 g
Sugars	3 g
Protein	4 g

Dietary exchanges: 1½ vegetable, 1 fat

Lemon Carrot "Coins"

SERVES 4 | ½ CUP PER SERVING

¼ cup water

4 to 5 medium carrots, cut crosswise into ½-inch slices (about 2 cups)

⅛ teaspoon salt

⅛ teaspoon sugar

1½ teaspoons snipped fresh tarragon

¼ teaspoon grated lemon zest

1½ teaspoons fresh lemon juice

Lemon and tarragon make carrots extraordinary.

In a medium saucepan, bring the water to a boil. Add the carrots, salt, and sugar. Cook, covered, on medium for 8 to 10 minutes, or until tender. Add a little water if needed so the carrots don't boil dry. Remove from the heat. If more than 1 tablespoon water remains, drain. Stir in the remaining ingredients.

PER SERVING

Calories	35
Total Fat	0.0 g
Saturated Fat	0.0 g
Trans Fat	0.0 g
Polyunsaturated Fat	0.0 g
Monounsaturated Fat	0.0 g
Cholesterol	0 mg
Sodium	129 mg
Carbohydrates	8 g
Fiber	2 g
Sugars	4 g
Protein	1 g

Dietary exchanges: 2 vegetable

Sweet-and-Sour Red Cabbage

SERVES 4 | ½ CUP PER SERVING

2 teaspoons olive oil

3 cups shredded red cabbage (about 12 ounces)

1 medium tart or slightly sweet apple, peeled and diced

3 tablespoons red wine vinegar

2 tablespoons firmly packed dark brown sugar

Be sure to try this dish with Pretzel Schnitzel (page 116).

In a medium nonstick skillet, heat the oil over medium heat, swirling to coat the bottom. Cook the cabbage, apple, and vinegar for 15 minutes, or until the cabbage is tender-crisp, stirring frequently. Stir in the brown sugar. Cook for 1 minute, or until the sugar is dissolved.

PER SERVING

Calories	75
Total Fat	2.5 g
Saturated Fat	0.5 g
Trans Fat	0.0 g
Polyunsaturated Fat	0.5 g
Monounsaturated Fat	1.5 g
Cholesterol	0 mg
Sodium	11 mg
Carbohydrates	14 g
Fiber	2 g
Sugars	12 g
Protein	1 g

Dietary exchanges: 1 carbohydrate, ½ fat

In-a-Hurry Curry Couscous

SERVES 4 | ½ CUP PER SERVING

¾ cup water

½ cup uncooked whole-wheat couscous

½ teaspoon canola or corn oil

½ medium red bell pepper, chopped

½ cup chopped onion

¼ cup plus 2 tablespoons slivered almonds, dry-roasted

½ teaspoon curry powder

¼ teaspoon salt

Tasty and quick, this dish will dress up the simplest entrée.

In a small saucepan, bring the water to a boil. Remove from the heat. Stir in the couscous. Let stand, covered, for 5 minutes. Fluff with a fork.

Meanwhile, in a large non-stick skillet, heat the oil on medium high, swirling to coat the bottom. Cook the pepper and onion for 10 minutes, stirring frequently. Stir in the remaining ingredients.

PER SERVING

Calories	179
Total Fat	6.0 g
Saturated Fat	0.5 g
Trans Fat	0.0 g
Polyunsaturated Fat	1.5 g
Monounsaturated Fat	3.5 g
Cholesterol	0 mg
Sodium	148 mg
Carbohydrates	27 g
Fiber	6 g
Sugars	2 g
Protein	7 g

Dietary exchanges: 2 starch, 1 fat

No-Guilt Macaroni and Cheese

SERVES 4 | ½ CUP PER SERVING

Cooking spray

4 ounces (about 1 cup) dried multigrain elbow macaroni or whole-wheat penne

⅔ cup fat-free milk

1 tablespoon all-purpose flour

¼ teaspoon dry mustard

4 ¾-ounce slices low-fat American cheese, quartered

2 tablespoons fresh bread crumbs, light whole-grain preferred (about ⅓ slice light bread)

PER SERVING

Calories	164
Total Fat	1.5 g
Saturated Fat	0.5 g
Trans Fat	0.0 g
Polyunsaturated Fat	0.0 g
Monounsaturated Fat	0.5 g
Cholesterol	6 mg
Sodium	229 mg
Carbohydrates	28 g
Fiber	3 g
Sugars	4 g
Protein	11 g
Dietary exchanges: 2 starch, 1 very lean meat	

No fuss, no frills, no guilt . . . this is the much-loved standby but with today's healthy twist.

Preheat the oven to 375°F. Lightly spray a 1-quart glass baking dish with cooking spray.

Prepare the pasta using the package directions, omitting the salt and oil. Drain well in a colander. Set aside.

In a medium saucepan, whisk together the milk, flour, and mustard. Heat over medium heat for 1 to 2 minutes, or until thick, whisking constantly. Add the American cheese, whisking until melted.

Stir in the cooked pasta. Spoon into the casserole dish. Sprinkle with the bread crumbs.

Bake for 10 to 15 minutes, or until the bread crumbs are nicely browned and crisp.

COOK'S TIP: Use a food processor to quickly turn fresh bread into bread crumbs.

Lighten-Up Mashed Potatoes

3 medium russet potatoes (about 1 pound total), peeled and cut into 1-inch cubes

¼ cup fat-free, low-sodium chicken broth

¼ cup fat-free milk or fat-free half-and-half

2 tablespoons light tub margarine

¼ teaspoon salt

⅛ teaspoon pepper (white preferred)

PER SERVING

Calories	110
Total Fat	2.5 g
Saturated Fat	0.0 g
Trans Fat	0.0 g
Polyunsaturated Fat	0.5 g
Monounsaturated Fat	1.5 g
Cholesterol	0 mg
Sodium	204 mg
Carbohydrates	20 g
Fiber	2 g
Sugars	2 g
Protein	3 g

Dietary exchanges: 1½ starch

Thanks to the fat-free chicken broth, fat-free milk, and light tub margarine, you can serve this family pleaser often.

Put the potatoes in a medium saucepan. Fill with cold water to cover by 2 inches. Bring to a boil over high heat. Reduce the heat and simmer, covered, for 15 minutes, or until the potatoes are tender when pierced with the tip of a sharp knife. Drain well in a colander.

Meanwhile, in a small saucepan, heat the remaining ingredients over low heat for 2 to 3 minutes, or until warmed through, stirring occasionally. (Or stir together in a microwaveable bowl, cover with wax paper, and microwave on 100 percent power [high] for 1 minute, or until warmed through.)

In a small mixing bowl, combine the potatoes and broth mixture. Mash with a potato masher or fork. Beat with an electric mixer on medium-high speed for 1 to 2 minutes, or until light and fluffy.

COOK'S TIP: This simple two-step process of mashing by hand and then beating with a mixer ensures that you'll have no-lumps-allowed potatoes.

Roasted Green Beans with Hazelnuts and Dried Cherries

12 ounces green beans, trimmed

 2 teaspoons olive oil

⅛ teaspoon salt

   Pinch of pepper

 3 tablespoons finely chopped hazelnuts

 2 tablespoons finely chopped unsweetened dried cherries

¼ teaspoon fresh lemon juice

PER SERVING

Calories	94
Total Fat	5.5 g
Saturated Fat	0.5 g
Trans Fat	0.0 g
Polyunsaturated Fat	0.5 g
Monounsaturated Fat	4.0 g
Cholesterol	0 mg
Sodium	78 mg
Carbohydrates	10 g
Fiber	4 g
Sugars	4 g
Protein	3 g
Dietary exchanges: 2 vegetable, 1 fat	

NUTRITION TIP:

Adding nuts to veggies and salads provides rich flavor and a crunchy texture.

This festive red-and-green dish is great for special occasions or just as an appealing way to prepare fresh green beans.

Preheat the oven to 425°F.

Put the green beans on a rimmed baking sheet. Drizzle with the oil. Sprinkle with the salt and pepper. Toss with tongs and arrange in a single layer.

Roast for 10 minutes. Sprinkle with the hazelnuts. Toss again to distribute the nuts evenly. Roast for 8 to 10 minutes, or until the beans are browned in spots and tender when pierced with a fork. Transfer to a serving bowl. Stir in the cherries and lemon juice.

Mini Veggie Pancakes

SERVES 4 | 2 PANCAKES AND 2 TABLESPOONS SOUR CREAM PER SERVING

1 large egg white

1 small sweet potato (about 6 ounces), peeled and shredded

1 small zucchini (about 4 ounces), shredded

1 tablespoon all-purpose flour

½ teaspoon dried oregano, crumbled

¼ teaspoon garlic powder

¼ teaspoon onion powder

⅛ teaspoon salt

Pinch of pepper

1½ teaspoons olive oil

Cooking spray

½ cup fat-free sour cream

PER SERVING

Calories	50
Total Fat	1.0 g
Saturated Fat	0.0 g
Trans Fat	0.0 g
Polyunsaturated Fat	0.0 g
Monounsaturated Fat	0.5 g
Cholesterol	3 mg
Sodium	69 mg
Carbohydrates	8 g
Fiber	1 g
Sugars	2 g
Protein	2 g

Dietary exchanges: ½ starch

Pancakes for dinner! Jazz up meat loaf, chicken breasts, or baked fish with this fun side dish that kids will love. The emphasis is on colorful veggies, which provide a broad range of nutrients.

In a large bowl, lightly beat the egg white.

Stir in the sweet potato, zucchini, flour, oregano, garlic powder, onion powder, salt, and pepper.

In a large nonstick skillet, heat the oil over medium-high heat, swirling to coat the bottom. Press some of the sweet potato mixture into a ¼-cup measuring cup. Invert in the skillet. Remove the cup and, using a spoon, slightly press the mixture to form a pancake. Repeat to make 7 more pancakes. Remove the skillet from the stovetop. Lightly spray the pancake tops with cooking spray. Return to the heat and cook for 3 to 4 minutes on each side, or until browned. Transfer to a plate. Serve each pancake with a dollop of sour cream.

VARIATION

If you want to vary the veggies, try 1 small yellow summer squash (about 4 ounces), shredded, and 1 large carrot, shredded (about 3 ounces), instead of the sweet potato and zucchini.

With either combination, you can omit the oregano and garlic powder and top each pancake with a dollop of unsweetened applesauce instead of sour cream.

NUTRITION TIP: For a heart-healthy alternative to bacon and eggs for Sunday brunch, serve these tasty little pancakes with an egg-white omelet.

Apricot-Nut Pilaf

SERVES 4 | ½ CUP PER SERVING

2 teaspoons olive oil

1 cup diced yellow onion

½ cup uncooked instant brown rice

½ cup water

½ cup low-sodium vegetable broth

10 dried apricot halves, diced

2 tablespoons dried currants

¼ cup shelled unsalted pistachio halves, dry-roasted

    Pinch of pepper

PER SERVING

Calories	155
Total Fat	6.5 g
Saturated Fat	1.0 g
Trans Fat	0.0 g
Polyunsaturated Fat	1.5 g
Monounsaturated Fat	3.5 g
Cholesterol	0 mg
Sodium	12 mg
Carbohydrates	22 g
Fiber	3 g
Sugars	10 g
Protein	4 g
Dietary exchanges: 1 starch, ½ fruit, 1 fat	

NUTRITION TIP:
Instant brown rice is one of the quickest whole grains to prepare and makes a great base for experimenting with add-ins. In addition to other nuts and dried fruits, such as pecans and dried cranberries, it works well with asparagus, peas, and carrots.

The flavor of brown rice, a terrific source of whole grain, is livened up with colorful dried fruit and crunchy pistachios.

In a medium skillet, heat the oil over medium heat, swirling to coat the bottom. Cook the onion for about 6 minutes, or until beginning to soften.

Stir in the rice, water, and broth. Reduce the heat and simmer, covered, for about 12 minutes, or until the liquid is nearly (but not completely) absorbed.

Stir in the apricots and currants. Cook, covered, for about 3 minutes, or until all the liquid is absorbed.

Stir in the pistachios and pepper. Fluff with a fork.

Creamy, Cheesy Spinach

SERVES 4 | ½ CUP PER SERVING

2 9-ounce packages spinach leaves, rinsed and patted dry

2 ounces low-fat cream cheese, cut into chunks, softened

¾ teaspoon salt-free garlic-and-herb seasoning blend

PER SERVING

Calories	61
Total Fat	3.0 g
Saturated Fat	1.5 g
Trans Fat	0.0 g
Polyunsaturated Fat	0.5 g
Monounsaturated Fat	0.5 g
Cholesterol	9 mg
Sodium	165 mg
Carbohydrates	6 g
Fiber	3 g
Sugars	2 g
Protein	5 g
Dietary exchanges: 1 vegetable, ½ fat	

Low-fat cream cheese enhances the taste and texture of the fresh spinach in this three-ingredient side dish.

Mound half the spinach in a large skillet. Cook, covered, over medium heat for 1 minute. Toss with tongs. Cook, uncovered, for 1 to 2 minutes, or until just wilted, tossing several times. Using the tongs, transfer the spinach to a large strainer set in a medium bowl. Discard any liquid remaining in the skillet. Still using the tongs, lightly squeeze any excess liquid from the spinach into the bowl. Repeat with the remaining spinach, reducing the uncovered time to about 30 seconds. (Since the skillet will already be hot, less cooking time is needed.)

Remove the skillet from the heat. Measure ¼ cup liquid from the bowl, discarding any excess. Pour into the skillet. Whisk in the cream cheese and seasoning blend until the mixture is well blended and creamy.

Fluff the spinach and stir into the cream cheese mixture. Heat for 1 to 2 minutes, or until blended and heated through, stirring several times.

NUTRITION TIP: Keep portions small for children, especially when they're not too sure if they like something. Too much food on a plate can turn kids off instead of inviting them to try new tastes.

Roasted Sweet Potato Fries

SERVES 4 | ½ CUP PER SERVING

Cooking spray

2 medium sweet potatoes (about 1¼ pounds total), peeled and cut lengthwise into ½-inch-wide strips

2 teaspoons olive oil

¾ teaspoon dried sage

¼ teaspoon salt

2 teaspoons maple syrup (optional)

PER SERVING (with syrup)

Calories	151
Total Fat	2.5 g
Saturated Fat	0.5 g
Trans Fat	0.0 g
Polyunsaturated Fat	0.5 g
Monounsaturated Fat	1.5 g
Cholesterol	0 mg
Sodium	224 mg
Carbohydrates	31 g
Fiber	4 g
Sugars	8 g
Protein	2 g

Dietary exchanges: 2 starch, ½ fat

Sweet potatoes are just that, a sweet source of energy-boosting nutrients and heart-smart fiber. These healthy "fries" are tasty even without the maple syrup, but it adds an extra dimension to their flavor.

Preheat the oven to 400°F. Lightly spray a large baking sheet with cooking spray.

In a large bowl, gently stir together the ingredients except the maple syrup. Spread the potatoes in a single layer on the baking sheet.

Roast for 20 minutes. Turn over. Roast for 10 to 15 minutes, or until tender and browned. Remove from the oven.

While the potatoes are still on the baking sheet, drizzle them with the maple syrup. Toss gently to coat.

COOK'S TIP: Once you open a bottle of maple syrup, store it in the refrigerator to prevent spoilage. It will keep for up to one year.

NUTRITION TIP: Sweet potatoes are low in calories and, like white potatoes, packed with potassium, an important nutrient for good heart health.

Asparagus Parmesan

Cooking spray

1 pound medium asparagus spears (about 12), trimmed

1 tablespoon olive oil

1 teaspoon salt-free lemon pepper

2 tablespoons shredded or grated Parmesan cheese

Using a salt-free seasoning perks up taste without adding sodium.

Preheat the oven to 400°F. Line a baking sheet with foil. Spray with cooking spray.

Place the asparagus in a single layer on the foil. Drizzle with the olive oil. Sprinkle with the lemon pepper.

Bake for 15 to 20 minutes, or until tender-crisp. Sprinkle with the Parmesan. Bake for 1 minute.

PER SERVING	
Calories	69
Total Fat	4.0 g
Saturated Fat	1.0 g
Trans Fat	0.0 g
Polyunsaturated Fat	0.5 g
Monounsaturated Fat	2.5 g
Cholesterol	2 mg
Sodium	45 mg
Carbohydrates	5 g
Fiber	2 g
Sugars	2 g
Protein	3 g
Dietary exchanges: 1 vegetable, 1 fat	

Orange-Kissed Broccoli

8 ounces broccoli spears, stems peeled if desired

1 tablespoon plain rice vinegar

Grated zest from 1 medium orange (about 1½ teaspoons)

¼ teaspoon Dijon mustard

¼ teaspoon grated peeled gingerroot

Fat-free spray margarine

A kiss of orange zest adds some zip and color to everyday broccoli.

In a medium saucepan, steam the broccoli for 4 to 7 minutes, or until tender-crisp.

Meanwhile, in a medium bowl, stir together the remaining ingredients except the spray margarine. Add the cooked broccoli, stirring to coat. Lightly spray with the margarine. Stir again.

PER SERVING	
Calories	21
Total Fat	0.0 g
Saturated Fat	0.0 g
Trans Fat	0.0 g
Polyunsaturated Fat	0.0 g
Monounsaturated Fat	0.0 g
Cholesterol	0 mg
Sodium	25 mg
Carbohydrates	4 g
Fiber	2 g
Sugars	1 g
Protein	2 g
Dietary exchanges: 1 vegetable	

Scalloped Potato Minis

SERVES 4 | ½ CUP PER SERVING

Cooking spray

3 medium russet potatoes (about 1 pound total), peeled, halved lengthwise, and cut crosswise into ¼-inch slices

1 cup fat-free, low-sodium chicken broth

½ cup fat-free half-and-half

2 teaspoons all-purpose flour

1 teaspoon onion powder

¼ teaspoon garlic powder

⅛ teaspoon pepper

¼ cup low-fat shredded Cheddar cheese

1 tablespoon shredded or grated Parmesan cheese

¼ teaspoon paprika

PER SERVING

Calories	132
Total Fat	1.0 g
Saturated Fat	0.5 g
Trans Fat	0.0 g
Polyunsaturated Fat	0.0 g
Monounsaturated Fat	0.5 g
Cholesterol	2 mg
Sodium	114 mg
Carbohydrates	25 g
Fiber	2 g
Sugars	3 g
Protein	7 g

Dietary exchanges: 1½ starch

NUTRITION TIP: This recipe is a good example of how simple substitutions can cut the fat, sodium, and calories in less-than-healthy but classic dishes.

Baking scalloped potatoes in custard cups cuts the cooking time and dresses up this low-fat version of traditional comfort food.

Preheat the oven to 350°F. Lightly spray four 6-ounce custard cups with cooking spray.

In a medium saucepan, bring the potatoes and broth to a boil over high heat. Reduce the heat and simmer, covered, for 10 minutes, or until the potatoes are tender when pierced with the tip of a sharp knife. Using a slotted spoon, transfer the potatoes to the custard cups. Increase the heat under the broth to medium low.

In a small bowl, whisk together the half-and-half and flour. Add the mixture, onion powder, garlic powder, and pepper to the broth. Increase the heat to medium high and bring to a simmer, whisking occasionally. Reduce the heat and simmer for 1 to 2 minutes, or until the mixture thickens, whisking occasionally.

Whisk in the cheeses. Remove from the heat and let them melt. Pour over the potatoes. Sprinkle with the paprika.

Bake for 20 minutes, or until the tops are golden brown and the mixture is heated through.

Squash with Carrot Matchsticks

SERVES 4 | ½ CUP PER SERVING

1 teaspoon canola or corn oil

½ cup chopped onion

½ cup matchstick-size carrots (about 1 medium)

2 medium yellow summer squash, thinly sliced

½ teaspoon sugar

⅓ cup shredded low-fat sharp Cheddar cheese

⅛ teaspoon salt

PER SERVING

Calories	56
Total Fat	2.0 g
Saturated Fat	0.5 g
Trans Fat	0.0 g
Polyunsaturated Fat	0.5 g
Monounsaturated Fat	1.0 g
Cholesterol	2 mg
Sodium	144 mg
Carbohydrates	7 g
Fiber	2 g
Sugars	5 g
Protein	4 g

Dietary exchanges: 1 vegetable, ½ fat

NUTRITION TIP: The small amount of sugar helps brown the vegetables and mellow the flavors, blending them without adding extra fat.

A beautiful mix of yellow and orange, this veggie combo will please your eyes and your taste buds.

In a medium nonstick skillet, heat the oil over medium-high heat, swirling to coat the bottom. Cook the onion and carrots for 3 minutes, or until the onion is beginning to lightly brown, stirring frequently.

Stir in the squash and sugar. Cook for 5 minutes, or until the squash is tender, tossing frequently as you would a stir-fry dish (using 2 utensils works well). Remove from the heat.

Sprinkle with the Cheddar and salt. Let stand, covered, for 2 minutes so the Cheddar melts and the flavors blend.

Lazy Cook's Applesauce

SERVES 4 | ½ CUP SERVING

2½ pounds medium Golden Delicious
    or Granny Smith apples, peeled,
    halved, and each half cut into
    4 cubes

⅓ cup water

3 tablespoons firmly packed dark
    brown sugar

1 tablespoon fresh lemon juice

2 cinnamon sticks (each about 3
    inches long)

PER SERVING

Calories	156
Total Fat	0.5 g
Saturated Fat	0.0 g
Trans Fat	0.0 g
Polyunsaturated Fat	0.0 g
Monounsaturated Fat	0.0 g
Cholesterol	0 mg
Sodium	4 mg
Carbohydrates	41 g
Fiber	3 g
Sugars	35 g
Protein	1 g

Dietary exchanges: 2½ fruit

Is there anything more comforting than homemade applesauce? The aroma of this easy recipe will fill the house, and you'll be comforted knowing your family is getting fiber, vitamins, and wholesome apple flavor.

Put the apples in a 3- to 4-quart slow cooker. Add the water, brown sugar, and lemon juice. Gently stir to coat.

Immerse the cinnamon sticks in the mixture. Cook, covered, on low for 5 to 6 hours or on high for 2 to 3 hours. Discard the cinnamon sticks.

Using a potato masher, coarsely mash the apples for a chunky, thinner applesauce. If you prefer a thick, smoother texture, pour through a fine-mesh sieve into a serving bowl after coarsely mashing. Serve warm or cold.

> NUTRITION TIP:
> Why not try something a little different in the morning? Spoon this delicious apple-sauce over oatmeal and sprinkle with some raisins.

Breakfasts, Breads, and Brunches

Tropical Mango Quick Bread

SERVES 16 | 1 SLICE PER SERVING

Cooking spray

2 cups all-purpose flour

½ cup sugar

¼ cup firmly packed light brown sugar

1½ teaspoons baking powder

½ teaspoon baking soda

½ teaspoon ground nutmeg

½ cup pineapple juice

½ cup light coconut milk

¼ cup egg substitute

¼ cup unsweetened applesauce

1 teaspoon rum extract

1 mango (about 8 ounces), diced (1 heaping cup)

2 tablespoons flaked sweetened coconut

For an afternoon tea party, this moist and aromatic sweet bread is a great favorite.

Preheat the oven to 350°F. Lightly spray an 8½ × 4½ × 2½-inch loaf pan with cooking spray.

In a large bowl, stir together the flour, sugars, baking powder, baking soda, and nutmeg. Make a well in the center.

Add the pineapple juice, coconut milk, egg substitute, applesauce, and rum extract to the well. Stir until just combined. Don't overmix.

Stir in the mango until just combined. Pour into the pan, gently smoothing the top. Sprinkle with the coconut.

Bake for 55 to 60 minutes, or until a cake tester or wooden skewer inserted all the way through the center comes out clean. Transfer the pan to a cooling rack. Let the bread cool for 5 minutes, then turn out onto the cooling rack. Let cool for 10 minutes before slicing. Wrap any remaining bread in plastic wrap and store at room temperature for two to three days or refrigerate for up to one week.

PER SERVING

Calories	119
Total Fat	1.0 g
Saturated Fat	0.5 g
Trans Fat	0.0 g
Polyunsaturated Fat	0.0 g
Monounsaturated Fat	0.0 g
Cholesterol	0 mg
Sodium	91 mg
Carbohydrates	26 g
Fiber	1 g
Sugars	13 g
Protein	2 g

Dietary exchanges: 1½ starch

COOK'S TIP ON CUTTING A MANGO: Lay the mango on its flattest side. Cutting horizontally, slice off the top half close to the center. (You won't be able to cut the mango exactly in half because of the way the fruit clings to the pit.) Turn the mango over so the pit side is down and cut off the other half. Trim off the peel and cut the remaining fruit away from the pit. Slice, dice, or chop the fruit as needed.

Berry Best Bran Muffins

SERVES 12 | 1 MUFFIN PER SERVING

1 cup unprocessed wheat bran

1 cup whole-wheat flour

½ cup sugar

1 teaspoon baking soda

¾ teaspoon ground cinnamon

¼ teaspoon salt

¾ cup low-fat buttermilk

½ cup unsweetened applesauce

2 tablespoons canola or corn oil

1 large egg

1 teaspoon vanilla extract

1 cup fresh or frozen blueberries (no need to thaw if frozen)

PER SERVING

Calories	121
Total Fat	3.0 g
Saturated Fat	0.5 g
Trans Fat	0.0 g
Polyunsaturated Fat	1.0 g
Monounsaturated Fat	1.5 g
Cholesterol	18 mg
Sodium	176 mg
Carbohydrates	22 g
Fiber	4 g
Sugars	12 g
Protein	3 g

Dietary exchanges: 1½ starch, ½ fat

No need for high-calorie, trans-fat-laden purchased muffins—make a batch of these instead. They taste great, and you can freeze any extras for up to two months. Reheat them in the microwave for a breakfast treat or an after-school snack.

Preheat the oven to 400°F. Line 12 muffin cups with bake cups.

In a large bowl, stir together the wheat bran, flour, sugar, baking soda, cinnamon, and salt. Make a well in the center.

In a medium bowl, whisk together the remaining ingredients except the blueberries until well blended. Pour into the well. Stir until the wheat bran mixture is just moistened. Don't overmix; the batter should be lumpy.

Using a rubber scraper, carefully fold the blueberries into the batter. Spoon into the bake cups to fill about three-quarters full.

Bake for 20 to 22 minutes, or until a cake tester or wooden toothpick inserted in the center comes out clean. Transfer the muffin pan to a cooling rack and let the muffins cool for 5 minutes. Turn the muffins onto the rack and let continue to cool. Serve warm or at room temperature.

COOK'S TIP: Look for boxes of unprocessed wheat bran in the cereal section of your supermarket. It's a versatile ingredient to have on hand to add fiber to muffins, quick breads, cookies, and breading mixes for fish or chicken.

NUTRITION TIP: Wheat bran is known as a tremendous source of fiber, omega fatty acids, and vitamins and minerals. Because it absorbs a lot of water and expands, foods that contain bran also can help you feel full and satisfied without adding lots of calories.

Apple Crumble Coffeecake

SERVES 8 | 1 2-INCH SQUARE PER SERVING

Butter-flavor cooking spray

2/3 cup uncooked rolled oats

2 tablespoons firmly packed light brown sugar

2 tablespoons plus 1¼ cups whole-wheat pastry flour, divided use

1 teaspoon ground cinnamon

2 tablespoons light tub margarine, melted and slightly cooled

2 teaspoons honey

2 medium sweet apples, such as Fuji, peeled and diced

¼ cup sugar plus ⅓ cup sugar, divided use

½ teaspoon apple pie spice and 2 teaspoons apple pie spice, divided use

2/3 cup fat-free milk

⅓ cup unsweetened applesauce

¼ cup egg substitute

2 teaspoons canola or corn oil

1 teaspoon vanilla extract

½ cup all-purpose flour

¼ cup toasted wheat germ

1 tablespoon baking powder

Here's a fragrant, whole-grain coffeecake to entice weekend sleepyheads out of bed. The rolled oats, apple, and wheat germ make this treat as good for them as it is delicious.

Preheat the oven to 350°F. Lightly spray an 8-inch square glass baking dish with cooking spray.

In a small bowl, stir together the oats, brown sugar, 2 tablespoons pastry flour, and cinnamon. Stir in the margarine and honey. Set aside.

Put the apples in a small bowl. Sprinkle with ¼ cup sugar and ½ teaspoon apple pie spice. Stir gently until well combined. Set aside.

In a large bowl, whisk together the milk, applesauce, egg substitute, oil, and vanilla.

In a medium bowl, whisk together the all-purpose flour, wheat germ, baking powder, remaining 1¼ cups pastry flour, remaining ⅓ cup sugar, and remaining 2 teaspoons apple pie spice. Pour into the applesauce mixture. Stir just to combine (no flour should be visible). Do not overmix.

Scatter the apple mixture over the batter. Gently fold in. Spread in the baking dish. Sprinkle with the oats mixture.

Bake for 35 to 40 minutes, or until a cake tester or wooden toothpick inserted in the center comes out clean. Let cool on a cooling rack for 10 minutes. Serve warm. Let any leftovers cool, then cover tightly with aluminum foil. The coffeecake will stay fresh until the next day.

PER SERVING

Calories	269
Total Fat	3.5 g
Saturated Fat	0.0 g
Trans Fat	0.0 g
Polyunsaturated Fat	1.0 g
Monounsaturated Fat	1.5 g
Cholesterol	0 mg
Sodium	199 mg
Carbohydrates	55 g
Fiber	5 g
Sugars	25 g
Protein	6 g

Dietary exchanges: 3½ carbohydrate, ½ fat

COOK'S TIP: Melting the margarine instead of crumbling it in cold lets you use less margarine while still making the topping nice and moist.

Peachy English Muffins

SERVES 4 | ½ ENGLISH MUFFIN AND SCANT ½ CUP PEACHES PER SERVING

2 whole-wheat English muffins, split in half

2 tablespoons low-fat tub cream cheese

1 15-ounce can sliced peaches in juice, drained and any thick slices cut lengthwise into ½-inch slices

½ teaspoon ground cinnamon and ¼ teaspoon ground cinnamon, divided use

¼ teaspoon ground allspice

¼ teaspoon ground nutmeg

2 tablespoons firmly packed light brown sugar

2 teaspoons light tub margarine

¼ cup uncooked quick-cooking oatmeal

These cinnamon-sparked treats will get your kids to the breakfast table in a hurry, and you'll know you're serving a nutritious combination of fruit and two grains.

Preheat the oven to 350°F. Line a baking sheet with aluminum foil.

Place the English muffin halves on the baking sheet. Spread the muffin halves with the cream cheese.

Put the peaches in a medium bowl. Sprinkle ½ teaspoon cinnamon, allspice, and nutmeg over the peaches. Stir gently. Arrange the peaches in a single layer on the cream cheese.

In a small bowl, stir together the brown sugar, margarine, and remaining ¼ teaspoon cinnamon. Add the oatmeal. Using your fingertips, rub the mixture until crumbly. Sprinkle over the peaches.

Bake for 25 minutes, or until the topping is firm and the peaches are hot. Serve while still hot.

> **NUTRITION TIP:** If peaches aren't a big favorite in your home, substitute another fleshy fruit, such as pears or apricots.

PER SERVING

Calories	176
Total Fat	3.0 g
Saturated Fat	1.0 g
Trans Fat	0.0 g
Polyunsaturated Fat	0.5 g
Monounsaturated Fat	0.5 g
Cholesterol	5 mg
Sodium	212 mg
Carbohydrates	34 g
Fiber	4 g
Sugars	19 g
Protein	5 g

Dietary exchanges: 1 starch, 1 fruit, ½ fat

Ricotta Pancakes with "Rainbow" Fruit

SERVES 4 | 2 PANCAKES AND ¾ CUP FRUIT PER SERVING

Cooking spray

⅔ cup white whole-wheat flour or all-purpose flour

½ teaspoon baking soda

⅛ teaspoon salt

1 8-ounce container fat-free vanilla yogurt

⅔ cup egg substitute

½ cup fat-free ricotta

3 cups mixed fruit, such as blueberries, diced strawberries, diced kiwifruit, and sliced bananas

PER SERVING

Calories	232
Total Fat	1 g
Saturated Fat	0 g
Trans Fat	0 g
Polyunsaturated Fat	0.5 g
Monounsaturated Fat	0 g
Cholesterol	6 mg
Sodium	387 mg
Carbohydrates	45 g
Fiber	5 g
Sugars	22 g
Protein	13 g
Dietary exchanges: 1 starch, 1 fruit, 1 fat-free milk	

These tender pancakes are a snap to prepare, and they start your day with a trio of nutrition heavy-hitters: whole wheat, fat-free dairy, and loads of fresh fruit.

Lightly spray a griddle with cooking spray. Heat on medium-high heat while preparing the batter.

In a food processor, pulse the flour, baking soda, and salt to combine.

Add the yogurt, egg substitute, and ricotta. Pulse several times to combine. Scrape the side of the work bowl. Pulse once or twice.

Spoon a scant ⅓ cup batter onto the griddle and gently spread to about 5 inches in diameter. Repeat as many times as the griddle will allow. Cook for 3 to 4 minutes, or until the pancakes are bubbly on the top and browned on the bottom. Turn over and cook for 2 to 3 minutes, or until browned on the bottom. Transfer to a warm plate and cover with aluminum foil to keep warm. Repeat with the remaining batter. Serve topped with the fruit.

NUTRITION TIP:

Mild-tasting white whole-wheat flour is lighter in color and texture than its regular whole-wheat cousin but has just as many nutrients. Try it in recipes that call for all-purpose flour, too.

Grab-and-Go Breakfast Pitas

SERVES 4 | 1 STUFFED PITA HALF PER SERVING

2 6-inch whole-wheat pita pockets

1 teaspoon canola or corn oil

¼ cup chopped green onions (about 2 medium)

⅔ cup soy-based sausage crumbles

1 cup egg substitute

2 tablespoons salsa (lowest sodium available)

PER SERVING

Calories	148
Total Fat	2.5 g
Saturated Fat	0.5 g
Trans Fat	0.0 g
Polyunsaturated Fat	1.0 g
Monounsaturated Fat	1.0 g
Cholesterol	0 mg
Sodium	425 mg
Carbohydrates	20 g
Fiber	3 g
Sugars	2 g
Protein	12 g

Dietary exchanges: 1½ starch, 1½ very lean meat

NUTRITION TIP:

Soybeans provide easily digested, high-quality protein and essential amino acids. Meat-free soy-based products that replace sausage, bacon, and burgers offer all the taste without the fat.

No waiting in a drive-through line for these portable pitas! The protein and whole wheat will keep you going through the morning—without the saturated fat, cholesterol, and sodium of fast food. (See photograph on page 194.)

In a medium skillet on medium-high heat, warm the pitas slightly, about 30 seconds on each side. Transfer to a plate and cover with another plate to keep warm.

Pour the oil in the skillet, swirling to coat the bottom. Cook the green onions for about 2 minutes, or until beginning to soften.

Stir in the sausage crumbles. Cook for about 2 minutes, or until just heated through.

Pour in the egg substitute. Reduce the heat to medium low. Cook for 2 to 3 minutes, or until set, stirring often.

Cut the pitas in half. Spoon the egg mixture into each. Drizzle with the salsa.

"Sugar & Spice" French Toast

SERVES 4 | 1 SLICE TOAST, ½ CUP BERRY MIXTURE, AND 2 TABLESPOONS SOUR CREAM PER SERVING

¾ cup egg substitute

4 slices light whole-wheat bread

1 teaspoon canola or corn oil

2 tablespoons sugar

1 teaspoon ground cinnamon

¼ cup all-fruit apricot spread

2 cups fresh whole strawberries, quartered

¾ teaspoon vanilla extract

½ cup fat-free sour cream or fat-free plain yogurt

The aroma of this cinnamon toast can create happy childhood memories.

Put the egg substitute in a shallow pan, such as a pie pan. Dip one slice of bread at a time in the egg substitute, turning to coat, letting any excess drip off. Transfer to a large plate.

In a large nonstick skillet, heat the oil over medium heat, swirling to coat the bottom. Cook the bread for 5 minutes on each side, or until golden.

Meanwhile, in a small bowl, stir together the sugar and cinnamon.

In a medium microwaveable bowl, microwave the fruit spread on 100 percent power (high) for 20 seconds, or until slightly melted. Stir in the strawberries and vanilla.

Sprinkle the sugar mixture on the French toast. Dollop the sour cream on the center of each slice. Spoon the strawberry mixture over all. Serve immediately.

PER SERVING

Calories	194
Total Fat	1.5 g
Saturated Fat	0.0 g
Trans Fat	0.0 g
Polyunsaturated Fat	0.5 g
Monounsaturated Fat	1.0 g
Cholesterol	5 mg
Sodium	235 mg
Carbohydrates	37 g
Fiber	5 g
Sugars	22 g
Protein	9 g

Dietary exchanges: 1½ starch, 1 fruit, 1 very lean meat

COOK'S TIP: This is a great choice when children have guests spending the night. Substitute ½ cup fat-free vanilla ice cream for the sour cream and fruit spread to make it a once-in-a-while "ice-cream-for-breakfast" morning!

Overnight Oatmeal

SERVES 4 | 1 CUP PER SERVING

⅓ cup fat-free half-and-half

1 tablespoon firmly packed dark brown sugar

1 teaspoon light tub margarine

1 teaspoon vanilla extract

Cooking spray

3½ cups water

2 cups uncooked rolled oats

2 medium sweet apples, such as Fuji or Gala (about 12 ounces total), cut into ½-inch pieces (about 2 cups)

⅓ cup raisins

2 teaspoons apple pie spice

¼ teaspoon ground cinnamon (optional)

This spiced oatmeal cooks while you sleep, so you can wake to a delicious-smelling kitchen and a heart-healthy breakfast that's ready to enjoy.

In a small bowl, stir together the half-and-half, brown sugar, margarine, and vanilla. Cover with plastic wrap and refrigerate overnight until serving time.

Lightly spray a 3- to 4-quart slow cooker with cooking spray. Put the remaining ingredients except the cinnamon in the slow cooker, stirring well to combine. Cook, covered, on low for 7 to 8 hours, or until thick and creamy.

To serve, stir the half-and-half mixture into the oatmeal. Spoon into bowls. Sprinkle with the cinnamon.

PER SERVING

Calories	274
Total Fat	3.5 g
Saturated Fat	0.5 g
Trans Fat	0.0 g
Polyunsaturated Fat	1.0 g
Monounsaturated Fat	1.0 g
Cholesterol	0 mg
Sodium	38 mg
Carbohydrates	57 g
Fiber	7 g
Sugars	24 g
Protein	7 g

Dietary exchanges: 2 starch, 2 fruit

COOK'S TIP: Do not substitute quick-cooking oatmeal for the regular rolled oats. They will not hold up in the slow cooker.

Super "Sundae" Breakfast Parfaits

2 6-ounce containers fat-free vanilla yogurt

1 8-ounce can pineapple tidbits in their own juice, well drained, juice reserved

1 medium banana, diced

1 teaspoon grated orange zest

1/2 cup coarsely crushed crunchy cereal

1/4 cup toasted wheat germ

1 cup frozen unsweetened pitted dark cherries, thawed, halved, and patted dry

PER SERVING

Calories	189
Total Fat	1.0 g
Saturated Fat	0.0 g
Trans Fat	0.0 g
Polyunsaturated Fat	0.0 g
Monounsaturated Fat	0.5 g
Cholesterol	1 mg
Sodium	90 mg
Carbohydrates	41 g
Fiber	4 g
Sugars	30 g
Protein	7 g

Dietary exchanges: 1 starch, 1 fruit, 1 fat-free milk

NUTRITION TIP: If your kids are stuck in a fruit rut, try chopping small bits of new fruits—papaya, mango, or kiwifruit—into this dish. It's usually easier to "audition" new foods when they're paired with already "approved" ones!

For an extra-special version of fruit and yogurt for breakfast, make this tropical treat. Top it with your family's favorite cereal; the crunchier the cereal, the more texture for the parfait.

In a medium bowl, stir together the yogurt, pineapple, banana, and orange zest.

Spoon the yogurt mixture into parfait glasses or wine goblets, then sprinkle with the cereal and wheat germ, and top with the cherries.

Desserts

Strawberry-Chocolate Pudding Cake 210

Spiced Applesauce Cake 211

Blueberry Crisp 212

Peach Crisp Minis 213

Mandarin Orange Cheesecake 215

Chill-Out Sundae Pie 216

Caramelized Pear Surprise 218

Oatmeal Raisin Cookies 219

Chocolate Toffee Brownies 221

Baked Cinnamon Apples with Orange Sauce 222

Chocolate-Berry Yogurt Parfaits 224

Chocolate-Berry Ricotta Parfaits 225

Strawberry-Chocolate Pudding Cake

SERVES 8 | ½ CUP PER SERVING

8 ounces fresh strawberries, halved

¼ cup plus 2 tablespoons sugar and ¾ cup sugar, divided use

¼ cup unsweetened cocoa powder and ⅓ cup unsweetened cocoa powder, divided use

1 cup white whole-wheat flour, whole-wheat pastry flour, or all-purpose flour

¾ teaspoon baking powder

¼ teaspoon salt

1 large egg

1 large egg white

1 teaspoon canola or corn oil

½ cup fat-free milk

1 teaspoon vanilla extract

1¼ cups boiling water

PER SERVING

Calories	218
Total Fat	2.0 g
Saturated Fat	0.5 g
Trans Fat	0.0 g
Polyunsaturated Fat	0.5 g
Monounsaturated Fat	1.0 g
Cholesterol	27 mg
Sodium	135 mg
Carbohydrates	46 g
Fiber	4 g
Sugars	31 g
Protein	5 g

Dietary exchanges: 3 carbohydrate, ½ fat

An intriguing combination of textures, this rich-tasting dessert forms cake on the top and pudding on the bottom. Studded with fresh strawberries, it's lavish yet low-fat.

Preheat the oven to 350°F.

Scatter the strawberries in an 8-inch square glass baking dish.

In a small bowl, stir together the ¼ cup plus 2 tablespoons sugar and ¼ cup cocoa powder. Set aside.

In a medium bowl, stir together the flour, remaining ¾ cup sugar, remaining ⅓ cup cocoa powder, baking powder, and salt.

In another small bowl, whisk together the egg, egg white, and oil until well blended. Whisk the milk and vanilla into the eggs. Pour into the flour mixture. Stir until just combined. Spoon over the strawberries.

Stir the boiling water into the reserved sugar and cocoa mixture until well blended. Pour over the batter in the baking dish.

Bake for 30 to 35 minutes, or until a cake tester or wooden toothpick inserted in the center comes out with only a few crumbs. Let rest for 5 minutes before serving. Serve warm.

Cover and refrigerate any leftovers for up to one day. To reheat an individual portion, spoon ½ cup pudding cake into a microwaveable dish. Microwave, uncovered, on 100 percent power (high) for 20 to 25 seconds, or until warm.

NUTRITION TIP: Cocoa powder contains much less saturated fat than regular chocolate. You can replace the chocolate in other recipes by substituting 3 tablespoons of cocoa powder plus 1 tablespoon canola or corn oil for 1 ounce of unsweetened baking chocolate.

Spiced Applesauce Cake

SERVES 16 | 1 PIECE PER SERVING

Cooking spray

1 cup all-purpose flour

1/2 cup whole-wheat flour

1/2 cup uncooked quick-cooking oatmeal

1/2 cup sugar and 2 teaspoons sugar, divided use

1/4 cup firmly packed light brown sugar

1 teaspoon baking powder

1 teaspoon baking soda

1 teaspoon ground cinnamon and 1/4 teaspoon ground cinnamon, divided use

1/4 teaspoon ground ginger

1/4 teaspoon ground nutmeg

1/4 teaspoon salt

3/4 cup unsweetened applesauce

1/2 cup fat-free milk

1/4 cup egg substitute

2 tablespoons light tub margarine

PER SERVING

Calories	106
Total Fat	1.0 g
Saturated Fat	0.0 g
Trans Fat	0.0 g
Polyunsaturated Fat	0.0 g
Monounsaturated Fat	0.5 g
Cholesterol	0 mg
Sodium	164 mg
Carbohydrates	23 g
Fiber	1 g
Sugars	12 g
Protein	2 g
Dietary exchanges: 1½ carbohydrate	

The applesauce, whole-wheat flour, and oats in this moist cake offer more fiber and longer-lasting energy than the simple carbs in most sugary baked goods—and the cinnamon-sugar adds a nice crusty topping, too!

Preheat the oven to 350°F. Lightly spray an 8-inch square metal pan with cooking spray.

In a medium bowl, stir together the flours, oatmeal, 1/2 cup sugar, brown sugar, baking powder, baking soda, 1 teaspoon cinnamon, ginger, nutmeg, and salt. Make a well in the center.

Add the applesauce, milk, egg substitute, and margarine to the well. Stir until just combined (the mixture may be slightly lumpy). Pour into the pan.

Bake for 25 to 30 minutes, or until a cake tester or wooden toothpick inserted in the center comes out clean. Transfer the pan to a cooling rack.

Meanwhile, in a small bowl, stir together the remaining 2 teaspoons sugar and remaining 1/4 teaspoon cinnamon. Sprinkle over the warm cake. Let cool for at least 15 minutes before turning out of the pan.

NUTRITION TIP:
Emphasizing portion control is part of providing healthy snack options. Cut a sample serving from snack cakes like this one so your children can see what one serving should look like when they help themselves.

Blueberry Crisp

SERVES 6 | 1 PIECE PER SERVING

Cooking spray

FILLING

5 cups (about 23 ounces) frozen blueberries, thawed and drained

½ cup firmly packed light brown sugar

2 tablespoons cornstarch

1 tablespoon fresh orange juice

TOPPING

½ cup uncooked rolled oats

⅓ cup firmly packed light brown sugar

¼ cup all-purpose flour

2 tablespoons sliced almonds

1 teaspoon ground cinnamon

1 teaspoon grated orange zest

1 tablespoon fresh orange juice

1 tablespoon canola or corn oil

This juicy pleaser updates the traditional fruit crisp by replacing butter or margarine with heart-healthy unsaturated oil. If you wish, you can top each serving with a quarter-cup of fat-free frozen vanilla ice cream or yogurt.

Preheat the oven to 375°F. Lightly spray an 8-inch square glass baking dish with cooking spray.

In a large bowl, stir together the filling ingredients. Spoon into the baking dish.

In a medium bowl, combine the topping ingredients. Sprinkle over the filling.

Bake for 30 minutes, or until the blueberries are bubbling and the topping is golden. Let stand for about 30 minutes to cool.

PER SERVING	
Calories	272
Total Fat	4.5 g
Saturated Fat	0.5 g
Trans Fat	0.0 g
Polyunsaturated Fat	1.5 g
Monounsaturated Fat	2.5 g
Cholesterol	0 mg
Sodium	10 mg
Carbohydrates	58 g
Fiber	5 g
Sugars	41 g
Protein	2 g
Dietary exchanges: 4 carbohydrate, 1 fat	

Peach Crisp Minis

Cooking spray

12 gingersnaps, crushed into about ¼-inch pieces

1 tablespoon plus 1 teaspoon chopped pecans

2 tablespoons unsweetened applesauce

1 tablespoon frozen orange juice concentrate, thawed, and 2 tablespoons frozen orange juice concentrate, thawed, divided use

2 cups sliced fresh or frozen unsweetened peaches (about 4 medium fresh or 8 ounces frozen), thawed if frozen, cut into ¾-inch pieces

½ teaspoon ground cinnamon

⅛ teaspoon ground nutmeg

1 teaspoon vanilla extract

¼ teaspoon almond extract

Gingersnaps are loaded with spice but not much fat, so they make a tasty and healthy base for the peach filling and do double duty as a crunchy topping.

Preheat the oven to 350°F. Lightly spray four 6-ounce custard cups with cooking spray.

Measure 2 tablespoons gingersnap pieces and put in a small bowl. Stir in the pecans. Set aside.

In a medium bowl, stir together the remaining gingersnap pieces, applesauce, and 1 tablespoon orange juice concentrate. Spoon into the custard cups. Spread to cover the bottoms. Transfer the custard cups to a baking sheet.

Bake for 15 minutes, or until set in the center (the texture will be like a soft gingersnap cookie).

Meanwhile, in a small bowl, stir together the peaches, cinnamon, nutmeg, vanilla and almond extracts, and remaining 2 tablespoons orange juice concentrate. Spoon over the set crusts. Sprinkle with the reserved gingersnap crumb mixture.

Bake for 20 minutes, or until the filling is heated through and the topping is golden brown.

PER SERVING

Calories	164
Total Fat	4.0 g
Saturated Fat	0.5 g
Trans Fat	0.0 g
Polyunsaturated Fat	1.0 g
Monounsaturated Fat	2.0 g
Cholesterol	0 mg
Sodium	138 mg
Carbohydrates	30 g
Fiber	2 g
Sugars	17 g
Protein	3 g
Dietary exchanges: 2 carbohydrate, 1 fat	

NUTRITION TIP: If you buy fat-free baked goods, remember that many of these products can be high in calories. Even when the fat content is low, you still need to pay attention to portion control and serving sizes.

Mandarin Orange Cheesecake

SERVES 12 | 1 SLICE PER SERVING

Cooking spray

1 cup finely crushed low-fat graham cracker crumbs (chocolate or cinnamon preferred) (about 16 squares)

4 ounces low-fat cream cheese, softened

1 cup sugar

2 teaspoons grated orange zest

1 teaspoon vanilla extract

2 15-ounce containers fat-free ricotta cheese

1 cup fat-free sour cream

¾ cup egg substitute

¼ cup all-purpose flour

1 11-ounce can mandarin oranges in water or juice, drained

PER SERVING

Calories	222
Total Fat	2.0 g
Saturated Fat	1.0 g
Trans Fat	0.0 g
Polyunsaturated Fat	0.0 g
Monounsaturated Fat	0.5 g
Cholesterol	14 mg
Sodium	254 mg
Carbohydrates	36 g
Fiber	1 g
Sugars	26 g
Protein	14 g

Dietary exchanges: 2½ carbohydrate, 2 very lean meat

> **KIDS IN THE KITCHEN:** Have your kids help arrange the mandarin oranges on top. And let them show their creativity!

This dessert makes a stunning presentation. The blend of fat-free and low-fat cheeses plus fat-free sour cream gives this cheesecake a richness and smooth texture and gives you a guilt-free, decadent delight.

Preheat the oven to 300°F. Lightly spray a 9-inch springform pan with cooking spray. Sprinkle the graham cracker crumbs on the bottom of the pan. Set aside.

In a large mixing bowl, using an electric mixer on medium-high speed, beat the cream cheese, sugar, orange zest, and vanilla for 3 minutes, or until light and fluffy.

Add the ricotta cheese, sour cream, and egg substitute. Beat on medium low until combined.

Add the flour. Stir to combine. Carefully pour over the graham cracker crumbs.

Bake for 1 hour to 1 hour 15 minutes, or until the cheesecake is set around the edges but still jiggles slightly in the center when gently shaken. Turn off the oven, leave the oven door slightly ajar, and let the cheesecake stand in the oven for 30 minutes. Transfer the pan to a cooling rack and let the cheesecake cool completely, 1 hour 30 minutes to 2 hours. Run a knife around the edge of the pan. Release the rim of the pan. Cover the cheesecake with plastic wrap and refrigerate for at least 4 hours.

Arrange the mandarin oranges in an attractive pattern on top of the cheesecake. Cover and refrigerate any remaining cheesecake.

> **NUTRITION TIP:** Rich desserts such as cheesecake don't have to be off-limits if you make lower-fat versions like this one. It's about trade-offs—if you have something high in calories and fat one night, serve chilled fruit or fat-free frozen yogurt for the next few nights to get things back in balance.

Chill-Out Sundae Pie

SERVES 10 | 1 SLICE PER SERVING

Cooking spray

1½ cups low-fat graham cracker crumbs

3 tablespoons fresh orange juice

¼ teaspoon ground nutmeg

1 quart (4 cups) fat-free frozen vanilla yogurt, slightly softened

1 medium banana, sliced

6 or 7 medium fresh strawberries, sliced

1 cup fresh blueberries

1 medium kiwifruit, peeled and thinly sliced (optional)

2 tablespoons fat-free strawberry topping

The warmer the weather, the happier everyone will be with this cooling fruit-filled pie.

Preheat the oven to 350°F. Lightly spray a 9-inch pie pan with cooking spray.

In a small bowl, stir together the graham cracker crumbs, orange juice, and nutmeg. Pour into the pie pan. Cover with plastic wrap and press with your hands to spread the mixture evenly over the bottom and up the sides of the pan. Remove the plastic wrap.

Bake for 10 minutes. Let cool on a cooling rack for 15 to 20 minutes.

Spoon half the frozen yogurt into the pie crust. Using the back of a large spoon, gently spread over the crust. Arrange half the banana, half the strawberries, half the blueberries, and half the kiwifruit in a decorative pattern on the yogurt. Repeat the layers. Drizzle with the strawberry topping. Cover loosely with plastic wrap and put in the freezer for 1 to 12 hours. Remove the pie from the freezer 5 to 10 minutes before cutting.

PER SERVING

Calories	175
Total Fat	1.0 g
Saturated Fat	0.0 g
Trans Fat	0.0 g
Polyunsaturated Fat	0.0 g
Monounsaturated Fat	0.0 g
Cholesterol	1 mg
Sodium	122 mg
Carbohydrates	37 g
Fiber	1 g
Sugars	26 g
Protein	5 g
Dietary exchanges: 2½ carbohydrate	

COOK'S TIP: For a patriotic red, white, and blue dessert, omit the kiwifruit. Perfect for Memorial Day or the Fourth of July!

Caramelized Pear Surprise

SERVES 4 | ½ PEAR AND 3 TABLESPOONS SAUCE PER SERVING

1 teaspoon fresh lemon juice

1 teaspoon water and ⅓ cup water and 2 tablespoons water, divided use

¼ cup sugar

2 large ripe but firm pears (about 7 ounces each, Bosc preferred), peeled, halved, and cored

1 teaspoon vanilla extract and ½ teaspoon vanilla extract, divided use

¼ teaspoon ground nutmeg

1 6-ounce container fat-free vanilla yogurt

¼ cup low-fat tub cream cheese, room temperature

PER SERVING

Calories	171
Total Fat	3.0 g
Saturated Fat	1.5 g
Trans Fat	0.0 g
Polyunsaturated Fat	0.0 g
Monounsaturated Fat	1.0 g
Cholesterol	11 mg
Sodium	101 mg
Carbohydrates	33 g
Fiber	4 g
Sugars	26 g
Protein	4 g
Dietary exchanges: 2 carbohydrate, ½ fat	

COOK'S TIP: Although any variety of pear will work for this dish, Bosc pears are firm and dense, so they are especially good for poaching or baking.

If you think serving fruit for dessert seems ho-hum, think again. With a sweet and creamy center nestled in a warm pear, this wonderful dish is truly elegant and special enough for entertaining.

In a cup, stir together the lemon juice and 1 teaspoon water. Sprinkle the sugar evenly on a medium plate. Set the plate beside the cup. Brush the cut surface of each pear with the lemon juice mixture. Immediately dip the cut surfaces into the sugar, pressing down and generously coating the cut sides only. Reserve 1 tablespoon of the remaining sugar, discarding the rest.

Heat a medium skillet over medium-high heat. Place the pears with the sugar-coated sides down in the skillet. Sprinkle the reserved sugar around the pears. Reduce the heat to medium and cook for 10 minutes, or until all the sugar has melted and both the sugar syrup and cut surfaces of the pears are golden brown (no stirring necessary).

Reduce the heat to medium low. Carefully stir ⅓ cup of the remaining water into the sugar syrup.

Stir in 1 teaspoon vanilla. Spoon some of the syrup over each pear. Cook, covered, for 10 minutes, spooning the syrup over the pears occasionally. Watch carefully so the skillet doesn't cook dry and the syrup doesn't scorch as the syrup thickens; if necessary, reduce the heat to low and gradually stir in part of the remaining 2 tablespoons water. Transfer the pears with the cut side up to plates, leaving the syrup in the skillet.

Stir the nutmeg and any remaining water into the syrup in the skillet. Cook for 1 minute, or until blended, stirring constantly. Spoon the syrup into the cavity of each pear half.

In a medium bowl, stir together the yogurt, cream cheese, and remaining ½ teaspoon vanilla until smooth. Spoon into the cavity of each pear half.

Oatmeal Raisin Cookies

SERVES 24 | 2 COOKIES PER SERVING

Cooking spray

²/₃ cup firmly packed light brown sugar

²/₃ cup sugar

3 tablespoons light tub margarine

2 teaspoons vanilla extract

¹/₃ cup unsweetened applesauce

3 tablespoons egg substitute

1 cup whole-wheat pastry flour

¹/₂ cup all-purpose flour

1¹/₂ teaspoons baking powder

1¹/₂ teaspoons ground cinnamon

¹/₄ teaspoon ground allspice

¹/₄ teaspoon ground nutmeg

1¹/₂ cups uncooked quick-cooking oatmeal

¹/₂ cup raisins

Soft and chewy, these spiced cookies are plump with sweet raisins. Applesauce replaces the moisture you'd get from the fats you find in other recipes, and whole-wheat flour and oatmeal add texture and boost the fiber. (See photograph on page 208.)

Preheat the oven to 350°F. Lightly spray 2 baking sheets with cooking spray.

In a large mixing bowl, using an electric mixer on medium speed, beat together the sugars, margarine, and vanilla for about 2 minutes, or until fluffy, scraping the side of the bowl as needed.

Beat in the applesauce and egg substitute. Scrape the side of the bowl.

In a medium bowl, whisk together the flours, baking powder, cinnamon, allspice, and nutmeg. Stir into the sugar mixture.

Using a sturdy spoon, stir in the oatmeal and raisins. Drop the batter by teaspoonfuls onto the baking sheets, keeping the mounds about 2 inches apart. With slightly moistened fingertips, slightly flatten the top of each cookie.

Bake for 10 to 12 minutes, or until the edges are just firm and the centers are still soft.

Transfer the baking sheets to cooling racks and let the cookies cool for 5 minutes. Transfer the cookies to the cooling racks and let finish cooling, about 10 minutes. Store any leftover cookies in an airtight container, using wax paper between the layers to keep the cookies from sticking together. The cookies will stay fresh for up to three days.

PER SERVING

Calories	112
Total Fat	1.0 g
Saturated Fat	0.0 g
Trans Fat	0.0 g
Polyunsaturated Fat	0.5 g
Monounsaturated Fat	0.5 g
Cholesterol	0 mg
Sodium	43 mg
Carbohydrates	24 g
Fiber	2 g
Sugars	14 g
Protein	2 g
Dietary exchanges: 1½ carbohydrate	

COOK'S TIP: Quick-cooking oatmeal has much smaller flakes than rolled oats. Using the quick-cooking variety gives these cookies the texture of a good oatmeal cookie without the need for too much fat.

Chocolate Toffee Brownies

SERVES 16 | 1 BROWNIE PER SERVING

Cooking spray

¾ cup white whole-wheat flour, or ½ cup all-purpose flour combined with ¼ cup whole-wheat flour

2½ tablespoons unsweetened cocoa powder

1 teaspoon baking powder

1 cup sugar

¼ cup light tub margarine

¼ cup egg substitute

1 2.5-ounce jar baby food pureed prunes

1 teaspoon vanilla extract

2 tablespoons toffee bits

PER SERVING

Calories	98
Total Fat	2.0 g
Saturated Fat	0.0 g
Trans Fat	0.0 g
Polyunsaturated Fat	0.5 g
Monounsaturated Fat	0.5 g
Cholesterol	1 mg
Sodium	66 mg
Carbohydrates	19 g
Fiber	1 g
Sugars	15 g
Protein	1 g

Dietary exchanges: 1½ carbohydrate, ½ fat

Two of kids' favorite flavors in one irresistible brownie! Add a glass of fat-free milk for a special-treat dessert or snack.

Preheat the oven to 350°F. Lightly spray an 8-inch square metal baking pan with cooking spray.

In a medium bowl, stir together the flour(s), cocoa powder, and baking powder.

In another medium bowl, using an electric mixer on medium speed, beat the sugar and margarine for 1 minute.

Add the egg substitute, pureed prunes, and vanilla to the sugar mixture, beating until combined.

Stir the flour mixture into the sugar mixture. Beat on low speed just until combined. Pour into the baking pan. Sprinkle with the toffee bits.

Bake for 20 to 23 minutes, or until a cake tester or wooden toothpick inserted in the center comes out clean. Transfer to a cooling rack and let cool slightly, about 5 minutes, before cutting.

> **COOK'S TIP ON TOFFEE BITS:** Check the shelves near the chocolate chips in the baking section of the grocery when shopping for toffee bits. Store leftover toffee bits in an airtight container in the refrigerator or freezer for up to six months.

Baked Cinnamon Apples with Orange Sauce

SERVES 4 | 1 APPLE AND 2 TABLESPOONS SAUCE PER SERVING

Cooking spray

4 medium Granny Smith or Rome Beauty apples

2 teaspoons grated orange zest

1 cup fresh orange juice

2 tablespoons sugar

2 teaspoons all-purpose flour

4 cinnamon sticks, each about 3 inches long, each broken in half

PER SERVING

Calories	138
Total Fat	0.0 g
Saturated Fat	0.0 g
Trans Fat	0.0 g
Polyunsaturated Fat	0.0 g
Monounsaturated Fat	0.0 g
Cholesterol	0 mg
Sodium	1 mg
Carbohydrates	36 g
Fiber	5 g
Sugars	28 g
Protein	1 g

Dietary exchanges: 2½ fruit

This apple dish is truly versatile, providing a fruit dessert, a comforting breakfast, or because it's not too sweet, an unusual accompaniment for savory meats, such as roast pork.

Preheat the oven to 350°F. Lightly spray an 8-inch glass baking dish with cooking spray.

Core the apples, cutting to, but not through, the bottoms. Cut a 1-inch strip of peel from the top of each apple. Set the apples in the baking dish.

In a medium bowl, whisk together the remaining ingredients except the cinnamon sticks. Pour over the apples, filling the cavities.

Put 2 pieces of cinnamon stick in each cavity.

Bake for 40 to 45 minutes, or until tender, basting twice. Check the apples often during the last 10 minutes so they don't overbake and the skins don't burst.

Drizzle with the sauce in the pan. Let cool for about 10 minutes so the sugary syrup isn't too hot.

Chocolate-Berry Yogurt Parfaits

SERVES 4 | 1 CUP PER SERVING

2 6-ounce containers fat-free vanilla yogurt

¾ cup fat-free sour cream

3 tablespoons fat-free chocolate syrup and 1 tablespoon fat-free chocolate syrup, divided use

½ teaspoon ground cinnamon

2 tablespoons bottled chocolate-hazelnut spread

1 tablespoon fat-free milk

2 cups mixed fresh fruit, such as blueberries and sliced strawberries and blackberries

2 low-fat graham cracker sheets (4 squares), crumbled

PER SERVING

Calories	279
Total Fat	3.0 g
Saturated Fat	0.5 g
Trans Fat	0.0 g
Polyunsaturated Fat	0.5 g
Monounsaturated Fat	1.5 g
Cholesterol	10 mg
Sodium	161 mg
Carbohydrates	53 g
Fiber	3 g
Sugars	36 g
Protein	10 g
Dietary exchanges: 1 fat-free milk, 2½ carbohydrate	

Chocolate-hazelnut spread and chocolate syrup add a decadent richness to this pretty parfait, which also provides a healthy serving of fruit.

In a medium bowl, whisk together the yogurt, sour cream, 3 tablespoons chocolate syrup, and cinnamon.

In a small bowl, whisk together the chocolate-hazelnut spread, milk, and remaining 1 tablespoon chocolate syrup.

Spoon ½ cup yogurt mixture and ½ cup fruit into each parfait or wine glass. Top with the graham cracker crumbles, then the chocolate-hazelnut mixture.

Chocolate-Berry Ricotta Parfaits

SERVES 4 | 1 CUP PER SERVING

¾ cup light ricotta cheese

¼ cup plus 2 tablespoons fat-free chocolate syrup

2 tablespoons bottled chocolate-hazelnut spread

1½ tablespoons fat-free milk

4 low-fat graham cracker sheets (8 squares), crumbled

2 cups mixed fresh fruit, such as blueberries and sliced strawberries and blackberries

In a small bowl, whisk together the ricotta cheese and chocolate syrup.

In another small bowl, whisk together the chocolate-hazelnut spread and milk.

Spoon the ricotta cheese mixture and chocolate-hazelnut mixture into parfait or wine glasses. Top with the graham cracker crumbles, then the fruit.

PER SERVING

Calories	241
Total Fat	3.5 g
Saturated Fat	0.5 g
Trans Fat	0.0 g
Polyunsaturated Fat	0.5 g
Monounsaturated Fat	1.5 g
Cholesterol	4 mg
Sodium	190 mg
Carbohydrates	44 g
Fiber	3 g
Sugars	25 g
Protein	9 g

Dietary exchanges: 1 lean meat, 3 carbohydrate

COOK'S TIP ON MEASURING CHOCOLATE-HAZELNUT SPREAD: Lightly spray your measuring spoon with cooking spray before you measure this spread, which is similar in consistency to peanut butter. The spread will more easily slide off the measuring spoon without sticking.

NUTRITION TIP: On those days when you want a special treat, it's good to know that it's okay to splurge once in a while, like with this extravagant dessert. It's not the occasional indulgence but the overall pattern of your daily food choices that matters most.

Cooking with Your Kids

Your kitchen is the heart of your home. It's one room where everyone wants to hang out, especially when you're cooking. Why not take the opportunity to turn your kitchen into a nutrition classroom and food lab? By doing so, you'll also create a fun environment for learning while sharing quality time.

Kids love having new experiences, learning different things, and—most of all— getting a chance to do grown-up stuff! Use your children's natural curiosity and their desire to be with you to teach them about important life skills such as healthy eating and cooking as well as to showcase unfamiliar foods. You can even bring geography into the kitchen by talking about the exotic countries where tropical fruits are grown or describing the vast fields of corn or waving wheat that make up much of the American heartland. Plenty of opportunities to incorporate other life skills, such as how to use math in the kitchen and at the supermarket, will pop up as well.

Involving kids in a hands-on way can open the door to getting them to try new foods and to give a second chance to foods they think they don't like. When your children watch the "magic" of cooking, it can also help them connect the image of fresh food with a prepared dish, which may reduce their resistance to trying that dish. For example, children who like raw carrots may lose their aversion to the same vegetable baked in a casserole if they helped prepare the food.

Sharing your joy in cooking and food preparation helps children develop a positive attitude toward healthy cooking methods and new foods and teaches them how to combine foods and flavors for meals that are both nutritious and delicious. Raise your children's awareness of good-for-you foods by encouraging them to be part of the creative process, which includes planning meals, making shopping lists, going grocery shopping, growing a garden, visiting a local farmer's market, and, of course, cooking!

Even the simple process of learning some basic safe kitchen skills, such as how to clean vegetables and stir ingredients, can help lay the foundation for a lifetime of thoughtful and healthy eating. Younger children will be proud of helping with grown-up tasks, and older children will enjoy the chance to contribute to a family meal.

Planning Meals

You can begin to get kids interested in food by having them participate in planning family meals for the week. You might start out by asking your kids what types of food they would like to eat for main dishes. If they say chicken, for example, flip to the different chapters that feature poultry. Older children can read the recipe titles and ingredients and pick one or two recipes that sound good. Read the recipe titles and ingredients aloud for younger children, and let them look at the photographs to help them decide. Once they select an entrée, help them choose one or two side dishes, such as a green vegetable or salad and a grain, that will round out the meal. As you are meal planning together, talk to your kids about how eating healthful foods helps them grow strong. Share with them how important it is for everyone to eat a variety of foods, especially different fruits and vegetables, to stay healthy.

Making Shopping Lists

Once you've created your meal plan, it's time to work together to make a shopping list. Have your kids look in the spice rack, pantry, and fridge to find which ingredients you have enough of and which need to be added to the shopping list. Younger children can search for ingredients they can identify by sight. Older children can look for the other ingredients and perhaps write out the list. This scavenger hunt right in your own kitchen will get kids involved with food in a fun way.

Going Grocery Shopping

Taking children to the grocery store can be another great opportunity to use food to get them involved in age-appropriate learning skills. As you shop, assign items or ingredients to look for: "Who can find the carrots?" or "Find me a yellow vegetable and a red vegetable for the salad." Encourage your kids to observe the vibrancy and variety of colors in the produce department as they hunt for what you've requested. You can even reinforce particular skills that your children are learning in school. If the color of the week is yellow or if the letter of the week is B, you might ask your kids to find three fruits or vegetables that are yellow or that start with B. Then incorporate some of this produce into your weekly meals or snacks. Older children can do the math to figure out how many cans or bottles you need to buy to have what the recipe calls for or even read ingredients labels to help you pick the brands with the lowest sodium and saturated and trans fats. Kids will not only enjoy these challenges but also feel good about being included in deciding some of what the family will be eating.

Growing a Garden

Consider planting a vegetable or herb garden with your kids. To get started, try planting tomatoes or basil; both are easy to grow and thrive almost anywhere in the United States. If you are limited on space, consider participating in a community garden.

Your children will have fun watching their garden grow and at the same time gain a better appreciation for food. Urge them to use multiple senses—sight, touch, smell, and, of course, taste—to enjoy the garden's bounty. As the garden grows, encourage the kids to use their senses to "play" with the food. Have them touch the produce and herbs to see what they feel like. Let them smell the herbs and watch the vegetables change color, size, and shape as they grow and ripen. When the produce is ready to be picked, encourage the kids to try the vegetables raw. For different flavor experiences, prepare dishes that include the same veggies in cooked form.

Visiting a Local Farmer's Market

A family field trip to a local farmer's market can be a real learning experience. Many suburbs and cities around the country have special areas where farmers bring their fresh produce to sell on weekends. Farmer's markets are great places to experience different varieties of fruits and vegetables and for kids to see which kinds are grown in your region. Pique your kids' curiosity by having them choose a fruit or vegetable they've never tried before.

Cooking Together

Kids can really get involved in the creative process when they are hands on in the kitchen. These experiences allow kids to learn about food in new ways. Cooking together can mean that in some way your kids help you prepare a meal. For instance, your younger children can tear the lettuce and help wash and dry the veggies for the salad. They can also whisk ingredients in a bowl to make the salad dressing. Older children can help with the salad by peeling the vegetables and cutting them up (with your supervision as needed). While cooking together, you can even reinforce math skills! For example, ask younger kids to help by counting out ten grape tomatoes for the salad. Kids learning fractions can measure the $\frac{1}{2}$ cup and $\frac{1}{4}$ cup ingredients you need for a recipe you are preparing.

Cooking together can also mean that your kids will prepare a recipe while you help them. To get started, try the recipes designed just for kids seven to nine years old on pages 231–236 and those for ten- to twelve-year-olds on pages 237–243. But don't leave out your younger and older children; it's never too early—or too late—to involve your kids in the kitchen!

Whether your kids are helping you prepare a recipe or you are helping them, have fun together and take advantage of those teachable moments. Being in the kitchen with your children can teach them valuable life skills about good food, good cooking, and good health.

Kids' Recipes

Sweet and Nutty Chicken Fingers with Honey-Mustard Dipping Sauce

SERVES 4 | 2 CHICKEN TENDERS AND 2 TABLESPOONS DIPPING SAUCE PER SERVING

Cooking spray

2 tablespoons honey

2 tablespoons prepared mustard

2 tablespoons firmly packed light brown sugar

2 cups whole-grain cereal flakes, crushed (about ⅔ cup)

⅓ cup chopped pecans, crushed (about 1½ ounces)

8 chicken tenders (about 1 pound total), all visible fat discarded

DIPPING SAUCE

2 tablespoons honey

2 tablespoons prepared mustard

2 tablespoons firmly packed light brown sugar

2 to 4 tablespoons water

PER SERVING

Calories	386
Total Fat	9.5 g
Saturated Fat	1.0 g
Trans Fat	0.0 g
Polyunsaturated Fat	2.5 g
Monounsaturated Fat	5.0 g
Cholesterol	66 mg
Sodium	376 mg
Carbohydrates	49 g
Fiber	3 g
Sugars	35 g
Protein	29 g

Dietary exchanges: 1 starch, 2 carbohydrate, 3 lean meat

What's not to love? Wrapped in a coating of pecans and whole-grain cereal, these lean tenders get dipped in a finger-licking-good honey-mustard sauce.

Preheat the oven to 400°F. Line a 13 × 9 × 2-inch baking pan with aluminum foil. Lightly spray the foil with cooking spray.

In a medium bowl, whisk together 2 tablespoons honey, 2 tablespoons mustard, and 2 tablespoons brown sugar. In a shallow bowl, stir together the crushed cereal and pecans. Set the bowl with the honey mixture, the bowl with the cereal mixture, and the baking pan in a row, assembly-line fashion.

Put the chicken in the honey mixture, turning to coat. Put 1 piece at a time in the cereal, turning to coat. Transfer to the baking pan.

Bake for 25 minutes, or until the chicken is no longer pink in the center.

Meanwhile, in a small bowl, whisk together the sauce ingredients except the water.

Gradually whisk in the water until the desired consistency. Serve the dipping sauce with the chicken.

COOKING SKILLS KIDS WILL PRACTICE:

- Measuring dry and liquid ingredients
- Crushing cereal and nuts
- Whisking together ingredients
- Stirring together ingredients
- Dipping chicken into liquid mixture
- Coating chicken with cereal mixture

Beef-and-Noodle Pinwheels

SERVES 4 | 1 PINWHEEL AND ½ CUP SAUCE PER SERVING

Cooking spray

4 dried multigrain or whole-wheat
   lasagna noodles

FILLING

1 cup fat-free ricotta cheese

¼ cup snipped fresh basil or
   1½ tablespoons dried basil,
   crumbled

2 large egg whites

SAUCE

1 teaspoon olive oil

8 ounces extra-lean ground beef

2 cups spaghetti sauce (lowest
   sodium available)

1 tablespoon plus 1 teaspoon
   shredded or grated Parmesan
   cheese

1 to 2 tablespoons snipped fresh
   basil (optional)

PER SERVING

Calories	274
Total Fat	5.0 g
Saturated Fat	1.5 g
Trans Fat	0.0 g
Polyunsaturated Fat	0.5 g
Monounsaturated Fat	2.0 g
Cholesterol	37 mg
Sodium	611 mg
Carbohydrates	30 g
Fiber	5 g
Sugars	10 g
Protein	28 g

Dietary exchanges: 2 starch,
   3 very lean meat

*Kids know that anything rolled up is just more fun! This super-lean
ground beef dish is good for them, too.*

Preheat the oven to 350°F. Lightly spray an 11 × 7 × 2-inch
glass baking dish with cooking spray. Set aside.

Prepare the pasta using the package directions, omitting the
salt and oil. Drain well in a colander. Set aside.

Meanwhile, in a medium bowl, stir together the filling ingredients. Set aside.

In a large nonstick skillet, heat the oil over medium-high heat,
swirling to coat the bottom. Cook the beef, stirring occasionally to turn and break it up.

Stir in the spaghetti sauce. Cook for 1 to 2 minutes, or until
heated through. Set aside.

Place the noodles on a clean work surface. Using paper towels,
pat them dry. Spoon the filling onto the noodles. Using the
back of a spoon, spread to the edges of the noodles. Roll up
each noodle, starting at a short end. Place with the seam side
down in the baking dish. Spoon the sauce down the center of
each.

Bake for 25 to 30 minutes, or until the filling is no longer glossy
and the sauce is lightly browned on top. Remove from the oven.

Sprinkle with the Parmesan and the remaining fresh basil.

COOKING SKILLS KIDS WILL PRACTICE:

- Snipping fresh herbs (with safety scissors)
- Measuring dry and liquid ingredients
- Stirring together ingredients
- Assembling and layering
- Sprinkling ingredients

Green Bean "Worms"

SERVES 4 | ¾ CUP PER SERVING

Cooking spray

12 ounces fresh whole green beans, ends snapped off

2 teaspoons olive oil

2 teaspoons sesame seeds

⅛ teaspoon salt

Call the beans "worms," call them "snakes" . . . either way, let the kids have fun with their food!

Preheat the oven to 425°F. Line a large baking sheet with aluminum foil. Lightly spray with cooking spray.

Put the beans on the baking sheet. Drizzle with the oil. Using a spoon or your hands, toss until well coated. Arrange in a single layer on the baking sheet.

Roast for 6 minutes. Stir the beans. Sprinkle with the sesame seeds. Roast for 6 minutes, or until just beginning to lightly brown. Remove from the oven. Sprinkle with the salt.

PER SERVING

Calories	56
Total Fat	3.5 g
Saturated Fat	0.5 g
Trans Fat	0.0 g
Polyunsaturated Fat	0.5 g
Monounsaturated Fat	2.0 g
Cholesterol	0 mg
Sodium	79 mg
Carbohydrates	6 g
Fiber	3 g
Sugars	1 g
Protein	2 g

Dietary exchanges: 1 vegetable, ½ fat

COOKING SKILLS KIDS WILL PRACTICE:

- Washing and drying green beans
- Snapping or trimming ends off green beans (with plastic or butter knife or safety scissors)
- Measuring dry and liquid ingredients
- Tossing and coating green beans with oil
- Stirring ingredients
- Sprinkling ingredients

NUTRITION TIP:

When fresh asparagus is in season, use it instead of green beans. Adjust the roasting time according to the diameter of the asparagus spears.

COOK'S TIP ON SNAPPING GREEN BEANS:

Hold the bean just below the stem end between the thumb and forefinger of one hand and at the very tip with the thumb and forefinger of the other hand. Gently bend and apply pressure at the tip, and the end will snap off. Green beans that are fresh will break very easily.

Fruit-on-a-Stick

SERVES 4 | 1 STICK PER SERVING

8 fresh blueberries or seedless grapes

8 mandarin orange segments or tangerine segments, drained if canned

8 pineapple chunks canned in their own juice (about $1/2$ 8-ounce can), 1 tablespoon juice reserved

$1/2$ large banana, cut into 8 slices

$1/4$ cup fat-free vanilla yogurt

$1/4$ cup fat-free frozen whipped topping, thawed in refrigerator

$1/4$ cup (about 1 ounce) dry-roasted unsalted peanuts, finely crushed

PER SERVING

Calories	102
Total Fat	3.5 g
Saturated Fat	0.5 g
Trans Fat	0.0 g
Polyunsaturated Fat	1.0 g
Monounsaturated Fat	1.5 g
Cholesterol	0 mg
Sodium	16 mg
Carbohydrates	15 g
Fiber	2 g
Sugars	11 g
Protein	3 g

Dietary exchanges: 1 fruit, 1 fat

Remember "nutty buddy" ice cream bars? This version, with its fresh and canned fruit, is just as yummy but much healthier—and it's more fun when you've made it yourself.

Using 4 skewers, put 2 blueberries or grapes, 2 mandarin orange or tangerine segments, 2 pineapple chunks, and 2 banana slices on each skewer in any order you wish. Put the skewers on a plate.

In a small bowl, whisk together the yogurt, whipped topping, and reserved pineapple juice. Using a pastry brush, liberally but gently "paint" the fruit with the yogurt mixture to coat. Sprinkle the nuts on all sides of the fruit.

COOKING SKILLS KIDS WILL PRACTICE:
- Washing and drying fruit
- Peeling fruit
- Cutting banana (with plastic or butter knife)
- Measuring dry and liquid ingredients
- Crushing nuts
- Assembling
- Whisking together ingredients
- Sprinkling nuts

NUTRITION TIP: Consider dry-roasting more nuts than you need for this recipe so you have some extra on hand. They will keep fresh for up to two weeks in an airtight container. When you are short on time, try giving your kids any cut-up or bite-size fruit, a small bowl of flavored fat-free or low-fat yogurt, and another small bowl of the extra nuts. The kids will have a blast dipping their fruit, such as raspberries, blueberries, blackberries, strawberries, cherries, and grapes, in the yogurt and then rolling it the nuts. They can use the nuts to coat apple and banana slices, too!

Pizza Faces

SERVES 4 | 1 PIZZA PER SERVING

4 6-inch corn tortillas

½ cup no-salt-added tomato sauce

1 tablespoon finely chopped fresh
   oregano or 1 teaspoon dried,
   crumbled

4 part-skim mozzarella string cheese
   sticks or 3 ounces shredded
   part-skim mozzarella cheese

4 pitted medium black olives,
   halved lengthwise

½ medium yellow or red bell pepper
   (halved lengthwise), cut
   lengthwise into 16 thin strips

¼ medium red bell pepper (halved
   lengthwise), cut lengthwise into
   4 strips

2 whole medium mushrooms,
   halved

   Cooking spray

PER SERVING

Calories	138
Total Fat	7.0 g
Saturated Fat	4.0 g
Trans Fat	0.0 g
Polyunsaturated Fat	0.5 g
Monounsaturated Fat	2.0 g
Cholesterol	20 mg
Sodium	305 mg
Carbohydrates	11 g
Fiber	2 g
Sugars	2 g
Protein	9 g

Dietary exchanges: ½ starch,
   1 vegetable, 1 medium-fat meat

This is the perfect food for a sleepover or party: The kids get the pizza they love, and you know they're eating a healthy dinner. Make it interactive by having everyone create his or her own funny face. (See photograph on page 226.)

Preheat the oven to 425°F.

Line a large baking sheet with aluminum foil. Put the tortillas on the baking sheet. Spoon 2 tablespoons tomato sauce onto each tortilla. Using the back of a spoon, spread over the tortilla, leaving a ½-inch border. Sprinkle with the oregano.

Pull the mozzarella strings from each stick. Slightly curl the strings. Decoratively arrange at the top of the tortilla for the "hair." Place 2 olive halves on each tortilla for "eyes," 2 yellow bell pepper strips for each "eyebrow," a red bell pepper strip for the "mouth," and a mushroom half for the "nose." Lightly spray the pizzas with cooking spray. Bake for 7 minutes, or until the mozzarella is melted.

COOKING SKILLS KIDS WILL PRACTICE:
- Measuring dry and liquid ingredients
- Snipping fresh herbs (with safety scissors)
- Washing and drying vegetables
- Cutting mushrooms (with plastic or butter knife)
- Sprinkling herbs
- Assembling

Sunshine Corn Salad

SERVES 4 | ½ CUP PER SERVING

½ tablespoon cider vinegar

1 tablespoon olive oil (extra-virgin preferred)

1 teaspoon snipped fresh parsley and 1 teaspoon snipped fresh parsley, divided use

⅛ teaspoon Dijon mustard

⅛ teaspoon salt

⅛ teaspoon pepper, or to taste

¾ cup frozen whole-kernel corn

1 tablespoon water

½ medium orange bell pepper, diced

½ medium yellow bell pepper, diced

½ medium yellow summer squash (about 2½ ounces), diced

1 tablespoon pine nuts, dry-roasted

PER SERVING

Calories	83
Total Fat	4.5 g
Saturated Fat	0.5 g
Trans Fat	0.0 g
Polyunsaturated Fat	1.0 g
Monounsaturated Fat	3.0 g
Cholesterol	0 mg
Sodium	79 mg
Carbohydrates	10 g
Fiber	2 g
Sugars	3 g
Protein	2 g

Dietary exchanges: ½ starch, 1 fat

COOK'S TIP ON SNIPPING FRESH HERBS: Put pieces of a fresh herb in a measuring cup or coffee mug. Using kitchen scissors (or safety scissors for young hands), snip the herb until the pieces are the desired fineness.

Like the colors of summer, this salad combines corn, bell peppers, and yellow squash for gorgeous visual appeal. What a delightful way to enjoy these garden vegetables.

In a medium serving bowl, whisk together the vinegar, oil, 1 teaspoon parsley, mustard, salt, and pepper.

In a small microwaveable bowl, combine the corn and water. Microwave on 100 percent power (high) for 2 minutes. Drain in a strainer. Run the kernels under cold running water for 30 seconds to cool. Pat dry with paper towels. Transfer to the serving bowl.

Add the bell peppers, squash, and pine nuts. Toss to combine. Serve sprinkled with the remaining 1 teaspoon parsley.

COOKING SKILLS KIDS WILL PRACTICE:
- Measuring dry and liquid ingredients
- Snipping fresh herbs
- Washing and drying vegetables
- Using a knife (with supervision)
- Whisking together ingredients
- Using a microwave
- Tossing ingredients
- Sprinkling ingredients

NUTRITION TIP: As soon as corn is harvested, its sugars begin to convert to starch. The sooner it's eaten or processed after it's picked, the better. That's why frozen corn can be just as sweet as—or sweeter than—corn that sits for days in the produce department.

Spinach Shells

SERVES 4 | 3 SHELLS PER SERVING

Cooking spray

12 dried jumbo pasta shells (about 12 ounces)

FILLING

2 10-ounce packages frozen chopped spinach, thawed, well drained, and squeezed dry

3 ounces fat-free cream cheese

1 tablespoon dried Italian seasoning, crumbled

1 cup spaghetti sauce (lowest sodium available)

1 cup (about 4 ounces) shredded part-skim mozzarella cheese

PER SERVING

Calories	260
Total Fat	5.5 g
Saturated Fat	3.0 g
Trans Fat	0.0 g
Polyunsaturated Fat	0.5 g
Monounsaturated Fat	1.5 g
Cholesterol	22 mg
Sodium	628 mg
Carbohydrates	34 g
Fiber	6 g
Sugars	7 g
Protein	20 g

Dietary exchanges: 2 starch, 1 vegetable, 1½ lean meat

Keeping pasta shells intact when you fill them is easy if you use a small spoon and take your time. The end result is a creamy vegetarian treat.

Preheat the oven to 350°F. Lightly spray an 11 × 7 × 2-inch glass baking dish with cooking spray. Set aside.

Prepare the pasta using the package directions, omitting the salt and oil. Drain well in a colander. Set aside.

Meanwhile, in a medium bowl, stir together the filling ingredients.

Using a teaspoon, stuff the shells with the filling. Place in 2 rows in the baking pan. Spoon the sauce down the center of each row. Sprinkle with the mozzarella.

Bake for 20 minutes, or until the mozzarella is lightly golden on the edges and the shells are heated through.

COOKING SKILLS KIDS WILL PRACTICE:

- Using the microwave (see Cook's Tip below)
- Measuring dry and liquid ingredients
- Shredding cheese
- Using an oven and stovetop (with supervision)
- Stirring together ingredients
- Assembling
- Sprinkling cheese

COOK'S TIP: To thaw the frozen spinach easily and quickly, remove from the package, place on a microwaveable rimmed plate, and microwave, covered, on 100 percent power (high) for 4 minutes. To squeeze dry, place the spinach in a strainer or colander. Using the back of a spoon, press the spinach until all the water has been drained. If you want the spinach really dry, you can also use your hands to squeeze the spinach by small handfuls, letting the water drip into the sink.

Shrimp-and-Veggie Packets

SERVES 4 | 3 OUNCES SHRIMP AND ½ CUP VEGETABLES PER SERVING

1 pound 4 ounces raw shrimp in shells (41 to 50 count), peeled, rinsed, and patted dry (about 15 ounces peeled)

4 to 5 ounces bite-size fresh or frozen broccoli florets, thawed if frozen

1 medium carrot

2½ tablespoons soy sauce (lowest sodium available)

1 tablespoon sugar

1 tablespoon cider vinegar

PER SERVING

Calories	124
Total Fat	1.0 g
Saturated Fat	0.5 g
Trans Fat	0.0 g
Polyunsaturated Fat	0.5 g
Monounsaturated Fat	0.0 g
Cholesterol	168 mg
Sodium	461 mg
Carbohydrates	8 g
Fiber	1 g
Sugars	5 g
Protein	20 g

Dietary exchanges: 1 vegetable, 3 very lean meat

> **COOK'S TIP:** Making carrot ribbons ensures that the carrots are thin enough to cook evenly. This dish cooks quickly, so it's important for all the ingredients to be fully cooked at the same time.

If you have more than one cook on duty for making this recipe, why not provide a variety of veggies, such as red bell pepper strips, snow peas, or green onions, and have each cook create a signature combination!

Preheat the oven to 425°F.

Cut eight 12-inch-square pieces of aluminum foil. Place the shrimp in the center of 4 of the foil squares. Put the broccoli on the shrimp.

Hold the carrot so it points away from you. Peel with a vegetable peeler. Make carrot ribbons by running the peeler down the carrot, letting the ribbons fall into a small bowl. Turn the carrot often as you work. Repeat until the carrot is too small to use. Put the ribbons on the broccoli.

In a small bowl, stir together the remaining ingredients. Spoon 1 teaspoon of the mixture over each serving. Save the rest. Top with the remaining 4 sheets of foil. Fold up the edges several times to seal securely. Place on a large baking sheet.

Bake for 10 minutes. Carefully open a packet away from you to prevent steam burns (you can use the tines of a fork) and check to see whether the shrimp have turned pink and are cooked through. If the shrimp are ready, carefully open the remaining packets. If not, continue baking for about 2 minutes. Spoon 2 teaspoons soy sauce mixture over each serving.

COOKING SKILLS KIDS WILL PRACTICE:
- Peeling shrimp
- Washing and drying vegetables
- Peeling a carrot
- Measuring dry and liquid ingredients
- Assembling and layering
- Stirring together ingredients
- Using an oven (with supervision)

Pumpkin Patch Smoothies

SERVES 4 | ¾ CUP PER SERVING

1 cup canned solid-pack pumpkin (not pie filling) (about ½ 15-ounce can)

1 cup ice cubes or crushed ice

1 6-ounce container fat-free vanilla yogurt

½ cup fat-free milk

½ teaspoon grated orange zest

¼ cup fresh orange juice

3 tablespoons sugar

2 tablespoons honey

½ teaspoon ground cinnamon

PER SERVING

Calories	146
Total Fat	0.5 g
Saturated Fat	0.0 g
Trans Fat	0.0 g
Polyunsaturated Fat	0.0 g
Monounsaturated Fat	0.0 g
Cholesterol	1 mg
Sodium	45 mg
Carbohydrates	34 g
Fiber	3 g
Sugars	30 g
Protein	4 g
Dietary exchanges: 2 carbohydrate	

Don't save these smoothies just for the fall months. This tasty and creamy smoothie is more than enough reason to have nutritious pumpkin around all year long.

In a food processor or blender, process the ingredients until smooth.

COOKING SKILLS KIDS WILL PRACTICE:

- Operating a can opener
- Measuring dry and liquid ingredients
- Zesting an orange
- Juicing an orange
- Operating a food processor

COOK'S TIP ON GRATING ZEST: Zest is tiny shreds of the colored part of citrus fruit skins. Using the small holes of a box grater or a Microplane, firmly stroke the skin of the orange over a medium bowl, turning the orange frequently. The raised edges of all these tools are very sharp, so be careful not to cut yourself. Do not use the white part of the skin because it has a bitter taste.

COOK'S TIP ON JUICING CITRUS FRUIT: Room-temperature citrus fruit will yield more juice than if it came straight from the fridge. If you didn't take the fruit out ahead of time, no worries! Prick the skin a couple of times with a fork, but don't go all the way to the flesh, then warm the fruit on 100 percent power (high) in the microwave for 10 to 20 seconds. Softening citrus fruit is another way to get more juice. Squeezing the fruit in your hands or gently rolling it on a countertop while exerting a bit of pressure will do the job.

Fruity-Tutti Pizza

SERVES 8 | 1 WEDGE PER SERVING

¼ cup canola or corn oil

¼ cup firmly packed dark brown
   sugar

2 tablespoons sugar

1 large egg white

⅓ cup all-purpose flour

½ teaspoon ground cinnamon

¼ teaspoon baking soda

1 cup uncooked quick-cooking
   oatmeal

   Cooking spray

4 ounces fat-free cream cheese,
   softened

3 ounces fat-free vanilla yogurt

3 ounces canned crushed pineapple
   in its own juice

¼ to ½ cup strawberry all-fruit
   spread

1 medium kiwifruit, peeled, halved
   lengthwise, and sliced

½ cup fresh blueberries or
   raspberries, patted dry

PER SERVING

Calories	233
Total Fat	8.0 g
Saturated Fat	0.5 g
Trans Fat	0.0 g
Polyunsaturated Fat	2.5 g
Monounsaturated Fat	4.5 g
Cholesterol	3 mg
Sodium	159 mg
Carbohydrates	35 g
Fiber	2 g
Sugars	22 g
Protein	5 g

Dietary exchanges: 2½ carbohydrate,
   ½ lean meat, 1 fat

Here's a fun way to make fruit into dessert. Any variety of fruit will work well, so you can let the chefs pick out what to use.

Preheat the oven to 375°F. Line a baking sheet with aluminum foil.

In a medium mixing bowl, using an electric mixer on high speed, beat the oil, sugars, and egg white until smooth.

In a small bowl, stir together the flour, cinnamon, and baking soda. Add to the sugar mixture. Using an electric mixer on low speed, beat until smooth. Stir in the oatmeal.

Using a rubber scraper, transfer the dough to the baking sheet. Lightly spray the back of a large spoon or your fingertips with cooking spray. Spread the dough into a 9-inch circle.

Bake for 20 minutes, or until just beginning to puff. (The crust will not appear to be done.) Transfer the baking sheet to a cooling rack. Let the crust cool completely, about 20 minutes. It will continue to cook while cooling.

Meanwhile, in a small bowl, whisk together the cream cheese and yogurt until smooth. Cover with plastic wrap and refrigerate until needed.

Pour the pineapple into a strainer. Drain well. Using a spoon, press against the strainer to remove any remaining liquid.

To assemble, transfer the crust to a round serving plate. Using a large spoon, spread the cream cheese mixture over the crust. Make a decorative pattern on top with the fruit spread, pineapple, kiwifruit, and berries.

Cut into wedges if serving immediately, or cover the uncut pizza with plastic wrap and refrigerate for up to 2 hours before serving.

COOK'S TIP ON PEEL-ING A KIWIFRUIT: Using a paring knife, cut a thin piece off each end of the kiwifruit. Gently cut off strips of the thin, fuzzy brown skin. Don't cut too deeply, or you'll remove some of the brilliant-green fruit underneath.

COOKING SKILLS KIDS WILL PRACTICE:

- Measuring dry and liquid ingredients
- Separating an egg
- Operating a can opener
- Peeling fruit
- Using a knife (with supervision)
- Rinsing and drying fruit
- Using an oven (with supervision)
- Using an electric mixer (with supervision)
- Stirring together ingredients
- Whisking together ingredients
- Assembling and layering

Appendixes

APPENDIX A: Good Choices in the Grocery Store—the Educated Shopper

In the process of feeding your family well, the art of grocery shopping is just as important as the cooking. Your choices dictate what staples and snacks you keep in your kitchen and what dishes end up on the family table, so it's crucial to know how to make the most of the time and money you spend buying food. With some simple steps, you'll be better prepared to shop smart.

You really do two kinds of shopping, one for the everyday basics that need replacing on a regular basis and one for the ingredients you'll need for the meals you intend to prepare. If you wait until the last minute to decide what's for dinner, you may be more tempted to eat out or heat up a packaged main dish. It seems so much easier to turn to these conveniences, but when you do, you may sacrifice nutritional control.

- **List #1:** Whenever you think of a staple, such as milk, that's running low, jot it down so you'll always remember to restock before you run out completely! Use your cell phone, computer, or a magnetic pad on the refrigerator—whatever you're most likely to keep close at hand.

- **List #2:** Spend a few minutes to decide on the meals you want to prepare and the snacks you'll need that week. Make a master list of the ingredients you'll need so you can shop once and have everything on hand when you start cooking. Check your pantry, fridge, and freezer for things you already have or staples you need to restock. This cookbook can simplify your planning process: Choose among the delicious options in Everyday Dinners, Busy Nights, Plan-Aheads, and Cook Once, Eat Twice. When you think ahead and organize your meal planning, you'll be pleasantly surprised to find how much money you can save by taking advantage of grocery specials, avoiding costly impulse purchases, and spending less on eating out.

Get Back to Basics

The more foods are processed to make them commercially viable, the more things are added that you want to avoid. It will benefit both your family's health and budget to limit the convenience products and focus on stocking your kitchen with "real" food.

Read Labels Before You Buy

All U.S. food manufacturers are required to provide the nutritional breakdown of their products on the Nutrition Facts label and to state the number of servings per package and how much of certain nutrients each serving contains. The information also shows the Percent Daily Value, which is based both on a daily intake of 2,000 calories and on the recommended daily amount for these nutrients. Each individual's actual calorie needs vary according to age, gender, and activity level. Everyone, however, should limit total fat, saturated fat, trans fat, cholesterol, and sodium to keep the risk of heart disease low. (For more information, visit americanheart.org.) Be sure to get enough fiber, vitamins, and other nutrients while keeping carbohydrates, sugars, and protein in balance to get the right amount for optimum nutrition.

Teach Your Kids

Help your children learn to be savvy shoppers, too. Have them help you find the products they like, then compare the Nutrition Facts labels with them to include them in the decision process. The numbers don't lie! If your children are old enough to read, they'll see for themselves the benefits of one choice over another.

Buy in Season and Bulk Up

Produce is usually fresher and less expensive when it's in season and grown locally. You also can save money by purchasing foods from the bulk food chains, cooperatives, and farmer's markets. Share the larger amounts with a friend or two. Another way to take advantage of buying in bulk is to make large batches of your favorite recipes and freeze family-size portions. When you're cooking dinner, prep extra of whatever vegetables you're using as side dishes so you'll have them handy for snacking, or prep several different veggies after shopping so they're ready to use in recipes and for snacks.

APPENDIX B: Good Choices in the Kitchen—the Smart Cook

If you use these heart-healthy techniques when you prepare most of your meals, you will eliminate many of the unwanted calories and much of the saturated fat, trans fat, and sodium from your family's diet. As you prepare the recipes in this book, you'll see how we put these same techniques into action.

Heart-Healthy Prep Techniques

- Before cooking most meat and chicken dishes, discard the skin and all visible fat. (If you're roasting a chicken, leave the skin on to prevent the chicken from drying out. Discard the skin before serving the chicken.) Be sure to scrub the cutting surface and utensils well with hot, soapy water after preparing raw meat, poultry, or seafood for cooking.

- To retain natural juices, wrap food in aluminum foil before grilling or in foil or cooking parchment for baking. Also try steaming food wrapped in edible pouches made of lettuce or cabbage leaves. Wraps keep in moisture and lessen the need for added sauces.

Heart-Healthy Cooking Techniques

- **Grilling or broiling.** Interchangeable in many recipes, grilling (cooking over direct heat) and broiling (cooking under direct heat) are favorites of health-conscious cooks. While the food cooks, the fat from meat, poultry, and fish drips away into the grill or the broiler pan, but the flavor remains. You can also grill or broil vegetables and fruit.

- **Braising or stewing.** Braising (for a pot roast with vegetables, for example) and stewing (for stews and chilis) are similar slow-cooking methods that tenderize tougher cuts of meat by breaking down the connective tissue. (Typically it's not necessary to braise or stew more tender cuts of meat.) Braising is also a good method for cooking firm vegetables, and stewing is good for some fresh fruits, such as plums and cherries, and for dried fruits.

- **Steaming.** Steaming retains the natural flavor, color, and nutrients of foods without adding fat. This technique works well for almost any food that can be boiled or simmered, including chicken breasts and vegetables. To add flavor, put herbs in the steaming liquid, which is usually water or broth. (When steaming, keep the water lower than the bottom of whatever is holding the food.)

- **Stir-frying.** Quickly cooking food by stirring constantly in a small amount of very hot oil seals in the natural juices of meats and seafood and preserves the texture and color of vegetables. Once you actually start stir-frying, everything moves quickly, so slice or dice each ingredient into uniform pieces (for more even cooking) and prepare any sauces first. In most cases, you can stir-fry in either a wok or a large skillet, so you don't need special equipment for this cooking method.

- **Roasting.** Another method that reduces the need for added fat, roasting uses the dry heat of an oven. When roasting meat, discard the visible fat and place the meat on a rack in a roasting pan to prevent the meat from sitting in its fat drippings. If needed, baste with liquids such as wine, fruit juice, or fat-free, low-sodium broth. After removing the meat or poultry from the oven, it's a good idea to let it "rest" for 15 to 20 minutes before you cut it (it will continue to cook slowly as it rests). Roasting also works well for most firm vegetables such as asparagus, carrots, and zucchini and for fruits such as peaches and bananas.

- **Microwaving.** Fast and easy, microwave cooking is especially healthy. It requires very little added liquid, so it doesn't leach nutrients from vegetables and fruits. Foods usually don't stick, so you don't need much added fat, and cleanup is easy.

- **Poaching.** Poaching is an excellent low-calorie way to prepare delicate foods, such as seafood, chicken, and fruit. To poach food, immerse it in an uncovered pan of almost-simmering well-seasoned liquid (the bubbles should not break the surface of the liquid). Although you can use water as the liquid, some more-flavorful choices are wine, fruit juice, or fat-free, low-sodium broth. After the food is cooked, remove it from the pan and reduce the remaining liquid (decrease the volume by boiling the liquid rapidly) to make a delicious sauce.

Heart-Healthy Kitchen Tips

Meats, Poultry, and Seafood

- After you roast or braise meat or poultry, refrigerate it, then discard any fat that has risen to the top and hardened. Save the defatted stock or drippings to use in stews, sauces, and soups.
- If you're using leftover marinade for basting or in a sauce, take precautions—be sure to boil the marinade for at least 5 minutes before using it. That will kill any harmful bacteria that the raw food might have transmitted.
- Instead of hiding fish in heavy batters and oils, grill, broil, or bake fish and use a few herbs and some citrus juice as seasoning.

Vegetables

- Cook vegetables just long enough to make them tender-crisp. Overcooked vegetables lose both flavor and important nutrients. When veggies have more natural flavor, you won't need to blanket them in butter or rich sauces.
- Cut down on cholesterol by using more vegetables and less poultry, seafood, or meats in soups, stews, and casseroles. Finely chopped vegetables also are great for stretching ground poultry or ground meat.
- When you make stuffing, substitute chopped vegetables for some of the bread.
- For added crunch in salads and casseroles, use unsalted dry-roasted or blanched nuts or water chestnuts instead of croutons, fried bacon, or fried onion rings.

Seasonings

- Substitute herbs, spices, and salt-free seasonings for salt as you cook, or season food at the table.
- Substitute onion or garlic flakes or powder for onion or garlic salt.

APPENDIX C: Good Choices Away from Home—the Best of Eating Out

Families on the go eat many of their meals away from home—now more than ever before. Given the large portion sizes served in restaurants and the prevalence of high-calorie foods that don't provide a lot of high-quality nutrition, even the most conscientious parent has a hard time knowing how to juggle the push and pull of convenience and cost as well as confusion about what to eat.

With a little research and planning, however, you can make better choices when you do dine out as a family. Start by checking the Web sites of take-out and fast-food places and the casual dining restaurants that your family enjoys. Print out the nutritional information for meal choices and compare the foods you tend to order with other options to see which are healthier. If you are a regular customer of certain restaurants, keep the printouts handy so you can refer to them quickly.

When you choose where to eat, steer the family to places you know offer healthier selections. Avoid all-you-can-eat buffets: It's very hard not to overeat and they make it much too easy for both kids and adults to pass up the good stuff for platefuls of all the unhealthy options.

Keep these tips in mind when you order:

- In general, the more vegetables the better. Request double portions of healthy vegetables and skip sides such as french fries or mashed potatoes, which may be loaded with butter and cream.
- Plan to share! It's good for your health, kids' smaller tummies, and your budget. Since so many places offer extra-large servings, it's perfectly okay to split an entrée or an entire meal. Or ask for a to-go box and plan in advance to take home part of your meal.
- Choose broiled, baked, grilled, steamed, roasted, or poached foods instead of high-fat fried options.
- Ask for extras such as dressings, cheese, and sauces on the side so you can choose how much to eat.
- Feel free to ask about ingredients or how a dish is prepared. Many places are happy to make substitutions or whip up a specially prepared dish, especially for children.
- Ask for whole-grain breads and rolls when available.
- Drink water or fat-free or low-fat milk instead of sugar-laden soda and juice drinks.

APPENDIX D: Good Choices for Choosy Eaters—Tips for Feeding Toddlers to Teens

Toddlers

Start by understanding that being picky is natural to toddlers, who are just learning to define their personal wants. Toddlers also experience a growth slowdown, compared to the rapid weight gain of their first year, so they need less food than you might think. It's normal for your toddler to go on food jags, have a hard time sitting still for meals, or want to nibble all day instead of eating three square meals. Think in terms of balancing nutrition for the week, not the day. Kids this age often will eat only certain foods at one time, whether determined by color, texture, or type. Here are a few ideas on how to avoid a power struggle while you encourage your little ones to eat well.

- Try letting toddlers graze as they busily go about their business. Set out a kid-level tray of healthy foods that will stay fresh for about an hour: steamed broccoli florets (trees); fat-free cheese cubes; carrot coins; fruit, such as apple, banana, or orange slices; slices of hard-boiled egg; avocado chunks; cubes of whole-wheat bread—you get the idea.
- Offer dips, toppings, and spreads for tactile appeal. Smeary, messy fun can broaden a toddler's interest and appetite. Try fat-free yogurt, peanut butter, unsweetened applesauce, guacamole, or other family favorites.
- Give your toddler a comfy place to sit still to eat. A low table and chair can help small children who find it uncomfortable to have their feet dangling in the air.

School Age and Older

When your child is eating away from home, you have several influences to consider. Since you can't be sure what your child will actually eat during the day, set up a workable schedule that allows for a nutritious breakfast. (It may help to prep breakfast foods the night before.) Then be proactive: Make it your business to know whether your child is actually eating the lunch you pack or is served in the cafeteria. Your child's teacher can be a great source of inside information about this. Find out what is being served for lunch in the school cafeteria. If you're not happy with the choices there, advocate for more nutritious options in schools. For more information, visit healthiergeneration.org.

Teenagers

There's a lot of pressure on teenagers these days, and most teens can easily fall into some bad eating habits. Skipping breakfast, indulging in high-calorie/high-fat processed snack foods, crash dieting, meeting friends at fast-food places, and drinking lots of high-calorie soda are the most common. Help your teens by making healthier snack options easily accessible, and reinforce the importance of eating well by being a good role model yourself.

Lunch Box Ideas for Everyone

A balanced lunch should provide the nutrients growing bodies and minds need to do well during the day. Instead of the packaged convenience foods that are typically high in calories, fat, and sodium, send your child to school with a lunch box that includes these basics:

- One serving of vegetables or salad and one serving of fruit (fresh, canned, or dried all count).
- One serving of a fat-free or low-fat dairy item such as a cheese stick, a yogurt cup, or some cottage cheese.
- One serving of meat, chicken, fish, eggs, peanut butter, beans, or another protein source.
- A healthy drink, such as water or 100% juice. (If you pack juice, make sure it's 100% juice. Many juice drinks contain no more than 10% juice and are mixed with a lot of sugar.)

Helpful Suggestions

- Use whole-wheat bread, pitas, or corn tortilla wraps for variety and added fiber.
- Make sandwiches with lean turkey or chicken breast instead of deli meats such as bologna or salami. Place lettuce, cucumbers, tomatoes, or shredded cabbage between slices of the meat or wrap them separately in plastic wrap to keep sandwiches from getting soggy.
- Use only a small serving of low-fat mayonnaise or skip it entirely.
- Send a salad as an entrée and include a lean protein, such as beans, grilled chicken, or hard-boiled eggs. Pack low-fat or fat-free dressing in a separate container. When you serve salad for dinner, make a little extra and pack it for lunch the next day.
- Put last night's whole-wheat pasta and sauce in a resealable portable container.
- Mix plain brown rice with canned beans or shredded lean meat for a high dose of protein and fiber.
- Pack hummus with fresh veggies and whole-wheat pita triangles or flatbreads for dipping.
- Add about ¼ cup salt-free, dry-roasted nuts for a hunger-busting snack.

Index

Note: Page numbers in *italics* refer to photographs.